CHRISTIAN BARRIERS
TO JESUS

Dr. Paul Pennington has done the global Christian community a great service by writing *Christian Barriers to Jesus*. Dr. Pennington points out an essential and clarifying truth, and he does so beginning with the title. Christians have erected barriers between the peoples of the earth and Jesus. Dr. Pennington has situated his book in the Hindu context. His experiences interviewing Indian people led him to further explore the reasons why Hindus and Christians know that traditional Christian assumptions stifle the growth of the gospel within Hindu communities in India and around the world. Throughout the book, Dr. Pennington points them out and then explains why they have become barriers. The greatest strength of the book is the grace and humility with which he deals with the problems and the solutions.

TIMOTHY SHULTZ
teacher and author, *Making Disciples among Hindus*

Christian Barriers . . . is a path-breaking work which examines systematically the obvious, and, the more subtle, factors that keep most Indian people from becoming disciples of Jesus Christ. It is an honest inventory of the legacy that "Christendom" has bequeathed on the Hindu people, and carefully documents why they reject the claims of Jesus Christ, our Savior and Lord. At a time when many Christians and mission agencies in India are being forced to discover (and re-discover) their true *raison d'etre*, Paul Pennington invites scholars and practitioners to get back to the "original fact of Jesus." Making this shift will not be painless, but is essential if Hindus are to hear—and see—the Good News, without the elaborate (and unnecessary) socio-religio-cultural stumbling blocks that have been unwittingly erected by Christians down the ages. Thank you, Paul Pennington, for calling us to return to our eternal, original foundations.

PETER IGNATIUS
President, Lakeview Bible College & Seminary
Chennai, India

The religious world of the Hindu and its labyrinth of unreached peoples has long presented the Christian movement with inscrutable barriers. But any radical incarnational witness to reduce these barriers will be sure to threaten the more conventional church life in India. Paul Pennington has chosen to journey alongside these churches and dialogue with them on their Christian responsibility for these barriers. The biblically reasoned curricula that has emerged, so long overdue, promises to free the log jam of misunderstanding surrounding incarnational witness among Hindus today.

BRAD GILL
editor, *International Journal of Frontier Missiology (IJFM)*

This is a paradigm-altering study. Standard paradigms of Christianity and church are part of the core problems addressed in this analysis of Christian barriers to Jesus. It hurts to break from long-accepted patterns of thought and practice, but this is part of the pruning that produces more fruit (John 15:1–10) and of the discipline that is painful for a season (Heb 12:11). Always Pennington is a faithful physician seeking to heal and restore, even when he deals with painful realities.

H.L. RICHARD
researcher and author of
Following Jesus in the Hindu Context and *Hinduism*

This book is a commentary on *Living Water and Indian Bowl*. The *prayashchitta* (atoning, reconciling offering) done by Paul Pennington will put the healing balm on the wounds of every Hindu Yesu bhakta and will encourage them to press forward, without minding what others say or think about them, to live with their birth right, to be a Hindu and a bhakta of the Nara-Hari Bhagavan Muktinath (the Man-God, the Blessed One, Jesus).

DAYANAND BHARATI
Yesu bhakta leader in India

CHRISTIAN BARRIERS
TO JESUS

CONVERSATIONS AND QUESTIONS FROM THE INDIAN CONTEXT

J. PAUL PENNINGTON

WILLIAM CAREY
LIBRARY

Published by William Carey Library
1605 E. Elizabeth Street
Pasadena, CA 91104 | www.missionbooks.org

Melissa Hughes, editor

Joelle Bridges, copyeditor

Joanne Liang, graphic design

William Carey Library is a ministry of
Frontier Ventures | www.frontierventures.org

Printed in the United States of America

19 18 17 16 15 5 4 3 2 1 BP 350

Library of Congress Cataloging-in-Publication Data
   Names: Pennington, J. Paul, author.
Title: Christian barriers to Jesus : conversations and questions from the Indian context /
   J. Paul Pennington.
Description: Pasadena, CA : William Carey Library, 2017. | Includes bibliographical
   references and indexes. |
Identifiers: LCCN 2017017190 (print) | LCCN 2017018688 (ebook) | ISBN
   9780878088584 (eBook) | ISBN 9780878085453 (pbk.) | ISBN 0878085459 (pbk.)
Subjects: LCSH: Missions--India. | Christianity and other religions--India.
Classification: LCC BV3265.3 (ebook) | LCC BV3265.3 .P46 2017 (print) | DDC
   266.00954--dc23
LC record available at https://lccn.loc.gov/2017017190

CONTENTS

FIGURES AND TABLES

FOREWORD

The explosion of Christianity as a truly world religion over the course of the twentieth century has brought new challenges to the mission endeavor of the twenty-first century. There are so many varieties of Christianity that many of us are getting familiar with the initially uncomfortable term "Christianities."

The many Christianities of the world still face a massive challenge in adequately representing Jesus Christ to the majority of the world which lives without a vital relationship with him. This book is focused on that challenge, and particularly that challenge in India among Hindus.

Author Dr. J. Paul Pennington is on an interesting pilgrimage. He has been a missionary in Africa, a teacher of missions in the USA, and in recent years has become familiar with the Indian scene. In all places, he has observed how Christians and churches are often their own worst enemy when it comes to representing Christ before others.

This book grows out of deep interaction with many Indian Christians. The problems it presents (the many Christian barriers to Jesus) have been identified and affirmed by Indian Christians, and the penetrating analysis presented here will stimulate readers in all contexts, not just Hindu contexts.

How Indian Christians can shed the baggage introduced to them by Western Christianity is a great challenge. Many of the voiceless Christians whose contributions are present in these pages would perhaps not have been able to face the radical ramifications of this situation without the biblical and existential probing of Dr. J. Paul Pennington.

Pennington has also kept his ears open to voices outside Christianity. He quotes with remarkable respect and humility some of the bitterest critics of Christ-church-gospel in India. This is commendable, as modern media makes even the most fringe voices altogether accessible to masses of people, and few can discern what is slanted and what is factual. And listening to and learning from even harsh and unfair critics is commanded by our Lord ("make peace quickly with your adversary on the way to court," Matt 5:25).

Yet there are also many voices beyond Christianity who hold Jesus in the highest esteem; people who are well-wishers towards the ideals of Christianity even if at times critics of Christianity in current practice. Pennington has particularly been heedful of these voices, and has found Indian Christians who are sufficiently humble and concerned with the glory of Christ to acknowledge the sometimes painful truths pointed out by these friends.

The end product, with historical and particularly biblical analysis, is this insightful study of Christian barriers to Jesus. Surely there is not a single sincere Christian who does not lament that at some point (for most of us, many points) their own person and their own church or Christianity proved a stumbling block that kept others away from Christ. We mourn ("blessed are those who mourn," Matt 5:4) and try to learn and improve.

But this book takes on deeper systemic problems that transcend the failings of individual Christians and churches and denominations. It is often addressing worldview issues, although thankfully it is intensely practical and never strays into philosophical ramblings. But it is worth asking, just how biblical is the standard "Christian" worldview? There is no simple answer here, and much depends even on one's definition of "worldview." But, as David Naugle said in his brilliant analysis of the history of the concept of worldview, "worldviews, in one way or another, are always works in progress" (Naugle 2005). Expect some shaking and refining of your Christian/biblical worldview as you read this book.

This is also a paradigm-altering study. Standard paradigms of Christianity and church are part of the core problems addressed in this analysis of Christian barriers to Jesus. It hurts to break from long-accepted patterns of thought and practice, but this is part of the pruning that produces more fruit (John 15:1–10) and of the discipline that is painful for a season (Heb 12:11). Always Pennington is a faithful physician seeking to heal and restore, even when he deals with painful realities.

May this book find a wide readership, and may it contribute to the development of new patterns of discipleship to Jesus that will break down barriers and reveal the Savior of the world who came to seek and save the lost, Jesus who still now on his throne appears "like a lamb that has been slain" (Rev 5:6). To him be all glory.

H. L. Richard
June, 2016

PREFACE

How did I end up writing a book about how Christianity keeps people from Jesus? It all began with a trip to India and many conversations over a great deal of tea and coffee. Christians and Hindus told me similar stories. When they described India's resistance to Jesus, the obstacles they described often shared a common thread. Indians did not seem to be turned off so much by Jesus or his teaching. More often they seemed to be alienated and offended by human traditions and practices that Jesus neither initiated nor condoned.

My Indian friends had been aware of and troubled by these issues for decades. They were actively pursuing alternative solutions in their seminary and churches. They knew of other changes they wanted to make, but sometimes felt hindered by the expectations of other missions and churches, foreign and Indian.

The more we explored the challenges, the more complicated the issues appeared. The questions became so complex that I recently suggested we may be a decade away from just adequately understanding the questions and barriers. We keep peeling layers of the challenge, only to uncover deeper, more complicated issues that still must be addressed. India's rich diversity and ancient traditions resist quick, simplistic analyses and solutions.

Unexpectedly, I found myself drawn into this surprising and challenging journey with our Indian colleagues. Together we continue to explore and address what we increasingly recognize as a multidimensional, complex network of *Christian barriers to Jesus*, hence the title.

What you hold in your hands is a first attempt at unpacking those conversations and questions, together with their implications. In the pages that follow I try to reflect what Indians have told me, and what our research has elaborated, about ways that Christianity keeps people from Jesus, sometimes actively alienates them from him. My colleagues

(Christians and *Yesu bhaktas*[1] alike) who recognized these barriers felt that these issues needed to be articulated and addressed scripturally for a broader audience.

I offer, then, this initial fruit of our efforts to identify these barriers and begin to understand them. We need much more conversation and field research to flesh out details; of that I am keenly aware. Where my recollection or representation of conversations is not completely accurate, I plead forgiveness. In the early days, I had no idea this challenge would become my focus. I was engaged in friendly conversations and did not always take notes. Only three years along did it become clear that what I was hearing required more intensive listening and more careful examination. I now have eight notebooks filled with reflections about these conversations and challenges, with significantly more material recorded electronically.

"THE OPPOSITE IS TRUE"

India is an incredibly complex nation. "Whatever you can rightly say about India, the opposite is also true" (Sen 2005). Amartya Sen's quote burdens me with nearly every paragraph I have written. While I am confident that I have described realities that are prevalent in too much of India, Christians and Hindus alike can and have pointed out contradictory experiences. I hope I have represented the situation fairly, but Sen's dictum will apply in specific places and contexts. Everything I say is both true, and in some cases, untrue simultaneously. In India, they have a way of answering some questions with what's called the Indian head wobble.[2] Your head does a small figure eight several times. It's not always a full yes or no. So ask me at any point, "Is that really true of India?" I may just do the head wobble.

I will reference the viewpoints of various Hindu critics of Christianity and its foreign nature and influence—Gandhi, Savarkar, Niyogi, Goel, Frawley, Malhotra, to name a few. Some would like to dismiss their views

---

1.   Believers in Jesus who stay in their Hindu culture and community and fellowship together in a *satsang* or *mandali* (Indian expressions of ekklēsia). The book will explain their choice in greater detail. *Yesu* is often pronounced "Yeshu."

2.   If you've seen it, you recognize it. If not, here's an Indian explanation: http://goindia.about.com/od/greetingscommunication/a/head-wobble.htm

as biased, unfair, and inaccurate. They do, however, voice concerns that often occur in discussions of Christian activity in India, whether in person or in the media. The perceptions they articulate are widespread enough that Christians should at least consider how to mitigate those sensitivities, where appropriate. At the same time, Sen's observation also holds true about these authors. What they say may be accurate in some situations and misrepresentation in others. We cannot adequately consider the barriers, though, if we ignore their voices entirely.

PERSONAL LIMITATIONS

This book is admittedly bound by my own geographical, cultural, and temporal limitations. My wife and I have had the incredible privilege of traveling to very different parts of India. We have experienced only a portion of India's rich and varied cultures over several years. What I share is primarily informed by where we have traveled and those we have encountered so far on this journey.

A friend of mine in India works in a place I have yet to visit extensively. He once told me, "You must visit our place before you finish the book. We have many examples of what you are talking about." Due to my schedule I have yet to visit him or so many others. We must publish what we know so far, though. Further trips and reader responses will, I am sure, lead to revised editions, as we refine and expand our understanding of these barriers. They will not, I am confident, undermine the premise of what I have written: Christian tradition is unnecessarily keeping people from Jesus and we must address the reality and causes of these Christian barriers.

We do not live in India so we are dependent on what our Indian acquaintances tell us and explain. To the extent that I have accurately represented these Christian barriers to Jesus, I am indebted to my Indian friends for describing and explaining them to me. They have expressed, at times, that our outside status helped approach these barriers from a fresh perspective. Our questions and conversations, along with our eyes and ears as visitors, allowed us to explore their familiar challenges from fresh vantage points.

Where we listened to them and improved our understanding, this book is a far better reflection of the challenges than my early drafts.

Where we have failed to hear, or understand properly, I apologize for any remaining misrepresentation or confusion and welcome correction and clarification. This version of the book is necessarily finalized. Its ideas and implications are a continuing work in progress.

DANGER OF OVERGENERALIZATION

This book describes barriers that certain Christian traditions can present to those who might be otherwise interested in Jesus. I do not mean to imply that all Christians in all places exhibit all the barrier-producing issues described in what follows. Some of the barriers are more prevalent than others. Some, where they do exist, are more problematic to Hindu society than others.

I also do not mean to imply that all Hindus are troubled by all the barriers I present. Some, in fact, have specifically told me that they do not see certain practices as confusing or offensive. They just recognize them as something Christians do.

These barriers seem to be common enough, however. Believers must at least consider whether they exist, how problematic they might be for their context, and how they should address them if they are identified.

It is impossible, I must add, to address every qualification, caveat, and alternate viewpoint. To do so would require a much larger volume. I am under no illusion that my presentation of these issues is complete, fully balanced, or the final word.

FOCUS ON HINDU CONCERNS

The reader will detect at points that I emphasize Hindu concerns and perspectives over Christian ones. I am aware that some Christians may perceive this as an insurmountable limitation. I readily acknowledge that possibility. Paul's policy, though, of "becoming all things to all people" requires us to step outside our comfort zone and look at how others perceive our faith and practice. Paul models this in the beginning of 1 Corinthians 9 (see detail in Chapter 8, p. 199). I have intentionally done that throughout this book for the sake of those Hindus who might want to follow Jesus but are prevented by the existing barriers. Given a choice between understanding Hindu concerns or preserving Christian tradition,

I am convinced that Jesus (friend of "sinners") and Paul ("all things to all people") would choose to understand and identify, rather than to preserve human traditions that alienated. If that is a limitation, I embrace it for the sake of Hindus who might otherwise never hear or consider the good news of Jesus.

HINDU AND HINDUISM

I have referred to Hindus several times now. Before I proceed let me briefly comment on my use of "Hindu" and "Hinduism." It is difficult, if not impossible, to fully define either because they are foreign-invented terms for India's very diverse cultural complexity. I have provided more detailed definitions of "Hindu" and "Hinduism" in Appendix A.

What is Hinduism? I like Timothy Paul's approach:

> A good starting place, perhaps, is to ask Hindu people to tell the world who they are and what they believe in their own terms. What Hindu people emphasize is that Hinduism is not a religion or a philosophy. It is a culture, or a way of life, that evolved over time in India. Furthermore, it is a uniquely Hindu culture, defining itself according to Hindu cultural dynamics; it is culture as Hindus define culture. (Paul 2011, 11)

It is unhelpful and unfair to equate Hindu or Hinduism purely with religion and then throw everything "Hindu" away (Pani 2001a, 24–25). Some Christians do this, but it creates unnecessary barriers to Jesus. Christians would not consider doing this with their own cultures even though those cultures contain many pagan elements from pre-Christian religions and cultures (e.g., Christmas, Easter, wedding customs, etc.).

In the New Testament, Greeks or Romans did not reject and leave their socioreligious communities when they followed Jesus. They navigated the challenges of living for him within their communities (see Chapter 1). In the same way, Hindus need not reject and leave their socioreligious communities to follow Jesus. They too, with the Lord's leading, can navigate what it means to be incarnational believers who remain with their people and live out their faith in Jesus within their own society as much as possible.

When I speak of Christian barriers that keep "Hindus" from Jesus I refer to members of Hindu socioreligious communities who do not know or do not follow Jesus. "Yesu bhaktas" are followers of Jesus who remain within their Hindu socioreligious community and culture. By culture they are Hindu, by faith they are disciples of Jesus. This book will explain how that choice is scriptural and possible, preferable even, for the majority of Hindus.

A WORD TO HINDU READERS

If you are a Hindu reading these words, I do not intend the descriptions or numbers in this book to target you in any way. I have used evangelical terminology and numbers to open Christians' eyes to how their traditions keep people from meeting Jesus who might be interested in him. I know Hindus who have deep interest in Jesus. In this book, I argue for Christians to stop treating Hindus as statistics and targets for their conversion and salvation agendas, or to increase their fundraising targets and efforts. I find these attitudes and practices offensive and actively condemn the harsh, disrespectful way Christians sometimes speak about and to Hindus in pursuing their evangelistic goals.

I do, however, fully believe that the *Marg* (Way) of Jesus, not the Christian religion, speaks to deep longings and needs in Hindu society and culture. My heart's prayer is that this book will open the door for interested Hindus to seriously consider his unique person, teaching, and claims, once they realize that these barriers do not come from him. I believe that Jesus is as troubled by these barriers as your Hindu community has been.

Having grown up in a Christian home and culture, I must acknowledge that it is an indelible part of my heritage. But I also offer this book as repentance (*prayaschitta*) for unnecessary offenses that Christianity has imposed on Hindus. I am sorry for ways that "my community" has at times treated and disregarded the Hindu community in its desire to evangelize and convert India.

Every time I have worked on this book, I have done so with a deep burden and prayer that it will remove these barriers for Hindus who want to follow Jesus. I pray that it helps Hindus realize that they do not need to follow Christian traditions to follow Jesus, and I pray that it helps

Christians remove these barriers so that Hindus who want to are able to meet and follow Jesus without abandoning their rich heritage of their Indian *sanskriti* ("culture").

FOCUS ON BARRIERS

If my focus on the barriers seems one-sided and unbalanced, the subject necessitated that focus. If I explored all the provisos, qualifications, and Indian nuances of these issues, it would take decades to compile the necessary encyclopedia. This book is not intended to provide in-depth analyses of the issue, but a shorter, introductory overview of the barriers and the hindrances they can present.

If readers are encouraged to dig, research, challenge, and explore more deeply on their own, this work will have succeeded. I will provide additional material in blog form that was cut from this book. Others have explored some of the concerns and I have referenced them where appropriate. My own ongoing research will, in the coming years, add nuance, as well as articulate solutions the Indian believers have developed.

The lack of solutions for each barrier may trouble some readers. These reflections, however, require careful and deep examination before we quickly pursue solutions based on a cursory review of the issues. In addition, my own recommendations as an outsider would often be detrimental for India. Frankly, Indians must develop the appropriate alternatives in their context after considering the barriers. In fact, they are already doing so.

ECCLESIASTES AND THE NEGATIVE FOCUS

A friend who read my first draft, recently commented on this version, "You really have softened the tone of these chapters now!" I'm glad he noticed, because I have endeavored to scale back my idealistic, at times pessimistic, evaluations of the barriers and the damage they can cause. My readers will not see the tears that I have wept, the continuing sorrow I feel, regarding much I have felt compelled to write and its implications for Christians and Hindus alike.

Ultimately barriers get in the way, they hinder, they impede. Before we can proceed, barriers must be removed or somehow overcome or bypassed.

Where these barriers, centuries of Christian tradition, keep Jesus from doing his will today and keep people from him, the time has come to remove them. We can't be content to polish the barriers, "redecorate" the barriers, "contemporize" the barriers, or "contextualize" the barriers. We can't even "reform" the barriers to remove some of their stigma, while keeping them primarily intact. We must recognize the barriers for what they truly are and get them out of the way.

Ecclesiastes says that "There is a time to plant and a time to uproot what is planted" (Eccl 3:2). Many are focused on planting more churches and more Christianity in India, and the more they do the more resistant India seems to grow. Susan B. Harper has noted, "Most cultural systems in South Asia have been influenced by Christianity, but South Asians have, on the whole, remained stubbornly hostile to evangelization" (Harper 1995, 14). My conversations and observations, along with my study of Scripture, lead me to wonder whether it's not actually time to "uproot what is planted." To take a painful look at what we are reaping and ask whether we are sowing what Jesus wants sown in Indian soil.

The next verse (Eccl 3:3) speaks of "A time to tear down and a time to build up." This book reflects the time to tear down. As will become apparent, the Christian assumptions about these barriers run deep, often less scriptural than we'd like to think. We cannot overcome these barriers by simply putting Indian wallpaper over Western walls that are both foreign and structurally flawed. Having spent my life in the church and Christianity, I have had to wrestle with myself and my own tradition with every sentence and paragraph of every chapter. It is deeply unsettling to realize that so much of what we do has nothing to do with Jesus or Scripture and everything to do with our own Western cultural preferences and concerns. Hindus find much of that foreign building confusing and off-putting. In some places, I'm convinced, we must completely tear down the old traditional models, and let the Lord build his *ekklēsia* as he wants in more culturally appropriate ways.

One more line of Ecclesiastes 3:2–8 is critical for our consideration: "A time to keep and a time to throw away" (Eccl 3:6). There is a time to keep and hold on to traditions that are meaningful to a particular culture in order to reach that society, but there is a time to throw those human inventions away when they are not appropriate for another time, another place, another culture, or another people. India's challenging context requires believers who will throw away what is no longer appropriate and necessary so that people can develop new traditions that are appropriate to keep in the Indian context.

Jesus and Scripture do not change. His good news is eternal. His ekklēsia is always his fellowship, his body, his family. Those we cannot, must not, throw away. But the ways we have packaged, explained, expressed, and embodied those for given cultures? Those are dispensable, despite centuries of Christian tradition to the contrary. If the findings of this book are at all realistic, we are going to have to throw away some dearly beloved traditions, if we truly want Hindus to meet and follow Jesus. That's what it took for Paul to "become all things to all people" (1 Cor 9:22). It will be the same for Christians today.

ACKNOWLEDGMENTS

To the Lord Jesus, who I now also know as *Sadguru* (Truth-teacher), *Prabhu Yesu* (Lord Jesus), and *Muktinath* (Lord of Salvation) through my Indian encounters.

Margaret, you have been a tremendous encouragement throughout the writing process, and have suffered too much neglect and book-related conversation. You have journeyed to India with me for most of our trips and provided extra eyes, ears, and needed perspective and insight. Your counseling credentials and expertise have opened doors for conversation with people we would not otherwise have met. In fact, if it weren't for your invitation to teach the counseling course at a seminary in India, we might not have gone in the first place. I could not have finished this without your listening ear, your insightful reading, your gentle encouragement, and your regular supply of tea and fruit snacks.

Peter and Cathy Ignatius, your passionate love for the Lord, for people, and for your country is an inspiration to those who know you. Your investment over the years in training servant leaders for India has produced remarkable fruit in quiet ways. The faculty you have brought together are an inspiring team who challenge and mentor students to see new, creative possibilities for ministry in the future. Our deep, intense conversations over these issues, have prodded, challenged, and inspired me. Thank you for the privilege of exploring the future together.

Anand and Esther Barnabas, you opened your hearts to us and have given us a home away from home spiritually, emotionally, and physically. Over cups of morning coffee, Esther's delicious food, even Anand's famous chutney, you have walked with us deeply on this learning journey. You have encouraged at times, questioned where needed, and clarified where we were unclear. Your love for our Lord and for people around you inspires and challenges us in our own walk with the Lord. You have been friends who "stick closer than a brother," and our lives are deeper and richer for the time we share together.

To my many Indian friends who have explored these Christian barriers with us over the past several years I owe you a deep vote of thanks. I cannot name most of you here without leaving out or offending some, but most of this book would not exist were it not for your continual, deep conversations over tea and coffee and countless meals. We have been blessed to travel to a variety of places in India and are deeply indebted for your gracious hospitality and challenging interaction wherever we have gone. Thank you for taking us into your hearts and homes and giving us the privilege of traveling with you at times on what is a complex and long-term journey.

I owe a deep debt of gratitude to many pioneers of incarnational faith in India. Much of my awareness of these alternative forms of ekklēsia and faith arose from reading the work of H. L. Richard and Dayanand Bharati. After my Christian friends identified the barriers themselves, I found myself often in tears as Bharati articulated the pain and alienation that Christians can foster when they force Hindus into Western Christian forms. He described from a Hindu perspective exactly what my Christian colleagues had identified. Richard's careful scholarship of various Hindu cultural ways of following Jesus provides a treasure trove of possible options to traditional church-based models. My Indian Christian friends asked for alternatives to what they had been doing. You two, now my friends, have helped us explore those alternatives together.

Finally, I can't begin to adequately express our gratitude for an anonymous couple who were burdened by these issues themselves. The Lord led us together, though we had never met, and your generosity and partnership has made this journey possible. We have been humbled and blessed by your encouragement and friendship through the initial years of this learning process.

INTRODUCTION

A Hindu once told the missionary statesman, E. Stanley Jones, "We have been unwilling to receive Christ into our hearts, but we alone are not responsible for this. *Christian missionaries have held out Christ completely covered by their Christianity*" (Jones 1926, 31; emphasis mine). This book will demonstrate that today's Hindus can say much the same about Indian Christianity. The barrier has not significantly changed in the century since those words were spoken. Substantial obstacles to Jesus remain despite significant contextualization, indigenization, and Indianization.

Today around 5 percent of India has any connection to Jesus (Center for the Study of Global Christianity 2013; Joshua Project 2016b). The percentage of Indians who identified themselves as Christian stayed at 2.3 percent between the 2001 and 2011 India censuses, unchanged, in fact, from the 1961 census (India Census 2001, 2011). According to Joshua Project, India's 2,013 "unreached people groups" represent four times as many as the next country on the list, China with 456 (Joshua Project 2016b; Joshua Project 2016a).

I was somewhat aware of these issues when we made our first visit to India in 2010. Our conversations about these challenges covered a wide range of causes. Few seem to have asked, however, whether Christianity itself might represent a significant factor in India's resistance.

Harold Netland concluded a discussion of world religions with this telling observation:

> It is significant that in spite of centuries of missionary effort, with a few notable exceptions, the Christian church has experienced little growth in cultures dominated by Islam, Hinduism, or Buddhism. Peoples shaped by the worldviews of these three religions have *proven to be remarkably resistant to the gospel*. Perhaps part of what

is needed in the coming decades is a *much more serious engagement with the sophisticated worldviews* underlying these religious traditions and *more creative ways of expressing the gospel* in these challenging contexts. (Netland 2000, 1031)

Christian Barriers to Jesus proposes that Netland's suggestion does not begin to address what is keeping these peoples from Jesus. We have not addressed India's resistance at a deep enough level. Fundamental assumptions about cultural separatism, Christian identity, and church present significant barriers that arise from cultural inventions rather than scriptural teaching. Other barriers, built on this foundation, compound the issues that alienate and offend too many Hindus in India today.

CHRISTIANITY, SOURCE OF RESISTANCE

Is it possible that Christianity itself is a significant factor in India's resistance and rejection? Over the past few years, I have frequently discussed with Christians and Hindus some of the dynamics that keep many Hindus from meeting and considering Jesus. Rarely has anyone identified Jesus as the direct cause for opposition. Instead, Hindus appear to be turned off more often by Christian and church traditions. These can at times actively alienate them from Jesus before they can meet or consider him. I have come to refer to these traditions as the "Christian barriers to Jesus."

What are these barriers that lead Hindus to reject Jesus before they really encounter him? In this book, we will focus on nine barriers that my Christian and Hindu friends have commonly identified. Each chapter will explain how that Christian practice can present an obstacle to Hindus. We will examine the Christian traditions and assumptions that contribute to that barrier. Then we will review these barrier-producing traditions by considering what Scripture teaches.

Christians follow these practices and traditions because they believe that God requires them or that Scripture teaches them; that's what the missionaries or early leaders told them. I know many Christians, though, who sense that these barriers are not what the Lord wants. I have found that the only way to help them address the barriers is for us to consider them in the light of Scripture.

FIVE COMMON THEMES

As my Indian colleagues and I have explored the Christian barriers to Jesus, five common themes have helped to examine the problems and solutions.

1. Search the Scriptures (Acts 17:11)

In examining the Christian barriers, we have often found that the root of the barrier lies in human Christian traditions. Sometimes these represent misinterpretations of Scripture, but often they represent non-biblical human inventions. So, we will look repeatedly at the traditions that seem problematic to Hindus and will examine what God's word says about them. The Berean believers were called "more noble" because they queried Paul's teaching, "examining the Scriptures daily to see whether these things were so" (Acts 17:11 NASB). They were commended, in other words, because they did not simply accept the word of the missionary or evangelist, even though he was an apostle. They examined the Scriptures to see whether his teaching agreed with God's revealed word.

If missionaries or evangelists or pastors asserted, "The Bible says . . ." many Indian believers simply accepted that teaching as permanent tradition. As we will see, that unquestioning allegiance to human interpretation and tradition drives many of the Christian barriers to Jesus. The people of Jesus in India and elsewhere need to be encouraged to "examine the Scriptures" and see if what their leaders and traditions say are true to God's word. Every chapter seeks to model this reexamination of what Scripture says in relation to common Christian traditions. I am deeply aware that my own interpretations may be flawed or inadequate. I hope, however, that believers will "examine the Scriptures" regarding my own analyses and come to conclusions that may be more faithful to Scripture than my own understanding.

I believe that the Scriptures are the inspired word of God, not simply human opinion and invention. They are, as Paul says to Timothy, "God-breathed" (2 Tim 3:16), not merely man-made. God used men, their temperaments, personalities, idiosyncrasies to write and did not override their uniqueness in doing so. However, at the end of the day, "men moved by the Holy Spirit spoke from God" (2 Pet 1:19–21). In this verse, and what precedes, Peter includes his own experience and writing as part of the "prophetic word."

The commands and principles of Scripture provide divine guidance for the questions and challenges all believers face. We must be sure that our faith and practice is rooted in his Word, not simply human opinion, invention, or tradition.

2. Jesus, Friend of Sinners (Matt 9:9–17; 11:19)

Many of the Christian barriers have arisen from subtle or overt expressions of extraction and separation from the surrounding culture. Jesus, faced with the separatist spirit of the Pharisees, repeatedly rejected their model of cultural extraction and disengagement. He engaged and associated so often that he became known as a "friend of tax collectors and sinners." The incarnation of Jesus required a fundamental perspective of identification not isolation, redemption rather than rejection. Where Christians manifest a spirit of extraction and separation from the culture around them, where they portray Jesus as primarily "enemy of sinners and culture," they misrepresent his fundamental relationship to the world (John 3:16–17), love and non-condemnation. Knowing Jesus' anti-separatist spirit, we are convinced that Jesus wants to be "friend of Hindus" today, not their enemy. Since the followers of Jesus are the only visible expression of Jesus to Hindus, does this not have direct implications about how we ought to view, relate to, and interact with Hindus?

3. Become All Things to All People (1 Cor 9:19–23; 11:1)

Paul followed Jesus' model of engagement rather than extraction. A former Pharisee himself, he abandoned that separatist culture and spirit. He engaged with the pagan, idolatrous culture of the Greeks and Romans so he could introduce them to Jesus. He did not adopt all their practices, in fact, he challenged certain ones. However, Paul articulated his principle of cultural engagement in 1 Corinthians 9:22: "I have become all things to all men in order that I by all means might save some." Paul, in other words, followed Jesus' model of incarnation and identification, not isolation. When we examine the Christian traditions that present barriers to Hindus, we repeatedly observe violations of this principle. Outside believers (whether cultural, social, or geographical outsiders) can bring their cultural traditions and assumptions about evangelism, preaching, worship, or benevolence and impose them on local believers without following Paul's principle. All too often, Christians have reversed the scriptural order and insisted that "all men become as us culturally to be saved."

4. Incarnational Believers (John 1:14; Phil 2:1–12)

This book arose from encounters with believers, Christians and Yesu bhaktas both, who know that Jesus wants them to live his life in respectful relationships with their majority culture around them, rather than extract and isolate from it. Some are Christians who recognized that certain attitudes and practices they once were taught are not reflected in the teaching or example of Jesus. They have been seeking the Scripture and the Lord for ways to better reflect his Way to the Hindus around them. Others are Yesu bhaktas who follow only Jesus but do so within their Hindu family, community, and society. I have come to term all these, "incarnational believers," believers who seek, to varying extents, to model and live out the life of Jesus among the culture in which they find themselves.

This does not denigrate or take away from the unique work Christ did in his incarnation, but since Paul tells us to have Christ's incarnational mind in us (Phil 2:3), I use it in that sense. What Christ has done must be fleshed out naturally within a given community, if the people are to genuinely meet and follow Jesus.

5. Gentleness and Respect (1 Pet 3:15)

As I talked with Christians and Hindus alike, I heard repeated accounts of Christians who spoke to or about Hindus with harshness and disrespect. In a challenging context of persecution, Peter instructed believers to explain their faith "with gentleness and respect" (1 Pet 3:15). A great deal of Hindu resentment toward Christianity would likely be alleviated if Christians would just apply Peter's injunction in the Indian context. In the pages that follow we will see specific instances where this principle could make a significant difference in Hindu-Christian relationships.

With those themes in mind, come join me as we explore some of the *Christian barriers to Jesus.*

ABBREVIATIONS

BIBLICAL ABBREVIATIONS

Old Testament

Gen	Genesis	Eccl	Ecclesiastes
Ex	Exodus	Song	Song of Solomon
Lev	Leviticus	Isa	Isaiah
Num	Numbers	Jer	Jeremiah
Deut	Deuteronomy	Lam	Lamentations
Josh	Joshua	Ezek	Ezekiel
Judg	Judges	Dan	Daniel
Ruth	Ruth	Hos	Hosea
1 Sam	1 Samuel	Joel	Joel
2 Sam	2 Samuel	Amos	Amos
1 Kgs	1 Kings	Obad	Obadiah
2 Kgs	2 Kings	Jonah	Jonah
1 Chr	1 Chronicles	Mic	Micah
2 Chr	2 Chronicles	Nah	Nahum
Ezra	Ezra	Hab	Habakkuk
Neh	Nehemiah	Zeph	Zephaniah
Esth	Esther	Haggai	Haggai
Job	Job	Zech	Zechariah
Ps	Psalms	Mal	Malachi
Prov	Proverbs		

New Testament

Matt	Matthew	1 Tim	1 Timothy
Mark	Mark	2 Tim	2 Timothy
Luke	Luke	Titus	Titus
John	John	Phlm	Philemon
Acts	Acts	Heb	Hebrews
Rom	Romans	Jas	James
1 Cor	1 Corinthians	1 Pet	1 Peter
2 Cor	2 Corinthians	2 Pet	2 Peter
Gal	Galatians	1 John	1 John
Eph	Ephesians	2 John	2 John
Phil	Philippians	3 John	3 John
Col	Colossians	Jude	Jude
1 Thess	1 Thessalonians	Rev	Revelation
2 Thess	2 Thessalonians		

COMMON ABBREVIATIONS

ESV	English Standard Version
f.	And the following verse, in Scripture references.
HYB	Hindu Yesu bhakta (Incarnational follower of Jesus within Hindu community)
IBMR	International Bulletin of Missionary Research
IJFM	International Journal of Frontier Missiology
KJV	King James Version
NASB	New American Standard Bible
NBBC	"Non-baptized believers in Christ" (Hoefer 2001b)— See Chapters 5–6
UK	United Kingdom
US	United States

INDIAN ABBREVIATIONS

SC   Scheduled Castes (official, respectful term for Dalit, Outcaste, Untouchable castes)

        May only be Hindu, Sikh, Jain, or Buddhist according to Indian law

ST   Scheduled Tribes (tribals who were not within the original religious communities)

        May be any religion by conversion from former animistic beliefs

OBC   Other Backward Castes/Classes (Disadvantaged castes and classes that are not SC or ST)

NOTES ON BIBLICAL LANGUAGES

This book often references what the original Scriptures say and how they apply to current cultural contexts particularly in India. Because of this, I reference Greek words together with words from various Indian languages.

Primarily I have chosen to transliterate as they are commonly represented using English letters. The following conventions are used for pronunciation of Greek words.

ē	ekklēsia (assembly)	like ay in say; the initial e, in contrast is like "eh"
ō	anthrōpos (man, person)	like long o in bone; the second o is pronounced like short o in not
u	sunagogē	like long u in tune (or oo in soon), not short u like rut
z	baptizō (immerse, baptize)	pronounced like dz in adze
ch	**Ch**ristos (Christ, anointed)	Not ch like church, but like ch in Scottish lo**ch**

CHAPTER 1

THE BARRIER OF CULTURAL SEPARATISM

Everywhere we looked, we saw colorful symbols of clay pots boiling over, smiling suns, and cows with brightly painted horns. My wife and I were on our first visit to India and had arrived in Chennai during *Pongal*, the Tamil harvest festival. Chennai traffic is challenging under normal circumstances; the evening streets were packed with vehicles and people coming and going for the festivities. We wanted to learn a little about what this festival and these symbols meant, so as we rode with an Indian couple, we inquired about what we were seeing.

After several questions, the wife suddenly responded from the back seat, "This is a Hindu festival. The Bible says, 'Come out from among them, and be separate. Touch no unclean thing.' We are Christians, so we have nothing to do with such things." With that, the conversation about Pongal ended.

That abrupt stop nagged at me. I sensed I had touched a nerve. The feeling with which she expressed herself conveyed a deep uneasiness. Our inquiries, it seemed, had pushed beyond her comfort zone.

ENCOUNTERING CHRISTIANITY'S CULTURAL SEPARATISM

Later I reflected with seminary professors and church leaders about the conversation and the uncomfortable conclusion. They indicated, in various conversations, that Isaiah 52:11, "Come out from among them . . . ," has at times defined how many Christians believe they should relate to the Hindu culture around them.

Described by Indian Friends

Indian friends described attitudes and behaviors from some Christians which cause levels of confusion, discomfort, or even offense to some Hindus. The following were a few examples:

- Say "Hindu" with a wrinkled nose and a tone of disdain
- Reject local cultural music as "the devil's music." Accept "Christian" music only (often foreign music in some form)
- Cheer against Indian sports teams or the Indian military
- Avoid Republic Day or Independence Day and refuse to sing the national anthem
- Forbid or discourage wives from wearing *bindi* (forehead dot), *mangalsutra* (wedding necklace), *sindoor* (red paste in hair part), and other jewelry
- Reject Hindu hospitality or offers of *prasad* (food offered at temple), *pongal* (rice), or *laddoo* (temple sweets) in impolite, offensive ways that foster resentment
- Refuse to carry a single piece of Hindu literature for study in colleges and seminary libraries
- Parents forbid children to enter a Hindu person's home because demons live there
- Engagement parties, weddings, and other social gatherings where Christian pastors learned they had Hindus in the audience and launched anti-Hindu diatribes that shamed and turned off Hindus

The spirit I experienced for the first time that night became more apparent in these diverse reports and observations. We now term it "cultural separatism." We have seen or heard its subtle or overt manifestations during every trip to India. Its effects play out at times in news reports of the tensions between Christians and Hindus in India. As I researched and explored the barriers examined in later chapters, this cultural separatism psyche intersected in various ways with each one. It sometimes appeared as a more understated disconnect or disregard for Hindu concerns. Some Christians, though, described overt disrespect or even disdain for the Hindu communities and traditions around them.

Confirmed by Other Indian Voices

These recurring oral accounts of cultural separatism were further confirmed from other Indian sources. In late 2012, an Indian missionary I have long known and respected asked me to read a short paper he had written about why India is so resistant to Jesus. He reiterated several of the items in the list above, but in greater detail. He articulated how these issues have prevented Hindu people from considering or following Jesus.

He confirmed what my Christian friends had observed. Many Indians admire Jesus and respect the Bible. Yet, despite this interest, Christian practices like those above actively keep people from considering Jesus. Sadly, he observed, the spirit of cultural separatism sometimes prevents Christians from even caring that these things might present a barrier. My friends shared his concern, but knew of many who seemed untroubled by the damage their separatist traditions could cause.

In early 2013, the reality of the Christian cultural separatism unexpectedly gripped and broke my heart. I picked up a small volume, *Living Water and Indian Bowl* by Dayanand Bharati. Ten or so pages into his book, Bharati had me in tears as he described the same cultural separatism and Christian barriers that my Christian friends had been identifying for some time. Bharati, though, wrote from Hindu experience. I heard and sensed from a cultural Hindu some of the hurt Hindus feel when exposed to Christians' cultural disregard and disdain. I repeatedly had to put the book down while I wept over further examples of how some Christians actively keep Hindus from Jesus by insensitive and unscriptural traditions.

I finished *Living Water* deeply burdened that cultural separatism was a far deeper barrier than originally suspected, so I purchased several copies and began sharing them with my Indian friends who had already expressed so much concern about these issues. They too began to wrestle at deeper levels with the sources and implications of this all-too-common separatist spirit.

Further research uncovered additional examples of how cultural separatism could keep Hindus from even meeting Jesus. A Christian leader interviewed his father, who had followed Jesus for much of sixty-five years. He asked his father in retrospect, "Would you still take the same course?" Yisu Das Tiwari replied "Christ is my 'ishta' [chosen God], he has never left me, I will never leave him, *but I would not have joined the Christian community*. I would have lived with my people and my community and been a witness to them" (Petersen 2007, 87–88; emphasis mine).

In a second example, D. D. Pani told of a young *Brahmin*[1] man who was studying in another Indian state. He met a Christian missionary there and decided to become a Christian. The missionary, wanting a quick conversion, encouraged him to make the choice without discussing with his parents. Afterwards, when he called to inform his parents of his unilateral decision, they told him never to come home. The missionary recommended that he should just leave his family and have nothing more to do with them. Several decades later, he has never returned to visit his family or village, even after marrying and having children. Pani concludes, "Many would call my friend's life a success story; I consider it a great tragedy" (Pani 2001b, 35).

The spirit of cultural separatism assumed that the family's view should be completely disregarded in a culture where family is intimately involved in every decision. The young man's decision to follow Jesus might have been mediated and discussed in respectful ways. The Christian separatist spirit ignored those possibilities. The missionary's disregard for family led to such insult and offense that the young man had no opportunity to even interact with his family about his desire to become a Christ-follower.

The separatist spirit also contributed to graver social consequences. Pani concludes, "Because he *abandoned his people*, his family and the people of his home locale have become *further polarized against the gospel*. They view him as a *traitor*" (ibid., 36; emphasis mine).

This is a sadly repeated tragedy in India. When Christians do practice such cultural separatism, Hindus rarely view it as an individual's neutral, harmless decision. To some Hindus, as Dayananda Saraswati once put it, conversion is an act of violence against family and community (Saraswati 1999) (detailed in Chapter 5, p. 112).

EXPLORING CHRISTIANITY'S CULTURAL SEPARATISM

In discussing the cultural separatism issues with my Indian friends, several factors became apparent. Believers who followed this spirit honestly

---

1. I will use *Brahmin* to refer to the highest caste in the Hindu system. Technically, some scholars now prefer *Brahman* as more in line with Sanskrit tradition. *Brahmin*, though, is more commonly used in the literature, even among Hindus, when referring to these communities.

believed they were serving and honoring the Lord in doing so. These attitudes and perspectives had been inculcated from generation to generation as the Lord's will for believers.

At the same time, though, a growing number of Indian Christians inherently sense that this cultural separatism is not what Jesus asks or Scripture teaches. The Lord seems to be challenging them to reexamine this long-held tradition with a closer look at God's word.

Ultimately, no matter how it is expressed, cultural separatism arises from a seemingly simple, yet incredibly complex question:

> *What should be the attitude of the followers of Jesus towards those who do not follow Him?* There is a wide variety of possible attitudes, all of which have been adopted by Christian people at different times. Do we despise them, fear them, shun them, tolerate them, condemn them, or seek to serve them? *What is the true responsibility of the church to the world?* (Stott 1976, 173, emphasis mine)

John Stott's question lies at the heart of this chapter and, in fact, the heart of this book. How should followers relate to those who do not follow Jesus? What is their responsibility, if any, to the majority culture that surrounds them? Out of Stott's list of responses, all but one, "serve," reflect some aspect of the separatist spirit.

SCRIPTURAL REFLECTIONS ON CULTURAL SEPARATISM

For some Indian Christians, like our friends at the beginning of this chapter, Isaiah 52:11 seems to provide the definitive answer to Stott's question. For them the church's true responsibility is to "*come out* from among them and be *separate.*" They primarily fear, shun, or condemn Hindus, although some grant a level of suspicious tolerance (see Stott above). Cultural separatism provides the reference point for any discussion of how these believers relate to the Hindu culture around them.

As we examined Scripture, though, we discovered that the word of God raised serious questions about the separatist tradition.

Isaiah 52:11—Foundational Verse for Cultural Separatism

Let's look first at that defining verse, "Come out from among them and be separate, says the Lord, and touch no unclean thing" (Isa 52:11). For many believers in Asia and the Middle East, this verse is interpreted to say that Jesus expects his followers to separate from the socioreligious community around them into a distinct Christian community (and often culture).

If Jesus understood this to be God's will, then we should see clear evidence of such cultural separatism in his own teaching and practice. We should also see this separatist understanding reflected in the lives of those who followed him.

Jesus and Cultural Separatism

On the contrary, Jesus clearly and repeatedly rejected the common separatist interpretation of Isaiah 52:11. The Pharisees personified the cultural separatism view of Isaiah 52:11. In fact, their name meant "Separatists" (Bromiley 1986, 1246; Bauer, et al. 1979, 853). Their traditions expected righteous people to avoid tax collectors, "sinners," [2] Samaritans, lepers, and Gentiles.

Jesus, however, ignored their separatist interpretation. He associated with all these people and more. When the Pharisees questioned him about violating the separatist tradition, Jesus indicated that they neither knew God's mercy nor his will (Matt 9; Luke 15).

He ate and drank with the "wrong" people so often that by Matthew 11 he was labeled a "*friend* of tax collectors and sinners" (Matt 9; Matt 11; emphasis mine). He stayed and ate with Samaritans on at least two occasions (John 4:39–43; Luke 9:51–56). He touched unclean lepers to heal them (Matt 8:3). Women touched him publicly, and he did not shame them or reject their calls for help. At every opportunity, Jesus, by his practice, challenged the separatist hermeneutic (interpretive framework) of the

---

2. The term "sinners" in these passages was a derogatory term used by the Pharisees for people who did not follow their restrictive laws and traditions. To the Pharisees they were the "wrong" kind of people. Their touch or shadow would defile you and require rituals and baths for purification. Eating with them was out of the question if you wanted to be a holy, righteous person. So, when Jesus is called a "friend of tax-collectors and sinners" He chooses to be a friend to those the separatist spirit said to avoid.

Pharisees. According to Jesus, their separatist understanding of Scripture was not God's will.

When Jesus associated with tax collectors and sinners, he was modeling the genuine separated and holy life that God intended. He did not exemplify extraction, isolation, separation, and self-protection. He instead modeled engagement, incarnation, and selfless service.

Today, I believe, he would live the same way in India among Hindus. Based on Jesus' life and example, I am convinced that Jesus would associate with Hindus so often and so well that he would be known as a "friend of Hindus." That is his starting point for the question, *how should believers relate to the culture around them?* It should also be the starting point for those who follow him today.

Jesus replaced the isolationist, separatist hermeneutic of the Old Covenant with an incarnational servant hermeneutic in the New Covenant. As Paul says in Ephesians 2:14f. Jesus destroyed the dividing wall that kept Jews and Gentiles separated by the Old Testament's law and commandments. The separatist hermeneutic and assumption of the Old Covenant died with Jesus.

In the New Testament, then, these Old Testament verses should be read from an incarnational perspective, not assuming the cultural extraction and separation of the Old Covenant. This hermeneutical challenge lies at the heart of the barrier of cultural separatism. Even Old Testament separatist passages like Isaiah 52:11 must now be viewed through the New Testament's incarnational lens (more on this below when we look at Paul).

As Jesus was finishing his time on earth, he specifically told his followers that they would disciple *all nations* (Matt 28), proclaim good news to *all creation* (Mark 16), announce forgiveness of sins to *all nations* (Luke 24), and be his witnesses not only to Jerusalem and Judea, but even to *Samaria and the ends of the earth* (Acts 1:8). In other words, he specifically commanded them to go to the very people the Jewish law and tradition had told them to avoid for centuries. Let's explore some examples of how that incarnational shift happened.

Undoing Jewish Cultural Separatism

In Acts 1–7 the followers of Jesus only came from the Jews living in and visiting Jerusalem. In Acts 8, however, a deacon named Philip decided to evangelize the Samaritans. We are not told why he was the one to do this.

No apostles initiated this outreach, even though Jesus had modeled compassion for Samaritans on several occasions. Jesus was moving his people to break down the old cultural separatism and fulfill Acts 1:8.

Then came Peter's turn. He initially lived by the Jewish separation rules: "No orthodox Jew would ever enter the home of a Gentile, even a God-fearer, or invite such into his home. On the contrary . . . 'no pious Jew would . . . have sat down at the table of a Gentile'" (Stott 1990, 185). God, however, did not allow Peter to persist in this cultural separatism.

In Acts 10 God used a sheet with "unclean" animals to first tell Peter that the old rules about unclean foods no longer applied: "What God has cleansed no longer consider unholy" (Acts 10:15 NASB). This happened three times (divine number) to make sure that Peter clearly understood that God meant business. The Old Testament food laws had partly been designed to keep Jews from eating with, thus associating with, Gentiles. They were part of the Old Covenant's separatist hermeneutic. Jesus had already taught that this law was obsolete (Mark 7:19). Now God dramatically reiterated that in the New Covenant the dietary exclusions that separated Jews from Gentiles were indeed gone.

The sheet was God's way of telling Peter and all believers, those separatist rules were finished, *the separatist hermeneutic* no longer applied. God knew he had to first challenge the hermeneutic, the separatist understanding of Scripture, before he could challenge Peter's separatist practice. Once God cleared up the obsolete interpretation, he then could direct Peter in a new, incarnational practice.

The next thing Peter knew, he had been invited by some strangers to come to the house of a Roman Centurion in Caesarea. Cornelius was a Gentile, an officer of the occupying imperial army. Upon entering this Gentile home, Peter realized the full implications of God's lesson from the sheet. He said, "You yourselves know how unlawful it is for a man who is a Jew to associate with a foreigner or to visit him; and yet God has shown me that I should not call any man unholy or unclean" (Acts 10:28 NASB). The sheet wasn't about food; it was about relationships with those outside the faith; it was how Jews were to relate with Gentiles. Cultural separatism was no longer God's will, cultural identification and incarnation was the new normal.

Paul and Jewish Cultural Separatism

So, what about Paul's experience with cultural separatism? Before he came to Jesus, Paul was himself a Pharisee, a separatist. He was raised and trained in the cultural separatism of that Jewish sect. Yet, when the Lord called him to be an apostle to the Gentiles (Gal 1:15f.; Rom 11:13), he embraced that call and engaged with the Gentile culture. We can't fully appreciate how much of a personal change Paul experienced to work among the people he had once despised and avoided at all costs.

Paul's Foundational Ministry Principle

In his ministry, Paul clearly followed a path of engagement with Gentiles, not extraction. his foundational ministry principle was, "I have become all things to all people, that by all means I might save some." (1 Cor 9:22 ESV). Paul specifically mentioned becoming as "one without the Law to those without the Law," a reference to Gentiles who did not have the Law of Moses.

Paul had to let go of his former Jewish separatism to "become all things" to the different Gentile groups where he worked. When he spoke with Gentiles, he used Greek (Acts 21:37), but he shifted to fluent Hebrew when speaking to Jews (Acts 21:40–22:2). He used his Roman citizenship at critical moments, rather than rejecting and denying it (Acts 16:37–39; 22:25–29). He engaged with the Gentile world. He stayed in their homes, he ate their food, he went to their bath houses. He adopted their way of life, as much as possible, so that they could see Jesus in his (Paul's) life within their context.

In "becoming all things to all people," Paul followed in the steps of his Master. Just as Jesus ate and drank with those who had once been considered unclean and untouchable, so did Paul.

"Come Out from Among Them and Be Separate"
(2 Cor 6:17)—Paul's Perspective

When Paul quoted Isaiah 52:11 in 2 Corinthians 6:17, was he telling the Corinthians to abandon, forsake, and reject their culture in its entirety? Was he instructing them to leave their family and community to join a separatist Christian cultural enclave (or "Christian colony" as some places in India have)? Absolutely not! That was the farthest thing from his mind. How do I know that? He explains what he meant in 1 Corinthians 5:9f.:

> I wrote to you in my letter not to associate with sexually immoral people—not at all meaning the sexually immoral of this world, or the greedy and swindlers, or idolaters, since then you would need to go out of the world. (ESV)

Paul told the Corinthians that they should *not* avoid the people of this world, including even idolaters. To do so would require leaving the world. This passage specifically says that believers are to associate with such people in the world (culture), not disassociate from them. Paul's discussion of a variety of cultural challenges in 1 Corinthians 8–10 only makes sense if the believers were engaged with their culture, rather than extracted from it.

2 Corinthians 6:17 clearly warns believers against joining too tightly with unbelievers and being influenced by them to turn from the Lord. "There were entangling alliances," Witherington comments, "from which the Corinthians needed to disengage themselves . . . These alliances involved *koinōnia* (participation, fellowship) with nonbelievers in pagan temples, and, worse, involvement with false believers" (Witherington III 1995, 406).

As with many Scriptures that seem to advocate opposite extremes, the will of the Lord is found in a Spirit-led balance between 1 Corinthians 5:9–10 and 2 Corinthians 6:17. Neither is the final word on how believers relate to the culture around them. We are called to engage and interact with the culture, not separate from it, but we are also called not to engage so closely with the culture that it draws us away from Jesus.

We have seen, then, that Isaiah 52:11 must not be used in the separatist spirit of the Old Covenant. Jesus rejected that spirit and called his followers to become incarnational rather than isolationist. That is not the only verse, though, that Christians use to inculcate a separatist spirit in believers. Let's look at one more example of how we must rightly interpret Scriptures commonly used for separatist teachings.

Leave Father and Mother (Matt 19)

A critique of insider movements uses Matthew 19:29 and other verses to assert, "Jesus was clear in his call that when we come to him we *abandon everything including family and possessions*" (Houssney 2010; emphasis mine). Some Christians in certain global contexts insist that Jesus taught such absolute abandonment or cultural separatism. It seems to have been standard teaching in Asia and the Middle East since the dawn of Protestant missions.

An early Indian convert, Dewan Appasamy, describes this family separation in his own testimony: "In those days missionaries did their best to prevent all social intercourse between Christians and the Hindus related to them, for fear that these Christians might relapse . . . The result was that they kept exclusively to themselves . . . and were cut off from all opportunity of influencing their Hindu relatives" (D. A. Appasamy 1924, 48). Notice how he admits (50 years after his conversion) that cutting off relationships kept Hindu relatives from meeting Jesus. This is the barrier of cultural separatism to the extreme.

Did Jesus really teach his followers to *abandon* their parents, their family, and their culture? You do not have to leave Matthew 19 to demonstrate that Jesus did not understand "leave" to mean abandon. In a discussion of divorce, Jesus quoted Genesis 2:24, "For this reason, a man shall *leave his father and mother*, . . . " (Matt 19:5; emphasis mine).

Do Christians anywhere in the world tell a husband that when he marries, he must abandon, forsake, and reject his father and mother before he can marry his bride? No one teaches that! Why? Because all Christians understand that Jesus did not, in fact could not, understand "leave" to mean "abandon" in Matthew 19:5. The new relationship must take priority over the parental relationship, yes, but abandon and forsake parents? Every believer knows that Jesus did not understand "leave" in that way!

If a man does not abandon his parents to marry his wife (verse 5), then he should not abandon his parents to follow Jesus either (verse 29).[3] Christians who teach cultural separatism from this verse misrepresent

---

3. If you checked your Greek, good for you! There are two words (*kataleipō*—19:5, *aphiēmi*—19:29). An Indian friend pointed out to me, though, that the two are used interchangeably as synonyms in Mark 12:18–22, both mean "leave," that's why they are both translated that way. Jesus likely had the same idea in mind in both places. If anything, *kataleipō* in verse 5 is the stronger word, so if it cannot mean abandon, then the weaker *aphiemi* cannot mean abandon in verse 29 (no dictionary gives "abandon" as a meaning of that word).

what Jesus understood by leave. He understood the same idea of relative relational priority, not absolute abandonment. The "abandon" interpretation does not come from Jesus (verse 5), but represents a return to the Old Covenant separatist hermeneutic that Jesus rejected and nailed to the cross.

Reread Scriptures with Incarnational Assumptions

Space does not allow exhaustive treatment of every scripture used to justify cultural separatism. Those above are the most commonly cited and provide representative examples. In these and most others, if you begin with a tradition of cultural separatism, you can read that into every passage. We call that method of Bible study *eisegesis* (reading into the text what we already assume that it says). This use of the Bible does not seek what Scripture says, but uses Scripture to bolster and proof-text existing tradition.

Jesus' engagement as "friend of sinners" and Paul's principle of "become all things to all people" both challenge the cultural separatism tradition. Read Scripture with the incarnational principle of Jesus and Paul in mind, and we see that cultural separatism has been imposed on numerous passages.

When Christians assert, "The Bible says . . ." to justify cultural separatism, they may quote the words of the Bible, but they make it mean what human tradition teaches. As with "come out from among them," their teaching may actually contradict the plain example and teaching of Jesus. Their teaching misuses Scripture to support human anti-cultural tradition.

What should be the fundamental relationship between followers and those who do not yet know Jesus? Between believers and the culture around them? The Old Covenant separatist spirit teaches people their primary responsibility is to

> Abandon or avoid,
>   Extract,
>   Forsake,
>   Isolate,
>   Reject,
>   Separate.

In contrast, the New Covenant's incarnational spirit, the spirit of Jesus, calls believers to

Associate not avoid;
Engage not extract;
Befriend not forsake;
Identify and incarnate not isolate;
Restore, reconcile, and redeem not reject;
Serve among, not separate from.

We have seen, then, that Jesus did not follow the spirit of cultural separatism. Peter and Paul were challenged to reject that spirit also. What about believers in general?

Did New Testament Believers Extract and Separate?

If New Testament believers were called to cultural separatism, then we should see them extract into a separate Christian culture just as Christians have been told to do in much of the world today, but did that happen? *Jews* did not extract into a separate Christian community on the day of Pentecost or later. Yes, Acts 5:13 says "None of the rest dared associate with them" (in the temple gatherings), but it also says that those same outsiders "held them in high esteem"—not that they despised and hated them. They did not leave, abandon, and reject their culture and community. In fact, the next verse speaks of multitudes who constantly joined their number. The "separation" here, if any existed, was more psychological, clearly not social or communal.

When they began to follow Jesus, they spoke the same language, wore the same Jewish clothes, mostly kept their same names,[4] ate the same Jewish food, followed the same Jewish laws, attended the same Jewish festivals, participated in the same Jewish times of prayer, and attended the same Jewish synagogues. How did Jews know they were different the day after Acts 2? Not by any of these common cultural markers. They were Jewish followers of Jesus, not extracted, separatist followers of Jesus.

---

4. Paul did switch from his Jewish Bible name to his Roman cultural name to build a bridge to his Gentile audience. He did not change names to separate himself from the culture and he did not change names at conversion.

Donald McGavran accurately portrays the early situation in his pivotal work, *The Bridges of God*:

> The early Church grew *within* Judaism. For at least a decade the Jews who were becoming Christians were not conscious at all of joining a non-Jewish religion. Had they dreamed that this was a possibility many of them would never have become Christians. Even after they were changed by fellowship with the Living Christ, they refused to accept Gentile Christians as full members of the Jewish Christian people. (McGavran 1961, 22–23)

No cultural extraction and separation took place. As Jewish believers in Jesus walked down the street, went to the market, or entered the temple at the hours of prayer, you could not visibly distinguish them from Jews who did not believe in Jesus. Any attitudes and behaviors that changed because of Jesus were expressed within Jewish cultural forms. Their allegiance to Jesus did not essentially separate them from their culture. Eventually, some Jews rejected them because they claimed Jesus as Messiah, but they did not separate and reject their culture and community as an inherent part of coming to Jesus. They continued to be socioreligious Jews who followed Jesus even when some Jews rejected them.

So, what about *Greeks or Romans* when they came to Jesus? Did they leave their culture and community and join a separate "Christian culture"? We have absolutely no evidence for that. Some Jewish believers insisted that Gentiles should separate from their culture and adopt Jewish culture (circumcision, food laws) to follow Jesus (Acts 15; Gal). The Jerusalem Council responded, though, with a resounding "No!" Greeks and Romans were to follow Jesus within their culture, not extract to someone else's culture. In other words, the Holy Spirit led the Jerusalem Council to choose cultural incarnation (within culture), *not* cultural separation (to a separate culture).

The New Testament, then, provides no evidence that the apostles taught *cultural separatism* for Jews, Greeks, or Romans to follow Jesus. They engaged with the non-believers in their culture, associated with them, socialized with them, and ate with them, even running the risk of food sacrificed to idols (1 Cor 10:25–27). We cannot derive cultural separatism from the examples of New Testament believers any more than we can from Jesus, Peter, or Paul.

In summary, then, the New Testament does not reflect the cultural separatism tradition that Indian Christians have been commonly taught.

PRACTICAL AND PASTORAL REFLECTIONS ON CULTURAL SEPARATISM

If the tradition of cultural separatism is not required of believers, how do we respond? What are the implications for those who follow and represent Jesus in places where separatism has been taught and has become a defining feature of what it means to be a Christian?

Undo the Mindset of Cultural Separatism

David Bosch, a South African missiologist, observed: "The Christian faith is intrinsically incarnational; therefore, unless the church chooses to remain a foreign entity, it will always enter into the context in which it happens to find itself" (Bosch 1996, 190–191). The tradition of cultural separatism, rather than being faithful to the Christian faith, counters this intrinsic incarnational impetus that Jesus both modeled and taught.

One implication of our study should be clear. Since Jesus actively opposed cultural separatism and chose engagement, we should follow his lead, not Christian tradition. The Way of Jesus is the way of engagement and incarnation, not a way of extraction and isolation.

Yes, we must teach people to love Jesus more than family and culture. However, we should also teach them that this does not require them to abandon, reject, and separate from their loved ones, or to initiate controversial stances that will antagonize and ensure that a break occurs. Jesus did not teach this, and neither should Christians.

"One of the hardest things in the world to unlearn is exclusiveness," observed William Barclay in discussing John 10:16 (Barclay 1972, 73). This chapter has illustrated that reality. When people decide to follow Jesus, whether Christians or Yesu bhaktas, we must specifically teach them not to be separatist and exclusivist. Given the human propensity to separation, this requires intentional and intensive coaching in how to incarnate the way and life of Jesus within culture, not extract to a separate, foreign culture. We must encourage believers, as much as possible, to live at peace with family and community (Rom 12:18), not to create tension and conflict whether inadvertently or intentionally.

Believers in the Workplace

The workplace provides a critical connection point where cultural separatism could be naturally overcome and engagement principles be worked out instead. I have Christian friends who once decried having to work in a "Hindu" company, who prayed and hoped for a position in a "Christian" company.

After wrestling with these considerations, they now recount how their workplace is their primary place of *seva* (service) to the Lord. As they go about their work in ways that honor Jesus, Hindus see their diligence, their integrity, and their selfless service to others inside and outside the company. As they interact and converse, instead of avoiding and isolating, they are seeing doors open for respectful conversation with those around them.

Believers in the workplace can naturally cross caste and communal barriers professional clergy often cannot (see Chapter 8, p. 203). If equipped with a non-separatist spirit, and a genuine relationship with Jesus, workplace believers can naturally introduce people to Jesus in India.

Incarnational Believers

Today, many Christians debate the legitimacy of what they term "insider" believers. This very terminology, however, betrays a separatist, extractionist psyche—a spirit, we have seen, that is counter to that of Jesus and the New Testament believers. By calling them "insiders," this term implies that "Christians" are, by nature "outsiders." For some Christians, being a true believer requires one to be an "outsider" believer; in other words, a separatist. Believers who stay "inside" the culture or community, or who retain respectful, close relationships, can be questioned for their lack of "separation."

The term "insider" has long use, but it is often used in disparaging ways by those who oppose respectful engagement with Muslim, Hindu, or other socioreligious cultures. Because of the separatist assumptions that underlie the term, I prefer "incarnational believers." They are following Jesus' call to incarnate his life within their culture, rather than to extract and isolate from it in an unscriptural way.

The issues around insider or incarnational paradigms are complex. For a positive articulation of why believers should be incarnational, see *Understanding Insider Movements* (Talman and Travis 2015), a compilation by the foremost practitioners and scholars in the field. This explanation of the incarnational paradigm was written to articulate the sound biblical and missiological grounds for such approaches in the face of charges that these are unfaithful departures from the way of Jesus.

Had Jesus chosen an "outsider" path, there might be no incarnation, no identification. By incarnating within human society and Jewish culture, Jesus became an "insider," not an outsider, yet he clearly challenged aspects of the culture that were not in agreement with God's will. Paul's principle of "all things to all men" calls cross-cultural workers, similarly, to become as incarnational as possible, rather than as separated and disengaged as possible. The Jerusalem Council rejected separatism and mandated that believers should follow Jesus within their cultural context and community, not extract to someone else's culture.

CHRISTIAN AND BHAKTA CONSIDERATIONS

If Jesus calls his people to imitate his incarnational spirit, not the Old Covenant's extractional one, all believers must consider the implications for their walk with the Lord and their relationship with the socioreligious community around them. The insider-outsider terminology is rooted in the Old Covenant separatist paradigm. It has also been used, in disobedience to Scripture, to label and judge believers who hold a different view of how they should live incarnationally (Rom 14–15).

We should instead view the incarnational paradigm as a spectrum. Christians who remain in their Christian community and identity will need to examine their stances in light of this scriptural understanding. This incarnational perspective has led some to address separatist attitudes and behaviors in order to better reflect the spirit of Jesus to those around them. At the same time, Yesu bhaktas lie further along the incarnational spectrum by remaining within their Hindu community and society to follow Jesus. They must navigate how Jesus wants them to live faithfully for him within that context.

In each chapter, then, I will suggest some implications of the incarnational paradigm/spectrum for Christians and bhaktas.

Christians

Just as the Apostle Paul "became all things to all men," followers of Jesus in India should continue to adopt that incarnational principle, not cultural separatism, as the starting point for their relationship to the culture around them. Paul faced a culture that had many issues. It had idolatry, religious practices, and many immoral and unjust elements. He did not avoid and extract from that world. He "became all things to all people," entered those cultures and communities, and incarnated the life of Jesus within those towns and cities.

My Indian Christian colleagues had recognized and been troubled for decades by the cultural separatism they had seen and experienced, sometimes in their own lives, more often in the practice of other Christians. They were working hard to remove the negative, anti-cultural spirit, where it existed, from their thoughts and speech. They actively pursued more meaningful ways to engage respectfully with Hindu people in their neighborhoods and workplaces.

They continue to dig deeper into these issues, to study and learn Hindu beliefs and practices, to seek bridges and openings to share Jesus in respectful ways. They more intentionally talk with Hindus to hear their diverse beliefs, to understand their diverse perspectives, rather than just give their "gospel" with no consideration of those with whom they speak (see Chapter 4).

They continue to courageously explore the implications of these questions regarding how they live, how they worship, and how they witness. This conversation is an ongoing, repeatedly disruptive process for all on this journey. At times, it has brought tears; at others, intense discussion. But all are committed to following the incarnational way of Jesus more carefully, rather than perpetuating Christian separatist traditions.

Because of the incredibly complex relationships between castes and communities in India, those considerations often lie near the surface of any discussion regarding interreligious relationships, even among Christians (see Chapter 3, p. 53). There are no quick and easy answers to these questions that have vexed Indian believers for generations. My friends continue to graciously and patiently walk with each other through complex discussions about what it means to live out the grace and good news of Jesus instead of the cultural separation and extraction of Christianity.

In some segments of Indian society, the best choice may be for followers to join a Christian community, but where this happens, they should be taught to do so in as incarnational a way as possible, rather than as separatist as possible. "As far as possible, be at peace with all men" (Rom 12:18) ought to guide discussions with family and community, rather than an antagonistic assumption of alienation and extraction.

Those concerns cannot be addressed overnight. They may take as long to overcome as some Christians and society at large took to create them in the first place. Where it exists, though, Christians must address and relinquish the separatist spirit first, before approaching Hindus. If Christians don't deal with that underlying spirit, Hindus will quickly detect it and continue to resent it.

Yesu Bhaktas

Bhaktas have made a more radical incarnational choice to follow Jesus as their *ishta devata* (chosen God)[5] within their Hindu family, culture, and community. For believers who have followed Jesus without separating from their culture, this chapter presents good news. It helps to show how this choice can be both scriptural and faithful to Jesus.

Even when they follow the incarnational path and follow Jesus within their community, this does not negate Jesus' warnings about the cost of following him. Some family or community members may find their choice to follow Jesus offensive. Their decision may not prevent family conflict that Jesus said could occur (Matt 10:21f.; Luke 12:51f.). I have a bhakta friend who lives with and cares for his aged Hindu mother. Despite his devotion to her, she finds ways to criticize him regularly for his choice to be a bhakta. The division often pains his heart. The choice to remain within their culture is not intended to nor will it avoid all opposition or persecution. They have made a scriptural decision, though, to live out their faith, whatever the cost, among their people, not away from them.

Just because they do not follow Christian tradition does not make bhaktas disloyal to the Lord or his word. Christian tradition is not the

---

5.   Hindu term for one's "God of personal preference" (Bharati 2005, 66) or "deity of choice" (Klostermaier 2003, 86). They can also have a *kul devata/devam* (family or clan god) along with village and more regional gods.

norm by which devotion to the Lord is measured. Only Scripture provides the standard for what the Lord finds faithful or unfaithful.

CLOSING REFLECTIONS

The separatist spirit of the couple at the start of this chapter kept them from exploring the significance of Pongal and the ubiquitous pot that symbolizes it. I had to ask Hindus and research Hindu writing to discover what that overflowing pot meant. Come to find out, the Pongal clay pot (Pongal *paanai*) represents a fragile human life. The overflowing, boiling rice signifies the blessing of God that the pot both contains and shares.

For believers, that calls to mind 2 Corinthians 4:7, "We have this treasure [God's glory and light] in earthen vessels (clay pots)." Had I ignored the festival as the couple implied, I would have missed that parallel entirely. An incarnational, respectful spirit, though, can see the pot as a conversational bridge from Hindu experience to the way of Jesus. Hindus and believers are speaking the same "clay pot" language here.

May the Lord help all his people, bhaktas and Christians alike, to be incarnational clay pots (*paanai*) of his glory and blessing to the people of India.

CHAPTER 2

THE BARRIER OF "CHRISTIAN"

I was flying back to the US from a visit to India when I struck up a conversation with the Indian woman sitting next to me. She disclosed that she was a Christian converted from a Hindu family with her mother and brother some fifteen years ago. Her father, however, remained staunchly opposed to Jesus because of many inconsistencies he saw in Christians and churches. "I just keep telling him," she stated, "don't look at Christians or churches, just look at Jesus."

I gently replied, "But what can your father do when he cannot see Jesus because of Christians and churches?" If her father, and millions of Hindus like him, are ever to meet Jesus, we must honestly examine the barrier presented by "Christian" and "Christianity" (we'll save churches for the next chapter).

"CHRISTIAN" IDENTITY CAN KEEP HINDUS FROM JESUS

Over the years several Indian friends have asked Hindus what they think about Christians, churches, and Jesus. What have they found? Hindus often express a positive view of Jesus' character and teaching, when they know about him. Some Hindus reject Jesus outright, but a considerable number have appreciated, even revered him and continue to do so today. "Though we are Hindus, we cannot help admiring the superior and exalted ethics which Christ brings to us," could still describe the sentiments of many Hindus (Sen 1884, 93).

Even when they admire Jesus, though, they may still identify negative perceptions about Christians or Christianity. Wherever I discuss this with Christian groups, they commonly acknowledge the pattern—respect for Jesus, but disrespect or disdain for Christians and Christianity.

This phenomenon is not unique to India or Hindus by any means. I know Western Christians who have faced anger or abuse when they mentioned the name of Jesus. Upon further investigation, though, the anger rarely derived from Jesus himself. They too recount instances where the person's antagonism arose from something Christians or churches had done, not from Jesus himself. We should not be completely surprised, then, if Christians and churches present a similar barrier to Jesus among Indians.

Jesus Is Not the Barrier

Many Hindus find aspects of the life and teaching of Jesus that resonate with their own spiritual aspirations, though their knowledge of Jesus is not complete. Gandhi and Vivekananda, for example, represent Hindus who speak highly of the character and teachings of Jesus, while not fully accepting his claims. They start, though, from a positive view of Jesus, rather than negative perceptions. Jesus himself, in other words, is not the primary barrier.

Nearly a century ago E. Stanley Jones, missionary statesman to India, reflected, "*I have dropped out the term 'Christianity'* from my announcements (it isn't found in the Scriptures, is it?), for it had connotations that confused" (Jones 1926, 26–27; emphasis mine). When he did, substantially more Hindus attended his roundtable discussions to learn about Jesus. Based on years of work with Hindus, the Kannans observed more recently, "Though high-caste people often have a high regard for Christ and the Bible, *they do not want to identify with Christianity*" (Kannan and Kannan 2001, 166; emphasis mine).

A long-term researcher into India's resistance to Christianity, H. L. Richard once observed, "The problem is . . . a default in every Hindu understanding that blends Christ, Christianity, church, and Western civilization. It is a package, and that is why they are so slow to come . . . *there is this whole Christian package*" (Gill 2009, 184; emphasis mine). Menezes and Menon, in an exposé of conversion practices, interviewed a theologian from Mumbai who said, "In the eyes of both militant and non-militant Hindus, *all Christians are the same*" (Menezes and Menon 1999; emphasis mine). From India's collectivist cultural perspective, the actions of a few Christians can be considered the responsibility of all. There is a tendency to ascribe communal guilt, rather than individual responsibility as in the West.

These examples indicate that Hindus will not consider following Jesus, if Christian and Christianity are required, no matter how much they admire him. Given India's challenge, I'm not sure that Jones went far enough. He dropped "Christianity" from his announcements because the name kept Hindus from hearing about Jesus, yet his book reflected his agenda to Christianize India. In his initial conversation with Gandhi about missionary strategy, he specified, "I am very anxious to see Christianity naturalized in India" (Jones 1926, 126). Not Jesus naturalized, but Christianity naturalized! He found it impossible to separate Jesus from Christianity's traditions and assumptions. Christianity, for Jones, was ultimately essential; he only temporarily removed the label to reduce confusion.

If India is ever to truly meet Jesus, we must address this assumption that Christianity is a proxy for Jesus and his teaching, and Christian an essential identity for his followers. Several aspects of India's resistance require us to fundamentally reexamine these associations. I believe we need to honestly ask and wrestle with what may seem an unsettling question at first:

Do you have to become a Christian to genuinely follow Jesus?

Christ Covered by "Their Christianity"

A Hindu man once told Jones, "We have been unwilling to receive Christ into our hearts, but we alone are not responsible for this. *Christian missionaries have held out Christ completely covered by their Christianity*" (ibid., 31; emphasis mine).

The man who originally said that referred specifically to foreign missionaries and "their Christianity." The foreign traditions, the denominations, the alien expressions, practices, and architecture of "their Christianity" hindered many Hindus from considering or following Jesus.

Some missionaries, Ziegenbalg and Carey for example, expended great effort to learn and understand Indian languages, cultures and religious beliefs, sometimes facing criticism from European supporters for doing so. Yet despite their efforts, they all taught that following Jesus required one to become a Christian, to adopt a Christianity that still reflected traditions from the missionaries' home cultures and communities. In effect, missionaries often answered our question, "Yes, you have to become a *Western-flavored Christian* to genuinely follow Jesus."

In the last century, most foreign missionaries have gone home. In India today, Christianity presents a vibrant mix of foreign and *desi* (local) influences. Indian Christians have made Christianity their own, and flavored it with their local and regional *masalas* (spices). In the face of charges that Christianity is foreign, believers have worked hard to establish that they follow an "Indian Christianity," a Christianity deeply rooted and indigenized in their own context. It is genuinely "their Christianity," not just that of someone's foreign culture.

Despite these efforts, though, H. L. Richard rightly observes that most Christian attempts at cultural adaptation in the twentieth century aimed for believers "to become both *fully Indian* and *fully Christian*" (Richard 1998, 106). Even with all this Indianization or indigenization or contextualization, the fundamental "Christian" barrier remains. A Hindu today could easily say, "Indian Christians have held out Christ completely covered by *their Christianity*." These Indian Christians seem to answer our question, "Yes, you have to become an *Indian Christian* to genuinely follow Jesus."

An Indian Christian himself, N. V. Tilak, once wrote, "India needs Christ, not so much Christianity" (ibid., 87). He dedicated his life to deeply contextualizing Christianity in Indian forms and expressions and still faced significant resistance. He ended up realizing that Christian identity itself could present a barrier, no matter how adapted to the culture one tried to make it.

STATISTICAL EVIDENCE FOR THE BARRIER OF "CHRISTIAN"

Segments of Hindu society today still seem troubled by Indians who practice "their Christianity," no matter how Indianized it might be. They continue to evidence a deep reticence toward the name or identity of "Christian" in any form. How do we know that the name "Christian" is a barrier in India? According to the 2011 Indian census, 2.3 percent of Indians were identified as "Christians" (India Census 2011).[6] A recent estimate indicates that 5.1 percent of India's population is somehow connected to Jesus (Joshua Project 2016b). If that number is at all reliable, then more than half of Indian followers of Jesus (2.8 percent) do not identify themselves as "Christians" for various reasons. In raw numbers, that represents about 30 million Indians who identify as Christians,

---

6.   The 2001 Census also returned 2.3 percent Christian (India Census 2001).

while 35 million follow Jesus without Christian identity. We must consider what drives this significant hesitation to assume a Christian identity.

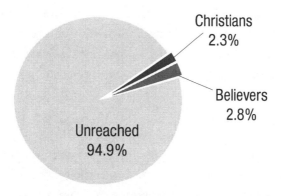

Figure 1. Christians, Believers, and Others in India

Several factors contribute to this significant avoidance of "Christian" identity in India. Christians have occasionally told me that they declared as "Christians," but saw the census-taker mark "Hindu" on the form. Conversations and research indicate that significant numbers keep their "Hindu" identity to preserve their access to government quotas for education and jobs. These positions are lost immediately upon conversion to Christianity or Islam (Government of India 2014, 62). Some likely do not declare as Christians to avoid persecution or family conflict. They may see themselves, or be labeled as, "Crypto-Christians" (Sharma, S. 2014).

A significant number of these believers, though, choose to follow Jesus only, yet remain within their Hindu cultures and communities as Yesu bhaktas. They will never take a "Christian" identity; in fact, they refuse to do so. Culturally and socially they are Hindus, but spiritually they follow Jesus alone. This is not the same as Hindus who put images of Jesus on their god shelf along with their Hindu gods, demonstrating India's prevalent pluralism.

The Yesu bhaktas, though, follow and worship Jesus alone, using Hindu cultural forms within their Hindu social and cultural communities. A bhakta leader pointed out to me, "If any Yesu-bhakta worshiped Muktinath (Jesus) along with other deities then it could be termed as 'syncretism,' and the *mandali* [ekklēsia, fellowship] would deal with it" (private email).

These believers are not practicing syncretism, despite some Christian claims; they are following Jesus within their cultural setting.

No matter the cause, all these options indicate that "Christian" is a problematic identity in India. This is India's ground reality. Right now, today, over half the believers in India answer our question: *"No, you do not have to become a 'Christian' to genuinely follow Jesus."* Are they being unfaithful to Jesus in making this choice, by not adopting the name or label of Christian?

Initial Definitions of Christian and Christianity

Later in this chapter, we will discuss scriptural definitions of "Christian" and "Christianity" and their contribution to the barriers. For now, let me provide initial working definitions in terms of common perception.

"Christianity" as I will use it in the next sections, represents *what Christians both believe and practice*. As such, it is not just the teaching of Jesus, but accumulated systems and expressions that have developed around that teaching since the end of the New Testament era. When most people think of Christianity, they do not just think of Jesus and his way; they also picture the forms, expressions, and institutions by which global believers have chosen to represent him. The systems of Christianity seem inseparable from the Savior they claim to represent. Different believers invest the institution and system with varying levels of authority and essentiality, further complicating our understanding of what constitutes "Christianity." Is it just what the New Testament teaches or is it also everything Christians have created since then—denominations and hierarchies, organizations, creeds and faith statements, doctrinal systems, liturgies and rituals, customs and expressions, rules and regulations?

I will use "Christian" initially for one who follows Christianity. Christians assert that the name "Christian" simply means "Christ-follower." Despite their assertions, though, few use it in this way. For many denominations, for instance, a true "Christian" is one who subscribes to their particular creedal requirements, or institutional expectations, or doctrinal formulations. Simply following Jesus is not enough; a believer must also associate with the right kind of church or churches to be a "genuine Christian."

For people outside Christianity, in addition, the name "Christian" can represent a conglomeration of connotations: church members, cultural traitors, Europeans and Americans in general, plus other considerations. Christians can argue against these associations, but, as we will see, this confusion about "Christian" presents a substantial barrier.

INADEQUATE RESPONSES TO THE "CHRISTIAN" BARRIER

Christians themselves recognize that this barrier of Christian identity requires some cultural and scriptural consideration. Let's first look at some ways believers have sought to address the Christian barrier in India.

Ignore the Barrier

Some Christians ignore the barrier altogether. They simply perpetuate their Christian traditions, assuming they are being faithful to Jesus in doing so. They might assert something like, "We are Christians and will continue to practice our Christianity as we always have. That is our Christian tradition."

Such Christians insisted that they need not adapt their expression to the culture around them, primarily ignoring Paul's principle of "becoming all things to all people." Some preserved specific languages (Syriac, Greek, Latin, English) while others maintained liturgical or architectural forms familiar to their own Christian culture.

Such cultural expressions of Christianity reached and will continue to serve certain segments and social groupings within India. At the same time, a substantial number of Hindus,[7] kept from Christ for centuries, may remain largely alienated from Jesus because the fundamental barrier of "Christian" remains unaddressed.

Like the Jewish believers in Jerusalem (Acts 15) who expected Gentiles to adopt their traditions, Christians can expect new believers to adapt to their cultural expression of faith in Jesus. Followers are expected to become "Christians" and to express their faith using the cultural forms of the Christians who convert them.

---

7.   According to the 2011 census, there were 960 million Hindus (India Census 2011). The Dalit populations of Hindus (200 million), are the originating communities for 75 percent of Christians (IDSN 2013). The remaining 760 million Hindus are primarily unresponsive to Christian approaches and expressions.

This issue of cultural forms, in other words, is not just a matter of Western forms. Indian Christians may be equally responsible for locking their Christianity into local cultural forms, then requiring new believers elsewhere in India to only follow "their Christianity" from another region or state.

Reform Christianity's Packaging

Some Christians, though, recognized that their cultural accretions kept people from Jesus. They addressed these at different levels both in India and elsewhere. Reformation, restoration, and even contextualization efforts attempted to remove layers of human tradition, to introduce people to a purer "Christianity." Recent movements to rethink, retool, reset, and re-church all reflect similar attempts to address Christianity's cultural baggage. They generally assume, though, that "Christian" is an essential core that must be preserved. In this view, some elements might need to be somewhat adjusted. Christian, though, remains an unquestioned core of what it means to belong to and follow Jesus.

In India, diverse groups have developed forms of "Indian Christianity," "Indian theology," or "Dalit theology" (Sumithra 1990). These movements identified and sought to address and remove, to some extent, Western, Euro-American assumptions inherent in traditional Christian forms and theologies. They too sought to identify and remove unnecessary cultural accretions *from* Christianity so that Indians might follow a more Indianized Christianity. However, they still assumed "Christian" as the essential identity for those who want to follow Jesus.

"Hindu-Christian" Responses

A few believers, like Sadhu Sundar Singh (Sharpe 2003), N. V. Tilak (Richard 1998), Brahmabandhab Upadhyay (Rao 2001), R. C. Das (Richard 1999), or Appasamy (Appasamy, A. J. 1927) sought to develop more Hindu-sensitive expressions of Christianity. Their contextualization to Hindu cultural forms and expressions crossed boundaries that many Indian and foreign Christians found uncomfortable, yet even they remained devoted to Christianity and certain Christian traditions.

Singh wore Indian clothing and spoke in Indian forms and language. "But," says Sharpe, "he was simply and patently Christian, using words and images and appealing to values which friends of missions could immediately appreciate and accept" (Sharpe 2003, 176).

"Das considered himself a 'Hindu Christian' and had great hopes for the Hindu Christian movement," summarizes Richard (Richard 1999, 16). But he remained tied to "traditional Christian orthodoxy" (ibid., 14). For Das, simply following the way and teaching of Jesus was not sufficient. These had to be "systematized, harmonized, . . . interpreted, and cultivated." The result of this process constitutes "the religion of Christianity or the Christian religion" to which all believers ought to belong (ibid., 141). He envisioned a time when Hindus, introduced to Jesus in indigenous ways, "will awake to find that they are *truly Christian in faith* though Hindu in religion (culture and life)" (ibid., 218; emphasis mine).

Rao's critique of Upadhyay could apply equally to all these attempts at "Hindu-Christianity." He suggests that they "should have been Hindu, no hyphen needed." Rao points us in a more radical direction when he concludes, "The main lesson of his [Upadhyay's] life is that discipleship to Jesus must be brought entirely into the Hindu ambient, without any 'Christianizing'" (Rao 2001, 199). Rao proposes that Upadhyay did not go far enough, rather than too far. From Rao's perspective, Upadhyay retained too much "Christian" identity, instead of relinquishing it to follow Jesus within his own Hindu culture.

These revolutionary Christ-followers still assumed Christianity at fundamental levels, and this prevented them from truly becoming incarnational disciples of Jesus within their own Hindu culture and community. While they followed differing approaches and levels of adaptation, all seem to answer our earlier key question: "Yes, but you should become a Hindu-Christian (or Christian-Hindu) to genuinely follow Jesus."

Even these attempts at deeply contextualizing Christianity did not significantly open the door for Hindus to consider and follow Jesus. The "Christian" barrier seems to have persisted. India's response to these Hindu-Christian approaches remains, "If Christian identity and Christianity are required, even if 'Hinduized,' we will not follow Jesus."

Hindus Resist All Forms of Christianity

So today, whether Christianity remains highly foreign, deeply Indianized, or somewhere between, Hindus continue to resist Christianity and Christian identity. A friend of mine in India demonstrates the Christian barrier like this. Beginning with his little finger, he enumerates several levels of Hindu interest in Jesus, from admiration for his teaching (*dharma*) up to recognizing that Jesus is God (index finger). "But from there," he says, pointing to the wide gap between his index finger and thumb, "*the gap is too wide for most to become Christians.*" He illustrates what various Indian Christians, past and present, have observed. The finger exercise assumes, though, that Hindus must become Christians to follow Jesus. Christians commonly assume that if Hindus refuse to cross that insurmountable gap, they lack commitment to Jesus.

In some situations, no doubt, Hindus truly hear the call to follow Jesus and respond, like the rich young ruler, by walking away from him (Matt 19:16–22; Mark 10:17–22). From my exploration of India's resistance, though, this does not always seem to be the case. Some Hindus do not primarily reject Jesus and his Way. They instead reject the identity of "Christian" and "Christianity" that has been inherently associated with him. They also reject the spirit with which Christians hold to and advocate their faith.

> The advance of the Gospel is significantly threatened by those who have been preconditioned to believe in the superiority (and universality) of the Western form of Christianity and in the relative inferiority of Indian culture. Unfortunately, this includes not only most of India's missionary forces (both Western and Indian) but also the bulk of the Indian Church. By listening to those who advocate such demeaning views, the West continues in its cultural bias. Tragically, most of these spokesmen were then—and are now—unable to distinguish between Hindu culture and Hindu religion. As a result, Hindu culture is viewed as evil, because the Hindu religion does not bring salvation. (Pani 2001a, 24–25)

Address the "Christian" Barrier in a More Scriptural Way

So, if "Christian" identity can present an obstacle, let's return to our key question: *Do you have to become a Christian to genuinely follow Jesus?*

Many Christians assert, "Yes, you must become a Christian." Yet the majority of Indian believers (our earlier statistics), answer "No, we cannot accept that identity." For all those who follow Jesus, the answer to this question should be firmly rooted in Scripture. Remarkably, we face a challenge precisely at this point.

Countless ministers, missionaries, evangelists, and witnesses have, for centuries, taught people something along the lines of, "The Bible says that you must become a Christian to genuinely follow Jesus." The church has taught this for so long, that both Christians and Hindus unquestioningly assume this is what the Bible says.

But does the Bible teach this? Are Hindus staying away from Jesus in disobedience to a clear requirement of Scripture—a command of Jesus or his apostles? Or are interested Hindus alienated from Jesus by a human invention? Uncomfortable as these questions might be, we need to consider carefully how Scripture answers this question.

What does the Scripture say about our key question: *Do you have to become a Christian to genuinely follow Jesus?* Surprisingly little. It does say enough, though, to provide a clear answer to whether Christian and Christianity are required identities for those who genuinely follow Jesus.

SCRIPTURAL REVIEW OF "CHRISTIAN" AND "CHRISTIANITY"

When I first had these conversations with my Indian friends, I had been teaching the Book of Acts for many years at a Christian university. Every semester we would reach Acts 11:26, where the label "Christian" was coined. I always pointed out that "Christian" was not used nearly as often in the New Testament as we use it today, only three times in fact (Acts 11:26; 26:28; 1 Pet 4:16). At the time that seemed like merely an interesting observation in my strongly Christian context. Today, though, I see Acts 11:26 as a critical key to addressing India's reluctance to follow Jesus.

Finding the word "Christian" in the New Testament is not easy. The three occurrences present an immediate contrast to the widespread use of the word today. These verses, while limited, do provide six details about the name "Christian" and how it was used in the New Testament era. With those in mind, we can better evaluate the modern prevalent use of "Christian."

Six New Testament Observations About "Christian"

Initially, the *lack of New Testament usage*, raises an immediate question, "Why does the name appear so infrequently?" If believers understood "Christian" as their essential identity, like Christians do today, we would expect them to use it widely in the New Testament. Compared to their use of other names (see Table 2, p. 37), "Christian" was clearly not significant to them.

Next, all we know about the origin of "Christian" is summarized in one phrase, *"The disciples were first called Christians at Antioch"* (Acts 11:26). This occurred some 17 years (AD 30–AD 47) after the momentous events of Acts 2 on the day of Pentecost (Witherington III 1998, 78). Prior to Acts 11:26, no believer used "Christian" because the name did not exist. They were "disciples" for years, and continued to use that designation for some time (Breen 2013). Significantly, though, even after "Christian" was coined, no New Testament believers ever used the name "Christian" for themselves in the rest of the New Testament. They continued to avoid the name.

Furthermore, *all three verses involve outsiders labeling disciples or believers "Christians."* Bruce observes, "In the NT it is applied to them *by non-Christians* (by Agrippa II in Acts 26:28 and by their prosecutors in 1 Pet 4:16)" (Bruce 1990, 274; emphasis mine). Marshall adds that the second two uses suggest "an element of ridicule" and that the believers "preferred to use other names for themselves" (Marshall 1980, 203).

In other words, Christ's followers never used "Christian" to refer to themselves or fellow believers (Wilken 1984, 33). This was true even of 1 Peter 4:16, where he instructed believers how to respond when Romans (under or before Nero's persecution) accused them of the crime of being "Christians" (Bruce 1990, 274; Robinson 1976, 150). Robinson, in fact, later explains Peter's injunction to mean, "Let commission of *this* 'crime' [being Christian] be all that they can find against you" (ibid., 157; emphasis original).

In addition, if "Christian" was an essential identity, *the apostles, of all people, should have modeled its use* as they do freely with other names for believers. Paul, though, never used it. Peter referred to it once as an outsiders' label (1 Pet 4:16). Even John, writing near the end of the first century, never used "Christian." He would surely have used the term if it had become a common self-designation by the close of the New Testament era. *No apostle used "Christian" to refer to themselves or to fellow believers.* Paul was at Antioch when the name was given in Acts 11:26 (see verse 25), so Paul's non-use of "Christian," particularly indicates that he did not see it as an essential identity for those who followed Jesus.

The New Testament, moreover, provides no definition for "Christian." Such is not the case for the names that were used by the followers of Jesus (brothers, disciples, believers, saints [holy people], etc.). Those descriptors are defined, and we see numerous examples of how believers lived out those essential identities. The fact that Jesus and his apostles felt no compulsion to do this with "Christian" further indicates that they did not see it as their essential identity.

Table 1. Six Contrasts between New Testament and Modern Use of "Christian"

New Testament	Contemporary
1. *Rarely used (3 times only)* Never essential identity	1. Most common identity Often claimed to be essential identity
2. Disciples first, "Christian" label only later (Acts 11:26; AD 47)	2. Believers typically "Christians" first, maybe become disciples later, if ever
3. *Coined and used only by outsiders* Never used by believers of themselves	3. Believers use label prevalently Outsiders also use it for believers
4. *Apostles never use "Christian"* for essential identity of believers	4. Leaders often insist on "Christian" and "Christianity" as essential identity
5. No definition for Christian in NT	5. Make up many definitions for "Christian" based on cultural, denominational, and other human traditions
6. *"Christian" is a human invention,* not a God-given name, hence not required	6. Christians commonly act as if "Christian" is God-given and required

The sixth observation arises from the first five. Some Christians claim that *God or Jesus* gave the name;[8] others assume this to be the case. However, the lack of use, the late invention, the outsider source, and particularly the lack of apostolic precedent all falsify this assumption. *The name "Christian" is a human fabrication, not a divine requirement.* Today's common usage, moreover, is also a human invention from after the close of the New Testament. The name "Christian," in other words, was not and is not an essential, divinely required identity for those who follow Jesus.

Are Believers Required to Use "Christian"?

"Christian" did not gain the prevalent usage it has today until the second century and after (Bruce 1990, 274; Witherington III 1998, 371). Later believers made it an essential element of their cultural packaging of Jesus, even though it was never New Testament practice.

The name "Christian," then, is as much a human invention as church buildings, pews, stained glass windows, Latin liturgies, European hymns, or American contemporary worship music. Like these, it is not an essential element of the Way or Faith of Jesus. Like these cultural inventions, it might carry deep sentimental value for believers in certain cultural contexts. At the same time, it represents an unnecessary and expendable impediment for believers and non-believers in other cultural settings.

How would the apostles and New Testament believers answer our key question: *Do you have to become a Christian to genuinely follow Jesus?* Scripture's answer is clear: "No, New Testament believers did not become Christians to genuinely follow Jesus." They avoided the name even after it was coined. That is what Scripture says, regardless of centuries of Christian claims to the contrary, and that remains Scripture's answer to this Christian barrier in India. If Jesus and his apostles did not require it, no believer should require it today.

---

8.   "The name was given by divine inspiration (through Barnabas and Saul)" (G. Reese 1971, 331f.); "Christian" is the one "God-given name by the apostles in the New Testament. The use of any other name is sinful, because it divides or denominates" (Nash n.d., 2).

What About "Christianity"?

If the New Testament, then, does not require Christian identity, what does it say about "Christianity"? Even less! That term never occurs in the New Testament. It was only coined in the second century by Ignatius (*Christianismos* = Christianism), in his *Epistle to the Magnesians*. After inventing it, he added, "He who is called by any other name besides this is not of God" (Srawley 1910, 68). Where did Ignatius get this? Not from Scripture, not from Jesus, not from the apostles. He made it up. As we have already demonstrated, the Bible does not teach that you must use Christian or Christianity.

Some might argue that Ignatius simply invented an alternative term for the Way of Jesus. Christianity, they allege, is convenient shorthand for "the faith once for all delivered to the saints" (Jude 3). I know Christians who want to simply use "Christianity" in this way, as a description for their faith in Jesus. After all, the Oxford Dictionary defines Christianity as "The religion based on the person and teachings of Jesus Christ, or its beliefs and practices" (OED 2016). How could that be problematic?

Other Christians have responded, "We have used it for so long, why does it matter? It doesn't hurt anyone if we use it. And it would be uncomfortable for us to stop using it."

However, when an identity without scriptural basis alienates nearly 1 billion Hindus—not to mention 1.5 billion Muslims—from Jesus, it is not a neutral, innocuous term. This "harmless" identity was, after all, a driving force behind Christendom and crusades, conquistadors and colonialism, apartheid and US slavery. India's resistance to this identity arises partly from its own painful encounters with some of those "Christian" associations.

Faithful Continuation or Unscriptural Departure?

If "Christianity" was just a neutral substitute for the Way or Faith of Jesus, perhaps we could justify using this non-scriptural term. In significant ways, though, Christianity carries traditions, connotations, and divisions that inherently convey negative perceptions to many Hindus. When Christians insist that believers accept "Christianity," they are not requiring a neutral identity, but an unscriptural identity encrusted with adverse baggage.

Some scholars even suggest that Ignatius did not simply invent a neutral substitute term for the Way of Jesus. David Bosch and philosopher Jacques Ellul both argue that the invention of "Christianity" represented a fundamental departure from or subversion of the Way that Jesus established (Bosch 1996, 50; Ellul 2011, 13). While they differ in details, both assert that the invention of "Christianity" signaled a departure from the informal, incarnational movement of Jesus to a formal, institutional religion (Bosch, 50; Ellul, 17).

Bosch and Ellul, I believe, are correct in their analyses. If they are, then Christianity has a deeper problem than simply negative or cultural baggage. The religion that Christianity has become is ultimately an unscriptural replacement for the movement Jesus intended. Instead of creating an alternate term, Ignatius helped replace the Way of Jesus with a separatist religious system Jesus never envisioned.

If this is true, then Indians who refuse to identify with Christianity are not being unfaithful to Jesus. They may be rejecting not only a human term, but an unscriptural religious system. As this chapter has illustrated, some Indians seem to have an aversion to "Christianity" while maintaining an interest in Jesus.

How, then, do we respond to the barrier of Christianity in India? We must answer our key question from the Scripture. Did Jesus ask followers to adopt Christianity? Did his apostles? Does Scripture anywhere ask this of believers? No. Therefore, we are not required to ask anyone to do so today. What would happen, though, if we simply introduced them to Jesus and his Way as revealed in Scripture, no Christianity required? India has been asking for this for centuries. How much longer will India have to wait for Jesus while Christians insist on a human "Christianity" that Jesus did not initiate?

NEW TESTAMENT ALTERNATIVES FOR "CHRISTIAN" AND "CHRISTIANITY"

When I discuss this barrier of Christian and Christianity, invariably the conversation leads to the question, "Then what should we call ourselves? Or what should we be?" Christians share an all-too-human desire to distinguish themselves from those around them. Without "Christian" and "Christianity" to serve that purpose, they find it hard to conceive of other legitimate identities. Yet the Scripture utilizes numerous terms that describe different aspects of what it means to belong to Jesus. Unfortunately, believers can sometimes emphasize a name for themselves with little scriptural support, rather than the numerous identities New Testament believers commonly emphasized.

What Names Should Believers Use?

In the New Testament, "when early Christians described themselves they spoke of being disciples, believers, saints, brothers and sisters, or followers of 'the Way'" (Witherington III 1998, 371).

The Book of Acts alone uses over thirty distinct descriptors for those who followed Jesus. Table 2 lists the four most common identifiers believers used in Acts (brothers/brethren, disciples, believers, saints) compared to the infrequent "Christian" (2 times by outsiders only). Paul never used "Christian," but he commonly used "in Christ" in various ways to describe the identity and character of believers. In fact, six times he refers to specific believers who are "in Christ" (Rom 16:7, 22; 1 Cor 1:30; 2 Cor 12:2; Gal 1:22; 1 Thess 3:8).

Table 2. Usage of Common Terms for Believers in Acts

Term/Identity	Frequency in Acts for Believers	Frequency in Acts for Non-believers
Brother/Brethren	32	17
Disciple	28	1
Believer	9	0
Saint	4	0
Christian (used by outsiders only)	2	0

New Testament believers did not feel obligated to limit themselves to one separatist term. Believers in India should not be required to do so either. In fact, these New Testament identities provide helpful guidelines for selecting scriptural and viable alternatives for believers in India.

Two Guidelines for Scriptural Identities

First, *choose a variety of terms that are readily understandable and translatable.* The top four scriptural names (Table 2) all made cultural sense to the broader community as well as to believers. This variety of terms highlighted different essential identities for those who followed Jesus. Rather than pick one, they used them all to call attention to those different aspects of their walk with the Lord. India would more likely resonate with that variety, than with one restrictive label.

Furthermore, we should *emphasize culturally neutral terms, rather than separatist terms.* The most common term for fellow believers in Acts was "brother" or "brethren" (32 total), but the believers used this same term seventeen times when addressing fellow Jews or God-fearers (Acts 13) who were not followers of Jesus. They avoided separatist terms (like Christian) and instead emphasized terms that built bridges to those around them.

Deissmann notes that brothers (*adelphoi*) commonly meant "*members of a community*" in the Greek world (Deissmann 1980, 107). My Indian readers may catch an implication of Deissmann's definition more readily than most of my Western readers. They live in a country where caste and religious divisions are euphemistically called "communities." Community disharmony and conflict, and community considerations provide a constant challenge in India (Richard 2007a). "Community" can be a very divisive, separatist concept.

It is instructive, then, that the New Testament uses "members of a community" (*adelphoi*) in very inclusive ways, rather than exclusive. Apostles frequently use the term to maintain identity as part of the Jewish community. In Paul's sermon in Acts 13, he broadens its inclusiveness to include the Gentile God-fearers at the back of the room (vs 26). Jews would not technically call them "brethren," because they had not taken circumcision and converted to the Jewish faith. Paul wants them to know that Jesus loves and wants them, so he calls them "brethren" also. Paul, I believe, is signaling here that God's incarnational community was getting bigger, no longer limited to the separatist confines of the Jewish "community."

What About Bhaktas?

Some of my incarnational believer friends in India refer to themselves as *Yesu bhaktas*, devotees of Jesus, Christ-followers, or some similar term. They also use common terms for disciple (*shishya, chela*) or servant (*dasa, doss*) of the Lord. The Bible does not have the Sanskrit term *bhakta*, obviously, so Christians might reject this name out of hand. But, as we've demonstrated, Christianity isn't in the Bible and we use it. Let me suggest a closer look at the word and its relationship to some possible New Testament connections.

A *bhakta* is a loving worshiper of God or follower of a teacher (guru). The word is impossible to define in a single English word, but conveys devotion, love, emotion, dedication, worship, and obedience among other ideas. Worshipers of Jesus should certainly exhibit these nuances in their relationship with him.

A bhakta is a person who practices *bhakti* toward God. Hawley provides a great definition for *bhakti* in his history of the Hindu *bhakti* movements:

> "Bhakti," as usually translated, is devotion, but if that word connotes something entirely private and quiet, we are in need of other words. Bhakti is heart religion, sometimes cool and quiescent but sometimes hot—the religion of participation, community, enthusiasm, song, and often of personal challenge, the sort of thing that coursed through the . . . Great Awakenings in the early history of the United States. It evokes the idea of a widely shared religiosity for which institutional superstructures weren't all that relevant, and which, once activated, could be historically contagious—a glorious disease of the collective heart. It implies direct divine encounter, experienced in the lives of individual people. (Hawley 2015, 2)

A *bhakta*, in other words, is *devoted to God*—defined by devotion. Interestingly, the English word "saint" intersects with *bhakta* at this very point. You can't see it at first (remember those church words that hide what the Bible says?). Christians usually hear "saint" and think of special holy people with halos, images in churches, or a special piety that is unattainable by ordinary believers.

The New Testament, though, calls all believers "saints" (*hagioi*). That word simply means "holy people." "Holy" still doesn't help us much, because even that word can sound unattainable or only for special believers. Many people probably think of "Holier than thou"! But what does "holy" (*hagios*) mean? Trench defines it as "*consecration and devotion* to the service of Deity [God]" (Trench 1978, 331; emphasis mine). Its first definition in the standard lexicon of biblical Greek is "*dedicated* to God" (Bauer, et al. 1979, 9; emphasis mine). A "saint," in other words, is someone dedicated and devoted to God. In this sense, the New Testament "saint" and Hindu "bhakta" intersect closely—both describe a person dedicated and devoted to God.

In suggesting these possibilities, I am not implying a one-to-one correlation between *bhakta* and "saint" (*hagios*). Jesus-followers would need to prayerfully examine Hindu religious connections related to *bhakta*. Rather than rejecting the term outright, though, believers should at least explore functional equivalents between Scripture and culture (de Waard and Nida 1986). This would be preferable to adopting supposedly "biblical" terms that simply preserve traditional church terminology.

What should believers call themselves? How should new Indian believers refer to themselves? They should examine the rich choices provided by Scripture and prayerfully select those that best explain what it means to follow and belong to Jesus in their context. If they follow the example of Acts, though, they will find the most culturally neutral names, rather than identities that separate them from the culture around them. They won't use "Christian" typically because it's scripturally unnecessary and culturally problematic.

If Not Christianity, to What Do We Belong?

In the same way, if we remove "Christianity" from our vocabulary, practice, and consideration, what would we call this thing that we follow? Since no New Testament believers used "Christianity," we again should investigate and utilize the terms they used. Scripture should guide us, not Christian tradition—the two are far from equivalent.

I will deal in the next chapter with the traditions and barriers around two common options, church (ekklēsia) and kingdom (*basileia*). The New Testament believers, though, did use *faith* (Acts 6:7; 14:22; 16:5; 24:24; Gal 1:23; Eph 4:5; Jude 3) and *way* (John 14:6; Acts 9:2; 18:25f.; 19:9,23; 22:4,14; 24:22) to describe what they followed and to what they belonged.

Christians might say that these terms are unclear, they do not make their Christian identity distinct, but that's exactly the New Testament's point. In contexts that were challenging and resistant, it was not wise to wave their difference like a banner, or more like a red cape before an angry bull. A neutral term, like "the faith" or "the way," allowed believers to know what they were talking about.

In using Way (*hodos*), Jesus and his followers used a common cultural term to identify "the faith." Jesus became their "Way" in the face of many competing ways in the first century. This language was natural to both Jewish and Greco-Roman culture to explain Jesus and what it means to follow him.

The same idea that Christ and his teaching is the Way or Path provides a similar bridge for understanding Jesus in the Hindu world. "Traditionally," H. L. Richard observes, "three *paths* to salvation are considered valid" (Richard, 2007b, 10; emphasis mine). They are called the *Trimarga* (Three Paths) in Sanskrit: "*karmamarga*, the path of works; *jñananmarga*, the path of knowledge; and *bhaktimarga*, the path of loving devotion" (Klostermaier 1989, 145). Hindus themselves, in other words, seek God through several paths.

So, when Indian believers refer to their life in Jesus as the *Yesu Marg* or *Panth* (Jesus Way or Path), they are using language familiar to Hindus. Their Bibles use these words already as one culturally understandable form to explain what it means to follow the "Way" of Jesus.

The collective terms "the Faith" or "the Way" are preferable to "Christianity" because 1) they are scriptural terms ("Christianity" is not), and 2) they build a neutral, understandable bridge to the culture, instead of reflecting Christianity's separatism.

THE KEY QUESTION

We have seen that Christian identity is problematic for many Hindus, even for many believers in the Indian context, so let us revisit our key question one more time: *Do you have to become a Christian to genuinely follow Jesus?*

Jesus did not teach it. Neither did his apostles. All evidence for the widespread use of Christian identity comes after the end of the New Testament. Scripture does not require anyone to become a "Christian" or adopt "Christianity" to live for Jesus.

CHRISTIAN AND BHAKTA CONSIDERATIONS

Look at Christian identity from the incarnational paradigm of Chapter 1. We must question the necessity for believers to adopt "Christian" or "Christianity" of any kind as their separatist identity. The New Testament does not require this, and the Indian context indicates many people reject it already for various reasons. Only Christian tradition claims it is essential.

Christians

Some communities in India, however, may choose to identify with "Christian" and "Christianity." Communities that have been culturally "Christian" for generations, for instance, present an interesting challenge. Some may be culturally Christians, but may not have a relationship with Jesus. Those who do truly learn to follow Jesus from Christian communities, will likely follow him in overtly "Christian" ways, since that is the only form they know. Like Jews who became followers of Jesus, the form of religion they once knew would take on new meaning as they encountered and followed the living Jesus within that.

This might hold true also for tribal groups who are primarily "Christianized" already. To follow Jesus in a way other than "Christian" would isolate the remaining believers from most of the culture which does follow Jesus. There may be segments of India's diverse communities for whom the Christian path might be more appropriate than a bhakta path. Believers in India would need to determine that for themselves; my suggestions from the outside would be completely inappropriate and ignorant of ground realities in specific contexts.

Some argue that the Dalits have no other option except to leave their community entirely and join the Christian community. As we will see shortly (Chapter 3—Church), this choice has not always led to greater freedom or equality for too many of their number. Where significant groups of Dalits have become Christian and more would follow them, this again may be an appropriate path. For many, though, the most incarnational option may still be the bhakta path.

If a Hindu expresses interest in following Jesus, or comes to visit your church, what should you do? Don't look at the Hindu as a target for Christian evangelism and conversion. Don't look at them as another potential Christian to add to the numbers.

From the last chapter and this one, we assume that people should stay with their family and community under normal circumstances, rather than making extraction essential. Based on that, our initial response would be to help them connect with a fellowship (*mandali*) of bhaktas who could disciple and encourage them from the start. We should start there, and prayerfully consider where on the incarnational spectrum the Lord wants them to follow him.

Yesu Bhaktas

Those who come to Jesus primarily from Hindu communities will usually be better directed to a mandali of Yesu bhaktas as soon as they develop interest in Jesus. Let bhaktas disciple and coach them in how to follow Jesus appropriately within their own culture and community. These followers would be, and indeed are, taught to set aside caste prejudices and discrimination as followers of the Lord. They know how to interact and relate appropriately across caste lines. They are encouraged to see all followers of Jesus as brothers and sisters in the Lord, part of his family, no matter the level of society from which they originate.

For readers who are Yesu bhaktas, I have prayed that this chapter helps set them free from anyone who tells them that they are not being faithful to Jesus if they do not become "Christians" and accept Christianity. I hope that this study will help them settle in their own hearts that they are being truly faithful to the Lord, that it will provide them with answers for those who challenge their choice to follow Jesus within their own culture and community.

CLOSING REFLECTIONS

An Indian friend of mine is a Christian who works gently and respectfully with Indians of various faiths. He does not push Jesus on people and does not engage in large, flashy evangelistic campaigns, but he and his colleagues work in creative ways to introduce Indians to Jesus. Some evangelists came to him one day and rebuked him for not aggressively making more Christians. He replied, "Let's say you have an audience of one thousand Hindus—*pukka* (real, genuine) Hindus, not Christians padding the audience. When you have preached, how many Christians will you make?"

They discussed among themselves and replied, "Maybe twenty!" He told me that in his mind he thought that estimate was high, but he gave them the benefit of the doubt.

"You take your twenty converts and make them Christians," he replied, "then I will work to undo the damage you have done to the 980, and will try to help some of them meet Jesus."

E. Stanley Jones once observed that Indians seemed to have made "an amazing and remarkable discovery, namely, that Christianity and Jesus are not the same—that they may have Jesus without the system that has been built up around him in the West" (Jones 1926, 13).

Sadly, in the last century Christianity has primarily rejected and shut the door on that discovery, insisting that India must become Christian to follow Jesus. The New Testament, though, has actually sided with the Indians' discovery all along. The original followers of Jesus had no "Christianity" to identify with Jesus, they just followed him. None of them saw Christian as an essential part of who they were.

Today we have an opportunity to set the record straight. Based on Scripture we can tell India, "You do not have to become a Christian or adopt Christianity. Christianity and Jesus are not the same! Just follow Jesus."

CHAPTER 3

THE BARRIER OF CHURCH

Arun and Sushimita converted to Christianity while working in the United States. The Christians there taught them to take strong stances against their Hindu family and community (cultural separatism). After a few years, they returned to India and initially followed the separatist practices with her family. The wife's family, consequently, had been antagonistic toward her and her husband.

Eventually, though, they began to wrestle with the barriers raised in the previous chapters. They recognized that part of the tension arose from how they had related to and communicated with her family. They sought to connect with her family in more respectful ways instead of offending them or staying away.

One day they invited me to their home for lunch. Their new engagement with her family had reduced the tension somewhat. Her father, though, remained resistant to their faith, although recently he had requested a study Bible in the local Tamil language. Eventually, the lady declared, "My father is a leader in his temple community. Nearly three hundred people follow his lead. If he were even to attend a church, much less join one, he would lose his influence with much of the community. But," she added, "if he could follow Jesus without church, many of them would take his lead. They might also follow Jesus."

Would that even be possible? Why would church attendance ever be a concern? Herbert Hoefer, from his research into Hindu views of Christianity and church, confirmed her sentiments:

> *It's membership in a church that is so contrary to Hindu piety*, so upsetting to Hindu families, and so threatening to Hindu politicians. If we can clearly state that one can convert to faith in Jesus and one can even be baptized, *without ever joining a church*, most of our difficulties with

the Hindu community and the political parties will be over. It's conversion into a new culture, it's baptism into a new community, that is the problem. (Hoefer 2001b, 223–4; emphasis mine)

Following Jesus without church? I know it's a major question and challenge. We will examine that issue shortly. Set that glaring question aside for a moment, though, and consider the implication of those statements. They raise a more foundational question? *Why is church such a problem that people would even consider avoiding it in the Indian context (and elsewhere)?* Some Christians may not like Hoefer's research,[9] or a more recent attempt by Dasan Jayaraj to update understanding of this phenomenon (Jayaraj 2010). We must still wrestle, however, with what causes so many Indian people to see church as problematic in some way.

Some Christians may quickly answer, "Hindus don't want to follow Jesus, so they don't want his church. Church is just their excuse." In their minds, the resistance to church is simply resistance to Jesus. Others have said, "They just wish to avoid persecution for Jesus' sake, so they avoid joining a church and identifying with Christians."

Other Indian Christians may point to situations where church was not a barrier. Chennai has several mega-churches that number in the thousands, occasionally tens of thousands. Those churches are not a barrier to at least some people. Christian friends can point to instances where Hindus came to church and met Jesus there. One told recently of a Hindu woman who asked to pray in the church building on her way to work. The building obviously was not a barrier for her, although he also tells of many Hindus who would not enter the same building, especially when services were being conducted. Other friends tell of Hindus who attended special occasions or Christian festivals at a church building, just not regular

---

9. *Churchless Christianity.* Bhakta friends and those who work alongside them are troubled by that title. They are not, and will never be, Christians, but they are genuine disciples of Jesus. While there are believers who do not associate with "church" as traditionally understood, they may very well find alternative, home-based forms of ekklēsia and fellowship both within a city and more regionally. They have a group of believers that gathers regularly; they just do not call it church. Christians don't like his title because it implies you can be a Christian without church, an idea they typically find unacceptable.

worship services. All these observations and qualifications demonstrate that this barrier is complex, not simplistic.

From my conversations, observations, and investigations, though, those Christian answers can be used to dismiss a reality that my friends regularly articulated. Church, as it is often known and expressed in India, is keeping a significant majority of Hindus away from Jesus, even when they might have an interest in him, so let's start there. What might Hindus find problematic about church and should we be at all concerned?

IS CHURCH A BARRIER FOR HINDUS?

A century ago, E. Stanley Jones avoided Christian churches as venues for his roundtable discussions to introduce Hindus and Muslims to Jesus. Why? Even then he noted, "There is a real prejudice against them [the churches]" (Jones 1926, 83). Jones' observation seems to hold true for many Indians even today. They still find church problematic, and demonstrate their concern in various ways.

Hindu attacks on church buildings and gatherings have represented a more violent reaction to church. I do not want to dismiss these issues, and originally included reflections about them. The more I investigated and researched, though, the more I realized that the reports of violence require much deeper research and reflection on that aspect of how Hindus perceive Christians and churches, and how some Christians portray these situations (see for instance, Bauman 2013). That will be a later project beyond the scope of this one.

Consequently, I have focused this chapter on more prevalent, non-violent Hindu concerns about churches.

AVOIDING CHURCHES

When Christians invite Hindus to church or talk about church, they receive a range of responses: "I can't go to church," "I find church uncomfortable," or "I don't want anything to do with church." Hindus, it seems, just avoid church far more frequently than any other response.

When asked politely, Hindus can identify a variety of traditions that contribute to the barrier of church. Hoefer's research, for instance, elicited the following:

- "Bad moral reputation of Christians
- "Dislike to join socially with Harijans [or caste Hindus, depending on caste origin]
- "Discomfort with patterns of Sunday worship
- "Feel sitting [in chairs] at worship is disrespectful . . . more comfortable to sit on floor
- "Feel inappropriate to wear shoes inside sanctuary
- "Cannot understand old Christian language
- "Dislike Western-style music—preferring *bhajans* (Indian-style worship songs)
- "Dislike changes in women's dress [e.g., Remove *tilak/bindi*, gold or jewelry, wear white sari—all signs of widowhood, insulting husband and his family while he is alive]
- "Dislike change of name [to Christian names—see Chapter 5 for this issue]
- "Loss of life-cycle rituals [up to sixteen such rituals, in Hindu traditions]
- "Reputation of Christians as unpatriotic" [anti-national] (Hoefer 2001b, 217–18; brackets identify my elaborations)

This is a rather short list that could be expanded significantly with additional interviews. I must point out that Hoefer did this research among cultural Hindus who believed in Jesus, loved Jesus, and wanted to follow Jesus at some level. They just could not or would not bring themselves to join a church to do so.

One Christian recounted that some of his own Hindu family members avoided his church wedding because of how the pastor and Christians would treat them. A pastor friend recounted instances where Hindus would not come to the church building during church services. They would only come to talk at times when services were not meeting, because they did not want to be seen by the community as attending or joining a church.

An Indian friend of mine tried for several years to start a more traditional church using school rooms and store fronts as meeting places. The people he worked with finally told him that they were turned off by rows, pulpits, and traditional worship. Formal church was a problem for them and their families. Today his ministry involves multiple house fellowships. One gathering is sometimes hosted by a Hindu family who want to learn more about Jesus, but who told my friend they could never come to a church. Hindus, Muslims, and Sikhs all come to learn in a neutral, non-threatening setting in homes.

Even some Christians have been hurt or turned off by one or more traditional churches. They want to follow Jesus, but church traditions and institutions get in their way. Repeatedly these people have told my friend that church is not an option for them. The barriers associated with church can affect Christians, not just Hindus.

As we saw in the previous chapter on Christians, a significant population of believers in India refuses to identify with Christianity and church. Both represent a powerful, barrier-building combination to Hindus. We must ask, then, why does church present such a challenge to Hindus?

WHY DO HINDUS AVOID CHURCH?

Embodies Other Barriers

Church is partly problematic because it embodies and inculcates so many of the other barriers to Jesus. Some churches emphasize the cultural separatism and Christian identity that we already saw can present barriers. Hoefer's comment at the start of this chapter illustrates the deep interconnection between the church and other Christian barriers: "It's *conversion* into a new *culture*, it's *baptism* into a new *community*, that is the problem" (ibid., 223–4; emphasis mine). The barriers in that one highlighted sentence are unpacked in Chapters 1, 2, 5, and 6. Church, in Hindus' minds, can reflect and represent all the barriers this book will explore. After all, it is the institution that fosters and inculcates them.

Set the other barriers aside for a moment. Let's focus on some deeper, unique challenges that church poses to Hindus. These barriers appear inherent in what church has become not only in the Indian context, but everywhere it exists today.

Embodies Division

Part of the barrier that church presents involves a set of divisive traditions that seem inherent in its DNA. I'm not referring to the "division" Jesus alluded to in Luke 12:51f. We can't evade the social division Jesus himself can cause. However, other divisive aspects of Indian church life neither originate from Jesus nor are they condoned by him. They can significantly contribute to Hindu resistance to Jesus.

EMBODIES FOREIGN DENOMINATIONAL DIVISION

Much of the denominational division is fully attributable to the West, to the foreign church. Jesus indicated that the unity of his believers was necessary for the world to believe and know that God had sent him (John 17:20–23). Earlier that same evening he indicated that all would recognize his disciples when they had love for one another (John 13:35). Yet a recent estimate claims that there are 42,000 Christian denominations globally (Johnson, et al. 2016). This denominational division can present problems for Hindus in several ways.

Confusion of Denominations

Jonathan Bonk once asked, "Can there be genuine Christianity without a gathered church?" He then reflected, "Answers to this question hinge on what we mean by 'church' and 'Christian.' For two thousand years, these deceptively simple terms have defied consensus as global estimates of 37,000 [now 42,000] Christian denominations and nearly 300 confessional councils worldwide attest" (Bonk 2005, 169).

When the Dalit champion Ambedkar was seeking a religious alternative for non-caste communities, he asked Bishop Azariah, "If we become Christians can we all be united in one Church wherever we live?" The bewildering denominational divisions caused Azariah shame because he could not promise unity within the church (Harper 2000, 313). If Ambedkar wanted to join the church, he would have had to choose one of many Indian denominations, and would have then belonged to a church divided within itself.

With India's strong sense of communal identity, church membership and denominational affiliation can present a barrier far more confusing than in Western contexts. How do Hindus begin to decide which church community is the right one to attend or join?

When Indian Christians, then, insist that a convert must join *the* church, they typically mean their church, as opposed to someone else's. An Indian seminary president recently told me of villages that had five different churches each with around ten members. The level of church and denominational division within India can be bewildering.

Foreignness of Denominations

The foreign nature of church denominations, even the "Indian" ones, is also troubling. Most denominational differences originated in foreign debates and cultural distinctives, not at all relevant to India. "As we have seen," suggests Darrell Guder, "'mission' had basically meant the Western expansion of *its own culturally conformed Christianity*, carried out in a complex relationship with colonialism. Implicit in mission was the formation of the institutional church, an extension of the territory of Christendom" (Guder 2000, 18).

For Catholics, it was "the *plantatio ecclesiae*, the planting of the church, under the pope and his bishops. . . . Protestant mission took a variety of stances regarding the institutional church, but the necessary result of their activity was invariably the *formation of an institution, normally modeled on the church tradition of the missionaries*" (ibid.). The denominations assumed that church, their version of the ekklēsia, should be the one that all believers in India followed. This assumption almost ensured that Hindus would perceive the church as a foreign entity.

Once churches become established, we don't often recognize how much cultural adaptation led to their original development. My daughter shared a blog post with me that highlighted how Western culture has imprinted itself on major denominational branches. The writer reflected, "[Jesus] wants to situate us in a larger life, which he calls the 'Reign of God.' But instead we make him into a Scholastic philosopher if we are Roman Catholic, into a moralist if we are mainline Protestant, or into a successful and imperialistic American if we are Evangelical" (Rohr 2016).

Traditions and denominations can embody fundamental cultural assumptions that are then imposed on believers in other parts of the world unwittingly, or sometimes intentionally. This subtle stamp of division and foreignness has maintained its imprint on Indian churches long after the foreigners left.

Along these lines, Brian McLaren suggests, "What we call Christianity today has a history, and this history reveals it as a Roman, imperial version of Christianity." He elaborates, "In this sense, we could refer to Roman Catholic and Roman Protestant Christianity—two wings of a project shaped in part by Jesus and the apostles and in part by Rome and its emperors" (McLaren 2012, 84). Church, as we will see, may reflect more of the Roman emperor Constantine than the scriptural concept of ekklēsia. When we dig deeper, church may be more essentially foreign than just the external trappings on which people usually focus.

Furthermore, when a church has headquarters or decision-making leadership in foreign countries, this exacerbates Hindu concerns about a foreign church operated to serve foreign interests and agendas. When the first churches came to India, they interacted with and remained answerable to church leaders and traditions from their originating countries. This was true with the Syrian churches in the fourth and fifth centuries. It was also true of the Catholics who arrived in Goa in the 1500s and who still owe allegiance to a Pope and hierarchy in Rome. The various Protestant groups also answered to foreign church bodies that had sent them from Europe and later America.

Even when the foreign churches handed leadership over to Indians, the "indigenized" structures maintained elements of the foreign flavor from the original denominations. Indian churches, even when indigenous for generations, can still be perceived by Hindus as alien, hence suspect. Consequently, denominations, as the foreign infrastructure of church, can present obstacles to Hindus. Even India's united churches reflect regional differences in the North and South that can appear foreign in different areas of the country.

Hindu "Denominations" (Sampradayas)

To be honest, Hindus have their own complex of *sampradayas* (traditions) that divide them—over three hundred and constantly expanding (Klostermaier 1989, 329). The debates between followers of Shiva and Vishnu, for instance, could be acrimonious, at times deadly (ibid., 333). The idea of church denominations, then, does not necessarily have to confuse Hindus if explained with such familiar examples. Different churches have followed, explained, and worshiped Jesus in different ways that were more natural to their culture and community. While they can be explained, though, church divisions along denominational lines still can pose a confusing barrier to Hindus. And when they embody foreign traditions, they are almost certain to raise concerns for many Hindus.

Denominational church challenges, then, can hamper Hindus from considering or following Jesus. From what I have heard and seen, though, a significant barrier arises from church divisions that reflect caste considerations. Some Christians will deny that this exists, but most I have talked with and read indicate that this is a very present reality in the church, one that creates challenges for Hindus.

PERPETUATES CASTE[10] DIVISION

Donald McGavran, once remarked with India in mind, "The structures of the Church and its modes of growth are heavily conditioned by *sociology* . . . The church always grows in a society" (McGavran 1979, 11). Caste is a major feature of Indian sociology, so it is not surprising that the Indian church has had, and continues to wrestle with, the challenge of caste. In an ideal world, caste would simply cease to exist in the church. Some Christian leaders assert that this has indeed been the case. Generally, though, Christians tell a very different story. Caste is an all-too-common reality within India's churches and presents a significant barrier to Hindus who might be interested in Jesus.

The Ongoing Presence of Caste

In 1984 the Evangelical Fellowship of India and the Asia Theological Association held a joint *Consultation on Caste and Church*. Three statements within this document tacitly acknowledged caste to be a problem *within* the church:

> Declaration 9: We confess and repent that on occasions and in places *we have permitted the evils of caste to influence the church* and to mar the beauty and unity of the body of Christ
>
> Declaration 10d: That local churches, theological institutions, organizations, leaders, families and individuals presently and periodically *evaluate the influence of casteism in their lives and take corrective measures to eradicate this evil.*

---

10. Since my Indian sources use "caste" regularly in the quotes, I am addressing this as a "caste" issue. More commonly Indians would use "community" as a less offensive term for the other "c" word. I am aware, from numerous conversations, that "caste" can be a sensitive and emotional topic. While I do not intend to unnecessarily offend, the "caste" language does illustrate the serious, offensive nature of "caste" consideration in the church. Where this causes hurt, I pray that it also causes soul-searching and healing.

Declaration 10e: That *wherever the evil of the caste system has permeated the church's worship and witness*, we seek corrective measures in the light of biblical teaching through the empowering of the Holy Spirit. Where guilty we must seek to humbly confess our sins and to accept and take disciplinary action.

(Editorial 1985; emphasis mine)

Robert Eric Frykenberg, long-time scholar of Indian Christianity and Hindu traditions, observed, "It is difficult to find any time in the history of Christians in India when caste has not been a burning issue. No problem has remained more persistent or enduring. No group of Christians in India seems to have been immune" (Frykenberg, Introduction 2003, 10).

Caste considerations are prevalent enough within the church that *Encyclopedia Britannica* even has an entry regarding "Christian caste." Its opening statement reflects what many Indian Christians have confessed to me, "Christian caste, in India, [is] the *social stratification that persists among Christians*, based upon caste membership at the time of an individual's own or of an ancestor's conversion. *Indian Christian society is divided* into groups geographically and according to denomination, but *the overriding factor is one of caste*" (*Encyclopedia Britannica* 2016b; emphasis mine). Note particularly that last phrase. It refers to *Christians*, not Hindus; "the overriding factor is one of caste."

"Has caste left the church? Unfortunately, such is far from the truth," concurs N. J. Gnaniah.

> Whenever a bishop's election happens in some mainline churches, caste emerges. Whenever a marriage happens, it comes out. Whenever an appointment is made by an institution, it comes out. Whenever a promotion to a job in a Christian institution is made, it comes out. Some people would rather marry a Hindu who belongs to the same caste than a Christian of another caste. It is sad, but true. (Gnaniah 2011, 165)

Unfortunately, it's not just an internal church problem. Caste distinctions within the church have directly impeded Hindus from considering or coming to Jesus.

Church Caste Considerations Keep Hindus from Jesus

In Gnaniah's experience—coming from a caste Hindu family himself—Hindus are interested in following Jesus, "when you explain the gospel in an understandable way." But, he adds, "the hesitation comes in joining the church, for any adherence to Christianity aligns one with a church made up of 'other caste people'" (ibid., 166). Some of my colleagues have corroborated Gnaniah's assessment. One of my Christian colleagues often points out that there are around three thousand *jatis* (castes) and twenty-five thousand *gotras* (subcastes). These revolve around deeply known rules regarding who you may or may not associate with, eat with, or marry. Indian believers face a formidable challenge in addressing these social distinctions as they impact church life and relationships.

If new believers are not the same caste as the church, they can feel uncomfortable associating with "another caste." I have also heard stories of the reverse. A church of one caste can make it clear that a person from another caste is not welcome (for instance predominantly Dalit churches toward higher caste converts).

A friend of mine told of a Brahmin couple who were interested in Jesus and began attending their fellowship. Several traditional Christians in the group, though, were not pleased with the presence of Brahmins in their midst. By ignoring them or subtly shaming them, the couple were eventually made to feel so unwelcome that they left the church. Such caste discrimination had nothing to do with Jesus, in fact it contravened his spirit of grace and engagement (Chapter 1).

Other Christians describe situations where a church accepted the person as a believer. However, the "wrong caste" convert would be discriminated against when seeking a spouse from among the Christians either for self or for a child (depending on age). Christian friends who married across caste have recounted the opposition they faced from their Christian families for doing so. They also point to the numerous Christian matrimonial (*shaadi*) sites where Christians include caste as one consideration, unless they specify "caste no bar" (caste not a consideration). Caste considerations for Christian marriages are a present reality.

Ironically, Christians might pay close attention to caste within the church, yet often display a level of disregard for caste sensitivities among Hindus, providing another source of offense. Gnaniah provides two examples. Couples were encouraged by Christian pastors to marry across caste, but without any discussion with or consideration shown toward their Hindu families. In both instances, because of this disrespect, the Hindu families refused to ever hear of Jesus. Many Indian Christians would simply claim victory for Jesus in the face of "unfortunate" opposition and persecution. Gnaniah's assessment, though, seems more realistic:

> In my opinion these young converts were not taught properly. The church and many pastors do not know or understand how to operate within the cultural realities of caste. Most evangelicals or those who do evangelism do not know enough about the social structures of Tamil Nadu . . . So they preach the gospel, win one or two, and rejoice. But if we don't teach and train new converts properly, *we lose the whole caste group*. It is a tragedy to win one or two, only to lose thousands. (ibid.)

Dr. B. R. Ambedkar was the foremost champion for Dalit rights and emancipation (Bhimrao Ramji Ambedkar 2016). He once asked the first Indian Anglican bishop, V. S. Azariah, "If we become Christians can we all be united in one Church wherever we live? And will we be entirely free from all Caste prejudice?" Azariah could not affirm either possibility, and reflected later, "I have never felt so ashamed in my life because I couldn't say YES to either question—I could only come away in disgrace" (Harper 2000, 313). This conversation occurred in 1936. Twenty years later, out of increasing disappointment with his people's options, Ambedkar led 200,000 Dalits to convert to Buddhism. The church's caste considerations and realities prevented hundreds of thousands of Dalits from considering Jesus as a path to freedom and reconciliation.

To be honest, most of today's church members originated from Dalit backgrounds (est. 75 percent). This represents around 10 percent of today's Dalit population. Church, then, has certainly not been a barrier to Dalits. Yet this Dalit influx has itself raised questions for Hindus.

Sandhya Jain, political researcher and columnist, illustrates Hindu awareness of the caste issues within the church. She points out that churches and missions have targeted Dalits (technically Scheduled Castes—SCs), promising them "equality and economic advancement." More recently, though, churches have been petitioning the government to provide educational and job benefits to Christian SCs because they continue to be disadvantaged.[11] This leads her to remark, "There must be a deep rot in the church if it cannot grant social equality and dignity to those whom it has pulled out of their traditional civilizational matrix [see Chapter 1], socially isolated by conversion [see Chapter 5], and then abandoned to wallow in fresh discrimination!" (Jain 2008).

Jain's recommendations may seem extreme, but they do indicate Hindu concern about caste prejudice within churches:

> There is no excuse for SC discrimination in the church, and it is high time the Government of India invoked existing laws against church clergy and laity for persisting abuse. An immediate crackdown should be made against exclusively dalit churches, followed by an action against churches with segregated pews for sitting, separate water for communion,[12] and separate burial spaces. (ibid.)

To the extent that she describes church caste realities, believers themselves ought to consider how Jesus would have them address such problems from within. I began this section with the 1984 Christian call to address caste challenges in the church. Twenty-four years later, Jain described the same caste-based discrimination, still not addressed. Jain articulates it, but Hindus like her can see what she has observed. Church discrimination, where it exists, can present an obstacle to Jesus.

These representative examples of caste barriers within the church should trouble true believers deeply. The ekklēsia, the body of Christ, breaks down dividing walls (Eph 2:14) and brings divided people together (Eph 2:15–19). Church, instead, can sometimes perpetuate social divisions that keep believers from fellowship with one another and that keep countless more from Jesus.

Please don't think I am singling out the Indian church here. This "caste" reality is one expression of a pervasive problem with the church construct.

---

11. The issue of government "reservation" (benefits) for Dalits is an ongoing debate that I cannot address here. Google "Christian Dalit reservation" for some sense of the intense feeling this issue arouses within India on multiple sides.

12. Refers to some churches that require separate vessels and juice ("water" is her confusion) for different castes when they take communion.

It's not just in India. At times, the Western church justified and legitimized slavery, anti-Semitism, apartheid, genocide, imperialism, colonialism, and segregation. These practices, sometimes even originated by church sanction, were justified by misuse of Scripture, and were only later corrected by concerned believers.

These considerations about denomination and caste offer representative examples of what could be a full book's worth of barriers related to church. Even if we dealt with these issues, however, my conversations and explorations have indicated that resistance to church lies deeper than any of these issues.

WHY IS THE WEST ABANDONING CHURCH?

Anyone familiar with Western Christianity is aware that the church has barriers of its own in the West. Indian critics note this fact, and point to the decline in church attendance and adherence. "To replenish these negative trends," says Malhotra, "the Churches have looked for the export market." As he sees it, India is the largest open market in the world for the church conversion business to make up for what the Western church is losing at home (Malhotra 2000).

We may not like such criticism, but look at it from a Hindu perspective for a moment. Why would they be attracted to a church that is being abandoned significantly in its home cultures (Europe and America)?

The Pew study of Religion and Public life in the US indicated that those who have no religious affiliation and never or rarely attend church rose from 15 percent to 20 percent just between 2007 and 2012 (Pew Research Center 2012). A US social survey, in addition, reported that people who changed to "No Religion" increased "from 8 percent in 1990 to 21 percent in 2014," including a 3 percent rise just between 2010 to 2014 (Hout and Smith 2015, 1). Another indicator of this shift away from church is the concurrent reduction in church attendance—24 percent of Americans attended weekly services in 2014, a decline from 30 percent in 1991 (ibid., 2). The West, in other words, increasingly finds church problematic and stays away.

Larry Kinnaman, of Barna Research, extensively researched reasons Christian young people are leaving and staying away from church in the

US (Kinnaman 2011) as well as what about church kept non-Christians away (Kinnaman and Lyons 2007).

A video publicizing *You Lost Me* asserted that the "leavers" must come back to church to connect with Jesus and "find what they are missing" (Baker Publishing Group 2012). In a similar vein a popular Christian speaker was asked whether a person could let go of church, but hold on to Jesus. His first sentence in response? *"If you do that, you are walking away from Jesus"* (Piper 2015).

Based on my India reflections about the church barrier, these responses are both short-sighted and ultimately unscriptural—despite the verses quoted to proof-text those answers (stay with me and I'll explain). The above studies (Kinnaman), and several others, suggest that if the current church is a required vehicle for Jesus, the "No Religion" respondents and many more are going to stay away in increasing numbers. They just don't want anything to do with church. Hindus and Muslims, who are completely outside the church, will continue to avoid it.

A more challenging alternative exists instead of the simplistic "come back to church" answers above. Whether people avoid or abandon church, this global resistance to church is not, and should not be automatically equated with resistance to Jesus or to his body or fellowship. I'm not sure all these people want to walk away or stay away from Jesus. What if they are walking away from churches and their associated institutional forms that keep them from Jesus, from his fellowship, from his ekklēsia? Currently they are afforded no alternative forms of ekklēsia. It's church or nothing. We need to reconsider that either-or option with a more scriptural alternative.

The church (no matter its origin) insists that it alone is the container for Jesus and his ekklēsia. Reject church, they say, and you cannot have Jesus either. Given no alternative, these people walk away from it all, unaware that the church may have given them a false, unscriptural choice.

If we truly desire to help Hindus, and many others, get past the "church barrier" and find Jesus, we must understand at a deeper level where the real barrier lies. It's not just external cultural forms, foreign worship styles, even denominational or caste divisions. At its heart, this barrier arises because common assumptions about church represent a human cultural tradition as foreign to the New Testament as it often seems to India (or many other places). The real barrier originated in the West.

Unless we recognize and address the church barrier at this level, church may just keep pushing more people away from Jesus, unnecessarily.

THE BARRIER OF THE TERM "CHURCH"

We must first understand the Greek word ekklēsia which is typically rendered "church" in English Bibles (except Acts 7:38; 19:32, 39, 41). Only then can we understand why church is a problem. The real barrier of church arises because the ideas inherent in that word are completely unrelated, and sometimes opposite, to the essence of ekklēsia.

DEFINING EKKLESIA

The word ekklēsia, interestingly, points us in an incarnational direction. In common Greek, it referred to a gathering, assembly, or meeting of people (Schmidt 1985, 397; Bauer, et al. 1979, 240–241; Liddell, Scott, and Jones 1940). The main idea of ekklēsia was a "convened assembly" (Deissmann 1980, 112), people gathered or meeting for some purpose.

Other words were readily available for religious gatherings, of which *synagogue* was a popular Jewish one. In describing his fellowship, though, Jesus and his followers avoided religious, separatist terms and used a neutral, widely used cultural term for the society of believers. Based on this reality, Schmidt suggests that we should ask "why the NT community avoids a cultic term for itself and selects a more secular one" (Schmidt 1985, 397). When believers used ekklēsia it did not flag them immediately as a separate and separatist religious "community." As a culturally neutral term for "assembly," it was not as likely to raise alarms.

The believers sought, as much as possible, to incarnate the way and life of Jesus within their culture and community. Using ekklēsia to describe their gatherings provided a neutral term, rather than a distinctive one. In *The Christians as the Romans Saw Them*, Wilken suggests that for the early Romans, ekklēsia suggested the political gathering of a city's citizenry to conduct city business (Wilken 1984, 33). Wilken further demonstrates that ekklēsia seemed situated among a variety of early clubs, associations, and societies, whether occupational, social, or occasionally religious (ibid., 35–47). These societies did not separate from the culture at large, but were subgroups, special-interest groups, *within* the broader culture.

Wilken observes that when the gatherings of believers were perceived as associations or societies, "such a characterization helped people to place the Christian groups within a familiar frame of reference and gave outsiders a sense of what went on in its meetings . . ." (ibid., 45). Because of this situation of ekklēsia within the broader culture, it was an incarnational not isolationist word term for Christ's followers.

The apologist Tertullian "uses the language of the association as a vehicle to present a portrait of the Christian movement to outsiders" (ibid., 45–46). In one chapter, in fact (Apology 39, cited in Wilken 1984, 46), Tertullian uses words for associations and societies commonly understood by the Romans, but not even ekklēsia. Rather than separating and isolating believers from the culture around them with separatist language, Tertullian intentionally chose "social and nontheological" language (ibid.) to situate the people of Jesus within their cultural milieu, to help others understand what the believers were about.

India today desperately needs believers who will grasp this incarnational language and approach in how they relate the fellowship of believers to Hindu society at large. The original choice of ekklēsia built a bridge to the Greco-Roman culture. "Church" is a bad translation, partly, because it does exactly the opposite today.

WORKING DEFINITION OF EKKLESIA

When the followers used it, ekklēsia was the association, meeting, and fellowship of believers, and it came to include the idea that it was a meeting of people associated with Jesus. I use it in this sense through the book, so let me provide my working definition of ekklēsia: *an incarnational fellowship of disciples of Jesus*. I choose these key words carefully, and need to explain why I have done so.

Incarnational

The word ekklēsia was not a separatist word in the first century. It afforded an incarnational bridge to the culture, not a barrier. It had familiar connotations and associations for people in the broader society. In addition, it was comprised of the New Covenant people of Jesus, who were to be recognized for their identification and incarnation as much as the Old Covenant people were for their isolation and separation. The body of

Christ should be incarnated within a socioreligious community as much as possible, rather than as separated from it as possible.

Fellowship

Almost anywhere else in the world, a good translation for ekklēsia would be "community," a group of people who share a common purpose or qualities. In India, however, we cannot use that word to render ekklēsia. See Richard's "Community Dynamics" for a summary of some of the problematic issues and terminology related to "community" (Richard 2007a). In India "community" is often the code word for "caste" or "religion." Ask someone about their "community" in India and you may offend them for insensitive prying. So, calling the ekklēsia the "community" of Jesus creates a separatist identity immediately, the opposite of what happened with ekklēsia in the New Testament.

I intentionally choose "fellowship," then, to emphasize an interactive gathering of people who share a common interest (Jesus). "Fellowship" also involves mutual concern and participation, rather than simply attendance at a meeting.

I also use "fellowship" because it allows the range of meanings that ekklēsia has in the New Testament. When believers gathered in one home, "the ekklēsia that meets in their house" (e.g., Rom 16:5), it was a house fellowship. Paul addressed the ekklēsia in a city also, implying that all the house fellowships were considered part of one city-wide fellowship. Other passages speak of all believers in every place as the ekklēsia. We can speak of a global fellowship or worldwide fellowship of believers and capture the essence of what ekklēsia conveys.

Disciples of Jesus

Part of the church's problem arises from the "Christian" issues in the previous chapter. I was talking with a business man one day and mentioned some people I know who do "church-planting." He immediately reacted, "Chennai does not need more church-planting; we have too many churches already. We really need disciple-making and equipping."

The ekklēsia of Jesus is only made up of disciples of Jesus. That's it. He doesn't look to see if a person has Christian on a census card, or is on a church roster, or was born into a Christian family. The *disciples* were not called Christians until nearly two decades after the Pentecost event

(Acts 11:26), but the ekklēsia was made up of disciples before "Christian" ever existed. It continued to consist of disciples after that point, because they still did not call themselves Christians.

Today churches make Christians and hope some eventually become disciples. Not so the New Testament ekklēsia. Our emphasis should be where Jesus put it in his commission (Matt 28:19f.), to "make disciples," not to "make Christians," or to make "church members." Those who become disciples become active parts of the incarnational fellowship. The ekklēsia was an incarnational movement of people, not a religious institution. That came later, as we will now discover.

Defining "Church"

As a child, I was taught a poem with hand motions:

> Here is the church. Here is the steeple.
> Open the doors. See all the people.

This poem explicitly inculcated the basic Western understanding of church. Church was a location (usually a church building with special architecture) to which people came. The steeple indicated that it was, in common parlance, a "house of worship."

Ministers have tried to counter this notion: "It's not the building; church is the *people*. You don't *come to* church; you *are* the church." For generations, though, their own Sunday school teachers have taught that poem, with endearing hand gestures to accompany it. The pastor's ineffective corrective just sounds like an adult talking in the Peanuts cartoons, "Mwah mwah, mwah mwah mwah mwah!" Thanks, pastor, but we know better! We learned it in Sunday school. No competition!

What is the problem with church then? That poem just hints at the real church barrier. We must examine common cultural understandings of church. To do so I consulted two standard dictionaries of the English language. The following chart compares the two sets of definitions (using the Oxford Dictionary's order).

Dictionary Definitions of "Church"

Table 3. Oxford and Merriam-Webster Definitions of "Church"

Oxford English Dictionary	Merriam-Webster Dictionary
"A *building* used for *public Christian worship*" (e.g., "They came to church with me")	"A *building* for public and especially Christian worship" ALSO "*Public, divine worship*" (e.g., Go to church)
"A particular *Christian organization*, typically one with its own clergy, buildings, and distinctive doctrines" (e.g., The Church of England)	"A *body or organization of religious believers*" (e.g., All Christians, a particular denomination, a congregation, or local gathering of believers)
"The *hierarchy of clergy* of a Christian organization, especially the Roman Catholic Church or the Church of England"	"The *clergy or officialdom* of a religious body" ALSO RELATED "The *clerical profession*" (e.g., He considered the church as a possible occupation)
"*Institutionalized religion* as a political or social force" (e.g., Separation of church and state)	
(Church, OED 2014) [Emphases mine]	(Church, MWD 2014) [Emphases mine]

These definitions illustrate six rather common assumptions about church. Let's first examine those assumptions, and then compare them to the New Testament understanding of ekklēsia.

- A Building or Location
- Public Christian Worship
- Hierarchical Clergy Who Preside over the Church
- Clergy Provide Ministry to the Church
- Institution and Denomination
- Specifically Christian Term (rather than culturally neutral term)

The first definition (shaded) is the one most commonly understood when the word is used. That's the idea that most readily comes to mind when people hear "church"—a building or location to which believers go.

Just what the poem taught! So, "church" is first and foremost a location (preferably a church building) for public Christian worship.

The other definitions provide additional nuances as to how "church" is often used, not only in English, but often when translated into other languages also. Christianity has certainly established a common global understanding regarding what it means by "church."

The dictionary definitions, though, only tell part of the story. Much of what we see above arose because of the history of the word itself. Therefore, it is helpful to take a quick historical journey to see where the word "church" and its associated ideas originated.

History of "Church"

Early English Bibles, like those of Wycliffe and Tyndale, translated ekklēsia as "congregation" prior to the Geneva Bible of 1560 (Hort 1914, 2). This emphasized the "people" idea of ekklēsia. In fact, Tyndale, in his preface, clearly indicated his view that the "congregation" was composed equally of all believers, not primarily the hierarchy of the clergy separate from the laity (Daniell 1994, 122). This was considered "damnable heresy" by the English church authorities on two counts: "the implied equality [of all believers] and the pernicious word 'congregation' instead of 'church'" (ibid.).

Tyndale was targeted as a heretic because he substituted understandable terms instead of "accepted ecclesiastical terms ('congregation' instead of 'church', 'elder' instead of 'priest', 'love' instead of 'charity')." For such unacceptable departures from church tradition, the English church had Tyndale "kidnapped and imprisoned, then garroted and burnt at the stake" (Wansborough 2015, 35). Tyndale presents a cautionary tale. He challenged the church's insistence that ekklēsia must be translated "church" and the church authorities killed him for doing so. Christians do not always take kindly to having their church traditions challenged with Scripture.

From the Geneva Bible forward, English Bibles typically have hidden ekklēsia behind "church." The church hierarchy (clergy) wanted to preserve its institutional and locational traditions against any attempt to return the ekklēsia to the people (congregation). The choice of word, seemingly so innocuous today, was an incredibly challenging and threatening cultural choice in 1536. Tyndale died for not using "church."

Why the big deal about church? Why was the church so insistent on its "church" tradition? That requires a little journey farther back in time. In the first two centuries of Christianity, ekklēsias met in homes or in available gathering places, whether public or private (school—Acts 19:10; mostly homes—Acts 2:46; 12:12; 16:40; 18:7; Rom 16:4f.; 16:23; 1 Cor 16:19; Col 4:15; Phlm 2). Early disciples had no dedicated church buildings (Schaff 1870, 372); in fact, they seem to have avoided special buildings altogether for two hundred years. We never read of people going *to* church or *to* "the Lord's house." The believers were the ekklēsia. They understood that they were "the Lord's house" (2 Cor 5:1; Eph 2:19; 1 Pet 2:5). They were *not* constrained by a physical location or building (John 4:20–24).

All that rapidly changed in the middle of the third century. Both physical buildings and church assumptions rapidly replaced New Testament ideas of ekklēsia. Church historian Everett Ferguson provides a synopsis of the history of church structures prior to and into the reign of Constantine:

> We have archaeological evidence of *halls being built for church meetings* at the end of the third and beginning of the fourth century. The great era of church buildings began with Constantine's patronage of the church in the fourth century. He commissioned basilicas to signal his support of the new religion and to advertise his reign. (Ferguson 2008; emphasis mine)

With and after Constantine (AD 313) the Roman and Greek Christians increasingly emphasized dedicated "church buildings" (North 1991, 83). This change to location-based church also involved a change from ekklēsia itself. Rutz, in *The Open Church*, describes the rapid transition in Constantine's era: "The church became less of a revolutionary band, and more of a static establishment. Eloquent preachers began to attract large followings . . . After this first flurry of church buildings in 327, we *ceased being an interactive family* and turned into an audience" (Rutz 1992, 9–10; emphasis mine).

These buildings, which became the center of Christian life and worship, were called *kuriakon* ("the Lord's place," "the Lord's house"). The Lord did not institute this tradition for the ekklēsia, and neither did his apostles. Church as a physical "Lord's house" was a Western cultural invention unknown for the first two hundred years of the ekklēsia.

Once it was invented, the clergy insisted that you had to go to the *"the Lord's house"* and receive ministry from the Lord's clergy, if you wanted to have a relationship with the Lord. They traded the informal, participatory house fellowships (1 Cor 14:26; Eph 5:19f.) for attendance at rhetorical presentations and liturgies performed by clergy, who increasingly separated themselves from the common believers in ways unknown in the New Testament.

The same dictionaries I cited before, provide the etymology (word history) of "church." The English word originated, after several language changes, from that old Greek word *kuriakon*, not from ekklēsia. The same path led to the Scottish *Kirk*, German *Kirche*, and Dutch *Kerk* (OED 2014; MWD 2014). This provides the backstory to our English word church and the powerful anti-ekklēsia connotations that it assumed. "Church" originated, in other words, from the time when the Western church turned the people-centered ekklēsia into a building-and ritual-centered religion, when the priesthood of all believers was unscripturally replaced by a hierarchical priesthood of the clergy (a contradiction of Matt 20:20–28).

THE SHIFT FROM EKKLESIA TO "CHURCH"

We can look at this shift from ekklēsia to church in several ways. It's possible to suggest that church inherently reflects the departure from the New Testament faith noted by Bosch and Ellul (see Chapter 2, p. 36). Some days, in a more despairing mood, I lean toward that option. From that perspective, the West replaced the ekklēsia with its own church, borrowing what it wanted from the New Testament, but incorporating much pagan tradition and human invention into an institution Jesus never initiated or intended.

However, we can also make a case that the church was partly the result of believers "becoming all things to all people" in their own cultural context. They adapted the ekklēsia in various ways to their cultures and communities, and, in the process, it accumulated layers of cultural accretions over centuries. Faced with new cultural contexts, they developed fresh expressions of the ekklēsia, or more often modified their previous adaptations to fit those new situations.

Some of their adaptations were faithful and legitimate. Others departed from New Testament principles. Most days, I'm more gracious and give it the benefit of the doubt. Unfortunately, once the initial adaptations were made, believers often assumed that the adaptations were normative for all believers. The resulting church, in future cultural encounters, often imposed their previous adaptations on new cultures, rather than starting with ekklēsia again.

Either way, the bottom line is the same. The "church" is actually a human cultural construct that attempts, with varying levels of success, to manifest the ekklēsia of Jesus. Some claim that their church is the ekklēsia of Jesus. They believe that what they practice now is what Jesus instituted and the apostles initiated. Every church that makes this claim, though, has so many additions beyond the New Testament that such claims are dubious. They have still added layers of cultural tradition and baggage to the original practice of Jesus and his ekklēsia.

This is, in fact, unavoidable. The New Testament specifies certain ordinances and practices, without providing the details of how they should be conducted in different contexts. Believers are forced to create expressions for a given location if they want to obey Scripture. Every church, then, is a unique mix of scriptural elements in varying degrees mixed with a significant portion of human invention and tradition. It is essential that they do this in a specific context. It's problematic when they impose their inventions and traditions on other believers in different contexts.

However we got from ekklēsia to church, we must stop and examine how different the two have become. Part of India's resistance may result from too much church and too little ekklēsia.

Comparing Church and Ekklesia

Let me set some of the key assumptions about church alongside some New Testament features of the ekklēsia of Jesus. This chart suggests that the West has taken some creative liberties with its church version of the ekklēsia. In fact, some of the standard features of church depart substantially from what Jesus and the apostles taught and practiced.

Table 4. Comparing Ekklēsia and Church Assumptions

Ekklēsia	Church
People (e.g., Rom 16:5) Believer is Sanctuary (1 Cor 6:19)	Location/Building Building is Sanctuary (Lord's House)
Live Life of Worship (Col 3:17) Participation & Interaction (1 Cor 14:26)	Focus on Coming to Public Worship Performance & Presentation
Priesthood of All Believers (1 Pet 2:9) Shared, Servant Leadership (Matt 20:20–28) Equipped to Do Ministry (Eph 4:11f.)	Clergy and Hierarchy are the Primary Priests Often Monarchical, Hierarchical Leadership Come to Receive Ministry
Non-religious Word for Assembly (Acts 19)	Exclusively "Christian" Word (separatist)

The ekklēsia was focused on people, not buildings, programs, or events. As we will see in Chapter 7, the early ekklēsia emphasized a personal life of worship, not just attending a weekly worship event. The early ekklēsia gatherings were informal, participatory, and equipped all believers to be ministers and priests. Finally, ekklēsia in the first century was a common cultural word with little or no religious significance. The Holy Spirit had words available for specific religious gatherings, but led the writers to use a neutral, non-religious term that had multiple senses in the surrounding culture. Using ekklēsia fit with several cultural patterns of association and did not flag the believers as some separatist group.

Church, as it exists today, cannot necessarily be considered an adequate—definitely not the best—expression of ekklēsia. It seems that there is room for improvement here, room to reexamine and rebuild from the foundation of the apostles and the prophets, instead of the foundations of Rome or Europe or America.

Fresh Expressions of Ekklesia

The Eastern and Western churches felt free to adjust the ekklēsia to their cultural likings. A long line of reformers and restorers have repeatedly sought to develop fresh expressions of the ekklēsia for their time and culture.

Where church particularly presents a barrier to Jesus because of its foreign nature, contextualizing church may be the wrong approach. We may need to let go of our church assumptions entirely. We need to instead encourage believers to start with only the essentials of ekklēsia as revealed in the New Testament. Then we should teach them to seek the leading of the Head of the ekklēsia, his Spirit, and his Word to develop a fresh expression of ekklēsia appropriate for their culture and community. We should not bind them to any church tradition or requirement. They are part of the ekklēsia of Jesus, his body, his family. That should be sufficient. They should not have to be part of a church, provided they become part of a scriptural and culturally appropriate form of ekklēsia.

"Church-planting" is also not a great idea in contexts that are rightly resistant to the foreign church construct. Some ministries don't call it "church-planting," but the groups they reproduce look, smell, and act like church more than ekklēsia. Whatever we call it, we need to focus on fellowships of believers that reflect the core values of ekklēsia, not the assumptions of Euro-American church.

Darren Duerksen has explored some of what this looks like in his work on *ecclesial communities* (Duerksen 2012; Duerksen 2015). The ways that these believers work out their fellowship, worship, witness, and instruction should be a natural interaction between the scriptural functions of ekklēsia and their own culture. Church expectations should not be imposed on them as normative. No matter how dear the practice might be to Christians in existing churches, much church tradition originated from Christian adoption of Euro-American cultural forms (Viola and Barna 2012). None of that tradition is essential.

Christian scholar and linguist, F. J. A. Hort, pointed to the same solution at the conclusion of *The Christian Ecclesia*:

> The Apostolic age is full of embodiments of purposes and principles of the most instructive kind: but the responsibility of choosing the means was left forever to the Ecclesia itself, and to each Ecclesia, guided by ancient precedent on the one hand and adaptation to present and future needs on the other. (Hort 1914, 233)

The European or American ekklēsia, should not presume to be the arbiter for how the ekklēsia should look in India. That's for Indian believers to decide with the Lord's leading.

My bhakta friends in different parts of the country also seek the Lord and Scripture in developing healthy expressions of the ekklēsia for their context and culture. Contrary to some accusations leveled against "insiders," the bhaktas I know meet regularly for fellowship in house gatherings (*satsangs*) but the whole *mandali* also meets regularly for larger encouragement, fellowship, and in-depth Scripture study. They have a regular, functioning ekklēsia, it just does not look like what Western Christians typically recognize as church.

How Does Ekklesia Address the Church Barriers?

How would fresh expressions of ekklēsia address the church barrier? Most obviously, it would remove the foreign, Western assumptions from church that Hindus (and others too) find so unappealing. If my analysis is correct, then believers have no obligation to maintain the cultural accretions of Western church tradition, any more than they are obligated to maintain, say English or Latin, as a church language.

Regarding denominational division, a fresh expression of ekklēsia removes much of the necessity for denominations, especially foreign ones. If a believer simply becomes a follower of Jesus in India, why does she have to owe allegiance to some organization that originated halfway around the world? Even if new denominations started in India as a result, at least they would be Indian, and, one hopes, closer to the New Testament ekklēsia. Since Christians elsewhere have felt free to create new churches for their contexts, why would it be inherently wrong for Indians to do the same in a much more diverse situation?

How would such an approach help resolve the caste divisions in the current church? The New Testament ekklēsia placed a high priority on fellowship and social reconciliation. The ekklēsia found ways to bring together and unify people from widely diverse backgrounds. This will take some incredible risk and creativity by Indians who know their own context. It will also require an incredibly delicate balance between maintaining respectful relationships with one's caste of origin, while also building new relationships across caste lines.

By not adopting "Christian" separatist identity, but emphasizing respectful, friendly relationships with the surrounding community, incarnational fellowships could lead to less suspicion, judgment, and condemnation. By not being pressured to "convert" out of community (Chapter 5), believers would have greater freedom to navigate and negotiate the still complex relationships with their Hindu family and broader community and society.

Is the Western "Church" Construct Normative?

Let me explicitly state what I hope has been clearly hinted at so far. The Western church paradigm is not, and should not be considered, normative for all believers in all contexts. Certainly not in India. The ekklēsia does not have to be expressed and propagated in forms the West has defined as church. The West created an institutional, building-based, meeting-based system as its expression. Indian believers are not obligated to start with those church assumptions and then wrap that in Indian garb (contextualization). They should, instead, be free to incarnate the ekklēsia of Jesus as faithfully to Scripture as possible, but in forms that reflect the values, traditions, and customs of their own heritage.

Neill, in his *History of Christian Missions*, points us in this direction. He speaks of a "disastrous theological error" in which global Christians assumed that the church was an amalgamation of "Anglicans and Methodists and Baptists, instead of the other way round, *the body of Christ being the great reality* of which Anglicans and Methodists and Baptists were recognized to be *fragmentary and very imperfect incorporations*" (Neill 1990, 383; emphasis mine).

Millions are abandoning the church in the West and rejecting the church in the East. That global resistance to church may have nothing to do with Jesus or his ekklēsia. They may just be alienated from Jesus by the "fragmentary and very imperfect incorporations" the church has retained from other times and contexts. Those incorporations are not essential. Only the ekklēsia is.

Incarnational paradigms in the Middle East and Asia, rather than being unfaithful to Jesus, may represent Jesus' call for his people to return to his ekklēsia. So many of those who might have followed him have been kept away or driven away because of the West's insistence that church is the only way to Jesus. We may actually be facing a new Reformation, hopefully more radical and scriptural than that initiated in Europe five hundred years ago.

Some will need to relinquish the familiar "old wineskins" of church. They will instead be led by the Lord to explore and develop fresh expressions and incorporations of ekklēsia in places where the church construct today keeps countless people away from Jesus.

Church Isn't the Only Term

In our discussion of church to this point, we have ignored another scriptural alternative. The New Testament uses nearly one hundred different metaphors and descriptors for the people of Jesus (Minear 2004, 268f). Minear's extensive discussion of these alternatives suggests that we aren't limited to ekklēsia to begin with. The West gravitated to "church" and created deeply seated traditions around that word. That does not mean that all believers in all places must follow that cultural emphasis.

Incarnational believers in other contexts are not obligated to adopt the West's emphasis on its one term of choice. Do you have to have "church" at the end of the name to make it legitimate? I don't think so. It would be just as scriptural to select one or more of the other descriptives for the fellowship or assembly—ones that resonate with Hindu culture—and then translate, explain, and utilize those. To "become all things to all people," Indian believers will need to consider these scriptural alternatives to church. They should be the ones to make the choice, though, and not Western churches or Westernized believers intent on preserving the church status quo.

CAN SOMEONE FOLLOW JESUS WITHOUT CHURCH?

Now, having addressed this church and ekklēsia concern, let us return to the question at the beginning of this chapter. Given the barrier that church can pose for various reasons, *can someone follow Jesus without church*? If you have stayed with me this far, you already have some idea of how I will answer.

People can follow Jesus without church, just not without a legitimate and appropriate form of ekklēsia. Who decides what that form will be? Jesus, his Spirit, and his people in that context. Not Westerners, not missiologists, not theologians, not even Westernized Christians from that location. Some Christians insist on aspects of church they deem essential, even though those features end up creating cultural barriers for incarnational believers.

These believers should follow Jesus without church. In fact, in many contexts *believers may be more faithful to Jesus if they are encouraged and taught to follow Jesus without church.* If Jesus is ever to incarnate within their culture and community, then the ekklēsia, the body of Jesus, must incarnate within their culture and community from the beginning.

I've written this chapter, in fact, out of multiple conversations with Christians and Yesu bhaktas. I know of Christians who try to tell bhaktas that they are not being faithful to Jesus if they do not join a church. I've been told of Christian evangelists whose "conversion" of bhaktas drove many more entirely away from Jesus. On the other hand, I know Christians who have encouraged believers to leave the church and return to their Hindu community where they really belong as bhaktas of Jesus. They are part of a *mandali* of believers, but not a "church."

If you choose to be part of a church, that is your prerogative, but no believer is obligated to belong to a church. They must participate in an appropriate expression of ekklēsia. For those who come to Jesus directly from a Hindu background, we want to encourage them to find a *mandali* and develop fellowship opportunities with like-minded believers. Under normal circumstances, they should not be brought into churches, even temporarily. That would unnecessarily compromise their relationships with their community and potentially damage their incarnational walk with the Lord.

So, based on these considerations, my friend at the start of this chapter was really thinking in the right direction. It would take time, prayer, and study, but if her father could follow Jesus without "church," if he could become a follower of Jesus and develop a fellowship of believers, they could become a faithful expression of ekklēsia without joining a church or adopting church traditions.

Ekklesia of One

What happens if only one person becomes a believer? We should see them as the seed of a new expression of ekklēsia. The Christian impulse to get them into a church, can be damaging. Do they need fellowship? Yes, but they need incarnational fellowship, not an extracting community. We should not force church membership to artificially create fellowship.

Instead, we should follow the New Testament pattern that the Holy Spirit used with a single new believer from a new cultural group (Acts 8:26–39). The Lord could have arranged a meeting in Jerusalem with one of the apostles there. He did not. In that instance, the man would have been made a Jewish believer, no doubt. Why did the Lord choose a deserted road instead? When Philip introduced the Ethiopian eunuch to Jesus, an amazing thing happened from the Western church perspective. The Holy Spirit took Philip out of there immediately after the eunuch's baptism. He had no chance to put him into a church fellowship or to coach him on "proper" worship and church practices.

The eunuch went on his way rejoicing as an ekklēsia of one with Jesus in his heart. It was up to him, led by the Lord and his Spirit, to live his faith and share his faith back home. Whatever form that ekklēsia took, it likely did not follow patterns that the Jerusalem church had established, or even those of the Pauline churches. However, I would contend, whatever form that fellowship took, it would be Ethiopian, not Jewish. It would be as much an ekklēsia as any Western church. It just would not look anything like what we think of as church. It didn't have to.

JUST TO BE CLEAR

In advocating for believers to follow Jesus without church but with ekklēsia:

- We are not saying that people should just be individual believers (just Jesus and me) with no fellowship (all believers should be part of an expression of ekklēsia as soon as possible).
- We are saying that people should be connected to a fellowship (they just do not have to join a church form of fellowship).
- We are saying that a believer can be in the body of Christ, the kingdom of God, the family of God, and his fellowship without being in a church.
- We are saying that such believers can and should follow Jesus in a culturally appropriate expression of the ekklēsia.

CHRISTIAN AND BHAKTA CONSIDERATIONS

Christians

The church model has resonated with some Indians and drawn them to Jesus in very meaningful ways. In my travels, I have worshiped with various churches who deeply love Jesus and who will never follow him in any other way.

Yet the issues inherent in church, and the Western traditions it represents (whatever word you use), continue to present significant barriers to billions of people globally, and to significant numbers of Indians. We cannot simply address the church barriers cosmetically, and ignore the deeper issues that create them. The Reformation kept church as its paradigm, Restoration Movements did so too. Renewal, re-church, rethinking, or reset attempts all perpetuate the same barriers, if they fail to question the deeper cultural assumptions around church itself.

Some of the church barrier can be removed by addressing its emphases and forms. Christians know these get in the way of too many people. Peter Ignatius, an Indian seminary president, has observed, "Astute students of Christian missions in India" have come to the opinion that "the Church today is not showing the original fact of Jesus, but it is showing itself with all its accumulated traditions and customs" (Ignatius 2016). He works with numbers of people who are seeking to make church incarnational in creative ways, in ways that emphasize the way and life of Jesus, rather than these "accumulated traditions and customs." Their creative exploration of various forms of ekklēsia is both refreshing and exciting to observe.

For those of you who are followers of Jesus, but know church is a barrier, I hope this chapter encourages you to consider fresh expressions of ekklēsia in your context. So many people are alienated by church that we must follow Jesus in prayerfully exploring and developing appropriate alternatives.

Yesu Bhaktas

Bhaktas have chosen to follow Jesus, but not join a traditional church. That decision may be more faithful to Scripture than some believers acknowledge. Jesus expects his followers to belong to an ekklēsia of some kind. They may use a variety of locally equivalent terms: mandali, sangam, sabha, satsang, or *darbar*. Hebrews 10:25 says that believers should not forsake gathering together. It does not say that the gathering must be a church. When believers are devoted to God's word, fellowship, Lord's Supper, and mutual prayer (Acts 2:42), the form of the gathering is irrelevant. When they meet in homes for satsangs focused on Jesus and his word, they have all that Jesus requires (Matt 18:20).

CLOSING REFLECTIONS

I am honestly of two minds as I close this chapter. I've spent sixty years in the church, over half of that in some form of church ministry. Sometimes, as I reflect on this chapter's contents, I can tell myself, the church is just the West's version of "becoming all things to all people." It was a perfectly valid contextual expression of ekklesia for Western culture. It's just not necessary for the rest of the world to follow our model.

Yet, the more I look at the scriptural and historical evidence in this chapter, I can't shake a nagging concern. The West's church model has departed fundamentally from the ekklēsia that Jesus instituted and that the apostles established in his name. I continue to be haunted by Bosch and Ellul's very real concerns related in the previous chapter (see p. 36).

The global rejection of church—abandonment in the West, avoidance among close to one billion Hindus—suggests that we who claim to follow Jesus must examine ourselves. Are we so committed to *our* church that we would keep millions away from Jesus in order to preserve church traditions and familiarity? Or will we love Jesus and his ekklēsia so much that we will listen to this global challenge? Will we allow him to initiate fresh expressions of his ekklēsia ("new wineskins") in places where church forms are not and maybe never were appropriate?

Did you catch that? *"Allow him"*? Who are we to think that we *allow* our Lord, the only Head of his ekklēsia, to do anything? In fact, through "non-Christian believers," "insider movements," "incarnational believers," and "missional communities" among others, Jesus seems to be challenging his ekklēsia to step away from traditional church models as the only forms. Christians are just having to catch up to his vision for the ekklēsia, instead of their church-focused understanding. The future will be both unsettling and incredibly freeing.

INTERLUDE
THREE FOUNDATIONAL BARRIERS

These first three barriers, *cultural separatism*, *Christian identity*, and *church*, form what I call the foundational barriers. The other barriers arise from and build off them, or contribute to them in various ways. Before we proceed, we need to review these foundational barriers from two perspectives. Let's briefly examine some common responses to the foundational barriers. Then we will briefly introduce the remaining barriers as they relate to these three.

RESPONSES TO THE THREE FOUNDATIONAL BARRIERS

Christians and Churches Adjust Their Separation Mentality

Some Christians and churches continue to maintain these identities. They try, however, in as many ways as possible to build respectful relationships to the culture around them. They intentionally seek to demonstrate that they are not against the culture or community in which they reside. They wrestle with how to appropriately associate with the predominantly Hindu community around them, rather than extracting from it. They will, though, always be Christians who associate with churches.

Churches Minimize Separation and Christian Identity, but Retain Church Identity

Other believers continue to worship and serve in a local church. They see themselves as active church members and identify with that expression of community and worship. When someone asks them about their relationship with Jesus, however, they avoid using "Christian" as a self-designation. That term is too polarizing in their context. Instead, they commonly call themselves Christ-followers, believers, disciples, or some other culturally neutral term.

Depending on the context, this may work. It does raise questions, though, from people who expect that the followers of Jesus must call themselves Christians. In some contexts, and India is one, such believers can be viewed with skepticism by the community at large.

As an example, various news sites reported in early 2016 that a group of believers were fined by their village council for disturbing communal harmony. When some of these believers were interviewed, they all asserted that they "were not Christians," but regularly went to church because they found the prayers helpful. Their frequent attendance at church gatherings and prayer meetings created the impression that they were Christians, even though they denied this (Ghatwai 2016). In one report, a US sponsoring pastor's inquiry into their welfare (see Chapter 8—Financial Dependency) raised suspicions about their claim to "not be Christian" (Williams 2016). This group had gathered to celebrate the Hindu harvest festival *Makara Sankranti*. Even this cultural affirmation was not enough to eliminate local Hindu questions about their identity.

Believers Change Terms, but Keep Christian and Church Forms

In some Indian languages, church is translated as *satsang*. The idea of "spiritual gathering" is closer to ekklēsia than "church." The things done in those *satsangs*, though, can clearly represent features of a typical church service—sitting in rows, leader up front, preaching. In other words, they change the labels to Indian terms, but use them to describe overtly Christian church forms and expressions. This can represent contextualization of church and its assumed essentials, but not necessarily incarnation of the ekklēsia for their context.

Some believers go further in their engagement with culture. They recognize that church is also a problem, so they instead meet in homes or neutral settings and call the gathering a *satsang* (or another Indian term for gathering). Some Christians though, co-opt even this form for more church-centered purposes. They do "satsang ministry," but this simply means developing both evangelism and worship based primarily on meetings. They also change the name, but still teach a discipleship that is primarily meeting-centered and attendance-based like Western church traditions. We will discuss why this is problematic for Hindus in the later chapter on worship (see p. 178).

Scriptural Alternatives to Separation, Christian, and Church

The above alternatives provide some possible ways believers have addressed the combined barriers of separatism, Christian identity, and church in India. Any of the above options may be perfectly legitimate, depending on the context, to reduce or remove the significant barriers.

India needs believers, though, who step completely away from the traditions of separatism, Christian identity, and church institutions. For many places and communities in India today, any version of the above responses will still present an insurmountable barrier to Jesus. Much of India will require the followers of Jesus to make a fundamental shift away from these Christian traditions. Believers need to begin with the Scripture studies in these chapters, then develop alternatives that are faithful to the Lord, but rooted deeply in the cultures and communities of India.

Instead of starting with Western Christian and church traditions, and then creating Indian modifications, I advocate for the more radical starting point. We should assume that the Christian tradition is a human invention, unless the Scriptures clearly teach it. No human invention from someone else's culture, no matter how old or hallowed, should be required or bound on Indian believers.

Believers should be encouraged, instead, to start with only Scripture, prayer to the Lord, the guidance of his Holy Spirit, and their knowledge of their culture. Looking to these, they should then ask him, and him only, how to incarnate the way and life of Jesus within their own culture and community. These believers will maintain as respectful and peaceful relationships as possible with their family and community. Instead of Christian identity, they will be genuine disciples and followers of the Lord: they will fellowship and worship with a scriptural and cultural expression of the ekklēsia.

OTHER BARRIERS BUILT ON THE THREE FOUNDATIONAL BARRIERS

Given these considerations of the foundational barriers, where do we go from here? Over the centuries, Christians have developed numerous traditions about proclamation, conversion, worship, and resourcing. These add additional barrier-producing layers to the first three. It is important to get the first three clearly in mind before you continue with the rest.

These additional barriers build on the separatist, Christian, church foundation in complex ways. They both draw from the three and foster increased expression of the three.

The six barriers discussed in the rest of the book fall into four main categories.

Proclamation Barriers

As my Indian friends and I explored the challenge of Christianity in India, a great deal of antagonism revolved around how the church proclaims its message. We will first examine how Christian understanding and explanation of the "gospel" induces confusion and rejection. Preaching traditions additionally reflect foreign cultural values and practices that are sometimes offensive and alienating in the Indian context. India needs believers who will proclaim the good news of Jesus in culturally appropriate ways, rather than mimicking the West's cultural forms as the only legitimate way to present God's word.

Conversion Barriers

Probably the greatest flashpoint for Hindu nationalists in India is the question of conversion. Do a Google search for "India religious conversion" and you will encounter a cross-section of perspectives on Christian and Muslim conversion, Hindu *ghar wapsi* (home coming, reconversion), and an incredible array of perspectives on these issues. When instances of communal conflict are reported in the Indian news, articles often indicate that conversion was a contributing factor to the tension. We will examine both how Hindus view conversion and what Scripture says about it. The results of that analysis will raise important questions about common conversion practices and rhetoric today.

The conversion issue also has led to confusion and tension around baptism. We will discover that human church traditions about baptism unnecessarily offend and alienate many Hindus. It is critical that believers properly examine conversion and baptism assumptions in order to address the barriers they often create.

Worship Barriers

The issue of foreign worship expressions could be a book itself. A great deal of Hindu resistance to Jesus revolves around common worship customs and traditions that often are human inventions, not scriptural essentials. The forms, in too many instances, arise from Western church cultures, and are sometimes inappropriate for the Indian context. This chapter calls for much greater attention to Indian forms and expressions rather than slavish conformity to foreign traditions as the essential norms for worshiping the Lord. In the process, it also highlights a deeper cultural problem where churches may emphasize public, corporate worship almost to the exclusion of private, personal worship. This unscriptural emphasis contributes to India's resistance to the good news of Jesus.

Resource Barriers

When Hindu critics are not reacting directly to conversion issues, their other common target is the foreign funding and benevolence enterprise of Christianity and its churches. In the concluding two chapters we will explore how the West's money imposes its own values and traditions on Indian believers in ways that enforce the previous barriers. These funds, from a skeptical perspective, are driving the Western agenda to convert Indians into members of a separatist, Christian, church community—a community both anti-Hindu and, in many ways, anti-Indian.

Believers in India and supporters in the West need to wrestle with the deep concerns that Western funds present to the Indian heart. In these chapters, we explore a biblical approach that encourages believers to fundamentally change their funding model when it presents a significant barrier to the society they claim they want to introduce to Jesus.

As you read, keep looking for ways that the foundational barriers of separatism, Christian identity, and church institutions, weave their way into these remaining barriers. Only then can we make the necessary adjustments to remove these Christian barriers to Jesus.

CHAPTER 4

THE BARRIER OF "EVANGELISM," "GOSPEL," AND "PREACHING"

Aaditya is the only believer in his Hindu family. The congregation where he attends has encouraged him, though, to maintain respectful and polite relationship with his family. While the family does not fully understand his decision to follow Jesus, they have not completely rejected him and he has not taken stances to intentionally alienate them.

The family had hoped to marry him to a Hindu girl, but Aaditya at least wanted to explore the possibility of finding a wife who shared his faith in Jesus. His mother respectfully conceded to his desire, searched for, and found, a young Christian woman from their same caste community. The families agreed to an engagement, as did the couple, so Aaditya and his family traveled to the girl's town for an engagement celebration.

The girl's family, being Christian, invited their pastor to bless the engagement celebration. This pastor realized that he had a captive Hindu audience and took the opportunity to confront them with the "gospel." He preached a sermon in which he attacked their Hindu beliefs, customs, and traditions in the name of Jesus. One phrase stood out to me from the groom's account: "Hindu gods kill; but Jesus gives life." The whole message was presented in a demeaning, condemning, negative tone, and with an arrogant spirit of Christian superiority.

When the celebration was finished, Aaditya later told me, the pastor approached him and said, "I am so happy I could give them the gospel tonight!" Sadly, the family heard no good news in his presentation of his "gospel." When Aaditya was alone again with his family, they surrounded him. They were embarrassed, shamed, confused, angered, and hurt. "Is this how all Christians talk? Is this how you see us? Is this what your Christian friends think of us?"

Because of the pastor's rude preaching, several of Aaditya's relatives told him they could not attend his wedding in a church setting, a painful choice given typical family closeness and support in India. They explained,

"If the pastor shamed us this way in a neutral place, how much worse will he speak to us in his own church?" In one evening, the pastor had damaged Aaditya's efforts at building bridges with his family by his inconsiderate and inappropriate "preaching" of a judgmental and inconsiderate "gospel."

EVANGELISM AS A BARRIER TO JESUS

It's a sad reality, but some forms of evangelism (spreading the good news) can alienate people from Jesus before they have a chance to meet or consider him. Consider the following examples I've learned from the Indian context.

Attacking Gods and Culture

Evangelism can pose a barrier to Hindus when Christians, like the pastor above, resort to attacking and condemning many aspects of Hindu culture and tradition. Some admittedly negative voices illustrate how staunch Hindus criticize Christian evangelism. T. R. Vedantham, an associate of Sita Ram Goel, once wrote, "The motivation for Christian evangelism is simple. Disrupt and destroy. The missions make no secret of it" (Vedantham, Swarup, and Goel 1983, 11). This concern with evangelism as "attack" repeatedly arises in Hindu criticisms of Christianity.

In 1999, an Indian magazine, *Outlook*, published an article, "The Zealots Who Would Inherit." Saira Menezes explored the "evangelical hardsell" that was intensifying anger among Hindu nationalists. She cited, as an example, a statement by Ralph Winter in *Mission Frontiers Bulletin* (Nov–Dec, 1994), "The Hindu World is the most perverted, most monstrous, most implacable, demonic-invaded part of this planet. . . . The perversion of Satan in this part of the world is just absolutely legendary . . ." (Menezes and Menon 1999). This quote was later added to Hindu activists' websites as an example of negative Christian publicity, even from widely recognized Christian voices (Frykenberg 2004, 108).

In 2014 scores of village councils in Chhattisgarh enacted bans on non-Hindu gatherings "to stop the forced conversion by some outsider religious campaigners and *to prevent them from using derogatory language against Hindu deities and customs*" (Dahat 2014).

Certain Hindus actively expose Christian evangelism practices. They track evangelistic activity and marketing through a number of sites: *hinduismtoday.com*, *crusadewatch.org*, *indiafacts.org*. The *IndiaFacts* site, for instance, posted a summary of its 2014 analyses of a number of evange- listic organizations (IndiaFacts Staff 2014).[13] That one link demonstrates the remarkable detail of Hindu research and monitoring in relation to Christian evangelistic activity.

Tracking Evangelism is a Hindu group that monitors Christian evange- listic activity in India. It has a Twitter account and a YouTube channel. Its Blogspot site includes the post, "Fundamentalism, Hatred, and Aggres- sion" (Tracking Evangelism 2014a). It provides a representative sample of the sense of attack Hindus feel from certain Christian evangelistic at- tempts. In recounting a Christian mission team's India visit, for instance, they use such phrases as:

"Spread hatred that Hinduism is a false religion . . ."

"Go to USA and brag about how many accepted Christ . . ."

"See how he is condemning Hindus and Hinduism" [after his unin- formed description of a first visit to a temple] (ibid.)

Near the end, the blog post observes: "Their hatred and fundamen- talism is astounding. If you try to raise objections to their hatred, they cry persecution, they say their religious freedom is being violated." The clos- ing criticism should trouble Christians, not please them, "Damning other people's religions, traditions and spreading this hatred is their definition of religious freedom" (ibid.). That sometimes appears to be the operating definition of evangelism for too many Christians.

It is not difficult to locate similar Hindu reports and exposés regard- ing Christian attacks against their faith. Westerners who engage in this anti-Hindu rhetoric might be excused for not understanding how cultur- ally demeaning such direct, antagonistic confrontations appear. Indians who have allowed Westerners to coach them and fund them to carry out such attacks, however, know much better how insulting such presenta- tions are in the communally sensitive Indian context.

Christians sometimes complain about Hindus attacking their religion, but they have no right to complain if they attack and condemn Hindu religion. Too many Christians, in pursuing their urgent evangelistic (confrontational) agenda, have blatantly disobeyed three teachings of Jesus, all found in Matthew 7.

---

13. Link at http://indiafacts.org/exposing-evangelism-indiafacts-impact-stories/

"The judgment you give is the judgment you will receive." (verse 2)

"Take the log out of your own eye, before taking the splinter from your brother's." (verse 5)

"What you want others to do for you, do also for them." (verse 12)

An Indian missionary I once met told me that he fires any worker who attacks Hindu gods. Others I have met certainly decry such offensive, confrontational approaches. Their stances, though, reflect awareness that confrontation can be a problematic, too common practice. They understand that evangelism does not require and should not be defined by anti-Hindu rhetoric and vitriol. That spirit misrepresents Jesus and instead manifests a judgmental, separatist spirit that Jesus clearly rejected (Chapter 1). He specifically says that he was not sent into the world to condemn the world (John 3:17). From my conversations and research, though, the non-confrontation policy of a few may not be common enough to minimize Hindu concerns.

Presenting Jesus in Confusing Ways

Sometimes the evangelism barrier originates in other Christian traditions about presenting the gospel. An evangelist, for instance, recounted how his invitation to gospel meetings commonly met with rejection in villages he visited. He told me, though, that when he sat under a tree in his *dhoti* (traditional wrap-around cloth men wear), he could carry on long, respectful conversations about Jesus even with members of the RSS or VHP (Hindu nationalist groups). Time and place, even attire, can affect how Hindus respond to believers' attempts to share their faith. Some Christians, as we will see, have not always paid enough attention to such considerations. Consequently, the very believers who were trying to introduce him have hindered Hindus from meeting Jesus.

Sometimes gospel presentations are done in ways that just make no sense to the hearers. Christians may attribute this to hard hearts or spiritual blindness. We need to explore, though, whether Christians jump to that explanation too quickly. What if Christian conceptions of evangelism and gospel are themselves confusing Hindus, even misrepresenting Jesus to them?

Rajiv Malhotra provides an intriguing, somewhat humorous, look at this possibility in a *Huffington Post* article, "Dharma's Good News: You Are Not a Sinner!" (Malhotra 2011b).[14]

The author describes repeated visits to his US home by Christian evangelists in training. As you read the article, it becomes apparent that Malhotra has been the subject of various evangelistic methods and presentations of the gospel over time. In the face of these continual approaches, his skepticism is fed by the witnesses' disregard for his own belief system (they only want to push theirs), their repeated pattern of approach, and their focus on sin, guilt, and "getting saved." After multiple encounters with evangelism, Malhotra still does not have a clear understanding of who Jesus is in terms he might understand. He seems to reject a Christian caricature of Jesus, not the real person.

I recently watched a video by a pastor who bragged that he just went up to Hindus in a Caribbean nation and presented the "gospel" the way he always does, with great success. People may have smiled and been polite, but I guarantee he did not help anyone follow Jesus that day. The following blog post describes the more likely result when well-meaning Christian evangelists use Western, one-size-fits-all methods for witness:

> A missionary friend of mine here in Nepal had a visitor from the States. This visitor was excited to witness to Nepalis. He went through the plan of salvation we all normally use in the States with a taxi driver who spoke English. He was about to lead him through the sinner's prayer when my missionary friend stopped him. He asked the taxi driver, "Do you believe Jesus is the only God?" "No," was the quick reply. This revealed the inadequacy of the plan he was using. (McTague 2013)

Canned presentations of the gospel, designed with Christian understanding and experience in mind, can, as with Malhotra or McTague, leave Hindus confused. Instead, we want to ensure that if they do reject Jesus, they actually met and considered him in the first place.

---

14. A separate video presentation expands on the evangelistic encounters that he describes in the article (Malhotra 2015): https://www.youtube.com/watch?v=gtyWUe-MjzY.

As we will see shortly, Christian evangelistic practices and gospel presentations, sometimes mimicked from the West, can get in the way of this understanding. The result? Evangelism and gospel presentations can keep Hindus from Jesus instead of introducing them to him.

"GOSPEL" AS A BARRIER TO JESUS

Sadly, if they are not aware, Christians may simply present their understanding of the "gospel" in a way that makes no connection to the hearer's worldview or situation. Why do Hindus reject Christianity as foreign? Gailyn Van Rheenen highlights at least part of the problem: "Too often we come with a good message, but little understanding of the people. Consequently, the Gospel, as we present it, makes little sense to the people, or they see it as foreign." (Van Rheenen 2006, 31–32). Since Hindus at times call Christianity a foreign religion, we must at least consider whether this foreign communication might not be partly to blame for the perception. Let me suggest two ways this can happen: hiding the good news, and explaining the good news using primarily "guilt" terminology.

Christians Forget Their Gospel Should Be Good News

At a fundamental level, the "gospel" Christians give has sometimes lost its essence. The definition of "gospel" in the Oxford English dictionary reflects this. Of its three key meanings, not one mentions good news: 1) "The teaching or revelation of Christ," 2) "The record of Jesus' life and teaching in the first four books of the New Testament," and 3) An adjective as in "gospel music" (OED 2015a). Dictionaries provide the common understanding of words. The church has so lost the core idea of gospel that many Christians, and the world at large, have no idea that the word means "good news."

Sometimes Christians seem to forget that they are supposed to be announcing incredible, joyful, wonderful good news. The English Bible words "evangelize" (*euangelizomai*), "evangelist" (*euangelistēs*), and "gospel" (*euangelion*) all relate to how we give, tell, or share good news. You can't see it in English, but the idea of "good news" (*euangel-*) underlies all three Greek words (Liddell, Scott, and Jones 1940; Bauer, et al. 1979, 317). This root usually included a sense of "joy" (Deissmann 1980, 366–367), of "good news, especially of a victory or some other joyous event" (Friedrich 1985, 267).

Jesus didn't preach an insipid, theological "gospel"; he announced joyous good news or glad tidings. So did Peter, so did Paul. Yes, they spoke of sin and judgment, but they emphasized the glad news that Jesus defeated sin, removed its guilt, took its shame, and broke its power. The sermons in Acts focus far more on the person and authority of Jesus than specifically on sin. References to him as Savior and Judge, though, clearly portray him as the One who deals with sin and frees humanity from its power and consequences.

In India, when Christians "give them the gospel," Hindus may have little sense that someone is offering incredible good news. Instead, Christians are known, too often, for attacking and condemning Hindus and Hindu traditions. The animosity engendered almost guarantees that many Hindus perceive Christians as purveyors of bad news.

Globally, one can read of Christians being defined by their judgment and condemnation, by what and whom they are against, rather than primarily by the One they are for. If the Hindus and Christians I have heard and read are any indication, this message of judgmental "bad news" is too prevalent in India.

Restoring the Good News

Three correctives are needed to address the "missing" good news. We must not allow the obscuring practice of translators to hide this foundational essence of who Jesus is. All leaders and believers should learn to see and think "good news" every time they read *gospel, evangelize, evangelist,* or *evangelism.* However, simply thinking this is not sufficient.

Rather than "give them the gospel" in traditional Christian ways, believers must also stop and consider. How is good news conveyed in their culture and community? For those who have been Christians for a long time, they must "become all things to all men," and ask how the Hindu communities around them would convey good news. The way Christians choose for "giving" the good news should be culturally appropriate for sharing good news, rather than bad.

Eugene Nida provides an example of a creative alternative from the Sumbanese of Indonesia. In their culture, people hold banquets to announce good news. The believers among this group have adapted their manner of evangelizing so as to fit the patterns of social life. It is quite in order for a person to give a feast and then to spend most of the night telling the people just why the feast has been given. Here in the leisure of evening hours and at the happy occasion of a banquet, people can listen to the plain, simple words of their host and ask questions. Furthermore, the guests are impressed that this new faith must mean something, or the host would not have spent so much in making it possible to tell his guests about his spiritual experience. (Nida 1954, 13–14)

This calls to mind a meal that Jesus attended, hosted by his new disciple Matthew Levi (Matt 9:9–17). Here too, Matthew took the opportunity to introduce Jesus to his friends. Jesus also became good news to many of those attending that feast. The good news of Jesus became especially meaningful for them when he specifically defended eating with them and confronted the Pharisees who avoided and regularly judged them as unworthy, undesirable "tax collectors and sinners."

Hindus can face a barrier when Christians forget the "good news" at the heart of their gospel, whether from Westerners or those who come to Christ and learn the "gospel" from them. This barrier can be compounded, though, when their presentation emphasizes foreign understanding of what the good news is all about, what really makes it good news.

Christians Focus Their Gospel on Guilt-Based Presentations

An evangelist in India recently asked me, "What is the most important element of the gospel?" He only asked so that he could give his own answer. He was not actually interested in hearing mine. Pursuing his agenda, he continued, "Isn't it that Christ came into the world *to save sinners?*" (1 Tim 1:15). This man was intent on "saving people from sin" as urgently as possible.

When he finally gave me a chance to reply, I asked in return whether Christ's *primary purpose* for coming was only to save sinners? Forgiveness of sins is not an end in itself. It is only part of a larger redemptive, restorative story: "God was in Christ reconciling the world to himself, not counting their wrongs against them" (2 Cor 5:19, my translation).

God deals with our sins so that we can be reconciled (reunited) to him, restored to fellowship with our Creator and Lord.

My friend's insistence on "saved from sins," illustrates a cultural myopia inherent in many Western explanations of the "gospel." The Christian anthropologist, Eugene Nida observed that different cultures respond to wrongdoing in three fundamentally different ways: "fear, shame, and guilt" (ibid., Nida 1954, 150). He added that Westerners tend to experience a guilt response, while shame and fear tend to be more prevalent responses in many other cultures. This insight, has tremendous significance for how we explain the good news of Jesus and what he has done for us.

3D Gospel: Ministry in Guilt, Shame, and Fear Cultures

Jayson Georges developed this perspective in *The 3D Gospel: Ministry in Guilt, Shame, and Fear Cultures*. He demonstrated that the Bible equally applies the work of Christ, the good news, to resolve issues of guilt, shame, and fear. According to Georges, a full understanding recognizes "three components of salvation": Guilt–Innocence, Shame–Honor, and Fear–Power (Georges 2014, 12). The book explores how different cultures resonate more closely with one or two of these components and tend to experience "the good news" in those terms.

Guilt-oriented cultures emphasize personal responsibility and liability for wrongdoing. Guilt cultures say, "I did wrong." These cultures tend to be more individualistic. Forgiveness and justification are meaningful metaphors for Christ's work in guilt-oriented cultures.

Shame-oriented cultures tend to be more collectivist in nature and the consequences of a person's wrongdoing reflect poorly on the group. Shame says, "I am wrong" or "I have wronged the group." In such contexts, issues of reconciliation, restoring honor and whole relationships, are important. The ideas of propitiation (a payment to restore honor), with its Hindu equivalent *prayaschitta*, can resonate more with an Indian shame-based society. The shame perspective is further explored and illustrated in "Have You No Shame?," a chapter in *Misreading Scripture with Western Eyes* (Richards and O'Brien 2012, 113).

Fear-oriented cultures tend to see wrongdoing as an offense against some person or spirit that then brings bad influences into a family or community. Fear cultures say, "I caused wrong" or "Wrong happened." These cultures seek power to overcome the source of the fear and can also use acts of propitiation to appease living or dead community members or spirits who were wronged.

WESTERN GUILT ORIENTATION

Western Christians, following the lead of Augustine and Luther, among others, highly emphasize the *guilt–innocence* dimension (Georges 2014, 13). Georges observes, "While theology from Western contexts addresses guilt and innocence, people in most Majority World cultures desire honor to cover shame and power to mitigate fear" (ibid.). All three are scriptural aspects of Christ's salvation. Different cultures, though, usually find one more salient than the others, based upon their culture's own primary guilt–shame–fear orientation.

My evangelist friend above (p. 92), along with too many Indian witnesses, follow the Western guilt preference in a country that is shamed and alienated by that emphasis. The Western guilt-centered presentation of the "gospel" focuses on one and only one dimension of the good news of Jesus.

Enoch Wan provides the most eloquent expression of this barrier I have encountered:

> Of course, the "whole counsel of God" (Acts 20:27) should be taught eventually in a discipleship program. But nobody should be alienated from the Kingdom of God because they are culturally unable to grasp the over-emphasized "forensic" aspect of the gospel and therefore, unprepared to accept the "penal substitution of Christ" as presented by Anglophone Caucasian Christians in evangelism. (Wan 2004)

When witnesses and evangelists focus on "beating people up" for their degradation and sinfulness, they cease to tell the good news and become bad news bearers instead. Think "Sinners in the Hands of an Angry God" or ". . . for such a worm as I." Unfortunately, when Westerners teach Indians guilt-based "gospel" methodologies, they can inadvertently coach their disciples to shame and offend people before those people have a chance to hear the glad news of Jesus.

"Hindus Do Not Know Sin"?

How much of India's resistance lies simply in this aspect of how we define "gospel"? I find a clue in the way several Indian Christians have told me, "Hindus do not know sin." When we explore this further, my Christian friends mean that Hindus do not "feel guilty" for sins the way Christians have been taught. I know of Indian gospel presentations that begin by emphasizing sin and guilt, so that they inculcate these "essential" senses into Hindus. Without guilt, the West's gospel presentations are commonly ineffective. They need to get sinners to feel guilty so that their "gospel" can work.

I was recently discussing this with a Hindu-background Christian. "That explains my experience," he suddenly exclaimed. "The Christians seemed so intent that we 'confess our sins,' that we found something to say to make them happy. Inside, though, I and my friends did not feel what they wanted. Now I understand why they wanted this from us, even though we felt no guilt."

Hinduism Has Deep Traditions of Sin

Hindus in fact have a deep-seated sense of sin. In his comparison of forgiveness in Christian and Hindu traditions, Hunter rightly observes, "Hinduism has concepts of sin (*paap*) and freedom from sin dating back to Vedic times. *Indeed, the Vedic hymns are most likely the earliest texts in the world documenting the human yearning for release from sins*" (Hunter 2007; emphasis mine). Hunter then describes various ways Hindus seek cleansing from sins: *yatra* (pilgrimage), *mela* (mass gathering), and *snanam* (ritual bathing), among others.

Let me attempt a broad generalization of an incredibly complex subject. Hindus tend to respond to wrongs in two ways simultaneously: shame and separation. If I do something wrong, the main consideration is how it shames my family and community, not just my personal culpability (guilt). In fact, my wrong can bring shame to all of them in the eyes of their larger community. For some wrongs, Hindus may ostracize individuals and "shame" them if a wrongdoing becomes public. The major concern, though, does not seem to be the wrongdoing itself, but the family or community shame and disruption that it causes. I am wrong because I have caused shame. Relieving the shame requires some act or payment of restitution to remove the shame and restore harmony and honor. In Hindu contexts, this reconciling payment is termed a *prayaschitta* (atonement). It removes the shame and allows reconciliation after separation.

Sin Causes Separation

On a deeper level, as Hunter notes, Hindus do have a sense of sin, and a "yearning for release from sins." From their worldview, they are separated from the divine because of the consequences of wrong they have inherited from past lives (*karma*) and wrong they continue to practice in this one. Life is a constant attempt from sunrise to sunset to undo this sense that "I am wrong," to undo the wrongness in me so that I might somehow be reunited with God. Ultimately, this sense aligns more with shame orientation ("something is wrong with me") rather than guilt orientation ("I did something wrong").

The answer for both shame and separation is reconciliation and reunion—with God and with the wronged community. The good news of Jesus has an incredible amount to say about reconciliation, reunion, and restoration. It does not just address sin and guilt issues. I do not advocate that we water down the good news to focus on these equally biblical emphases. I only suggest that India needs a more scriptural and appropriate presentation of the good news. Those who limit the "gospel" to primarily sin and guilt are themselves misrepresenting the manifold grace of God by focusing on one dimension as their only starting point.

When Christians present Western expressions of the "gospel" that emphasize guilt and condemnation, Hindus may find such language confusing at best, repulsive and immoral at worst. Discussions of the good news of Jesus (how he removes the reality and effect of sin) would be just as scriptural if they began with shame concerns, rather than guilt. Since shame and separation are the salient cultural senses for Hindus, India needs believers to understand and take to heart the significant passages that address shame–honor issues. Then Jesus will more likely become good news to many Hindu hearts.

Jesus' Approach to Shame-Based Culture

What might a more shame-based approach look like? We need only examine Jesus' way with people to see this clearly in action. The Jews had God's law and a sense of sin and guilt. As Easterners, they also shared a common shame-based culture. So, how did Jesus relate to and speak with the people of his day and culture? With the common, ordinary folk, He rarely confronted and attacked their sin, guilt, and depravity. Instead, he ate and drank with them. When presenting his good news, he often used parables, proverbs, metaphors, and similes. He introduced spiritual truth in oblique, non-confrontational ways (shame-aware), rather than in direct, confrontational ways (guilt-focused).

With whom was Jesus direct and confrontational? With the scribes, Pharisees, and Sadducees. Those who practiced a condemning, law-centered, guilt-based righteousness were addressed directly with condemnation and guilt-based rhetoric.

When we limit the "gospel" to a Western guilt orientation, we may fail to address the heart and soul of people who are more in tune to shame or fear orientations. We are not presenting the full good news of Jesus. I wonder how much of India's resistance might be attributed to this misplaced emphasis on aspects of Christ's work salient to some in the West, but more problematic for many in the East?

Enoch Wan articulates the intersection of Western guilt orientation and legal explanation as an issue in communicating to the Chinese particularly. His perspective, though, applies as much to India as elsewhere in the East:

> Western culture has a Greco-Roman, politico-legal base and Judeo-Christian ethical foundation. The Greek social system of city-state, the Roman law, etc. have been well developed for "millennia" in the West. The influence of the Judeo-Christian value system and moral code has left its mark in the mind and heart of people in the context of western civilization, so much so that anthropologists who have conducted cross-cultural comparative studies have classified the western culture as a "guilt culture" in contrast to the "shame" culture of the East. (Wan 2000)

Only Indian believers can navigate the shame tendencies of their culture and find the appropriate scriptures that apply the work of Christ to that part of their experience. This will require believers to take off the Western guilt-based glasses with which they have been taught to read so much Scripture. They will first have to intentionally read Scripture from shame-based considerations until they begin to see the wealth of material there.

Interestingly, there is not a single reference to "guilt" in Romans 3:21–30, though it has been used to emphasize guilt since Augustine and his Augustinian heir Martin Luther. Every word used there might, just possibly, fit a shame/restoration understanding better than the common guilt/forgiveness framework.

We have seen, then, that Hindus may be alienated when Christians evangelize with an attacking spirit, when they hide the good news behind Christian jargon, or when they explain the good news in foreign, confusing ways. Sometimes, though, preaching itself gets in their way.

"PREACHING" AS A BARRIER TO JESUS

"When we preach the gospel, they do not listen. What can we do?" That deceptively simple question arose after a presentation to a Bible college audience in India about some of the Christian barriers. That phrase, "preach the gospel," can carry layers of Christian assumptions, church traditions, and cultural baggage accumulated over centuries.

When we begin to examine those layers, we come face-to-face with a set of challenges that can, too frequently, keep people from hearing the good news of Jesus. Come dig through some layers with me. Let's see what we find.

A friend recently described a church wedding where the pastor recognized there were Hindu guests in the audience. Like the engagement party incident (start of chapter), this pastor also attacked and shamed them publicly. My friend had to restrain his Hindu brother-in-law who wanted to go and berate the pastor for his unwarranted, disrespectful "fanaticism."

It is not hard to imagine such pastors going home at night feeling pleased with themselves for having "made the most of the opportunity" and for having "preached the gospel," but all they preached was anti-Hindu bad news. It is hard for me not to see Jesus weeping for their crass disobedience to the Golden Rule: "Do unto others as you would have them do unto you" (Matt 7:23). Their preaching tradition taught them to violate Peter's explicit instruction to speak "with gentleness and respect" (1 Pet 3:15). Would Jesus be pleased at the preacher proclaiming him as an enemy of Hindus, instead of one who longs to be *their* Friend and Savior too?

Jesus isn't responsible when such preaching drives people from Jesus before they have a chance to meet him for who he is. These encounters provide sad examples of the barrier of preaching in India.

Western Preaching Assumptions

Preaching may also present an obstacle, though, for a deeper reason. Christianity in India seems to derive its understanding of preaching significantly from Western traditions. Certain adaptations may be made for Indian cultural values and audiences, yet the underlying assumptions that drive preaching may prioritize Western traditions more than Eastern.

Western Assumptions About the Meaning of Preaching

The word "preach" in English is primarily defined as "deliver a sermon or religious address to an assembled group of people, typically in church" or to "publicly proclaim or teach (a religious message or belief)" (*OED* 2015b). In other words, English church tradition primarily limits "preach" to religious messages and exhortations, whether in church or in other settings. It usually assumes a religious context and/or content.

On the contrary, the New Testament words that are translated "preach" made no religious assumptions about either the context, the content, or the presentation. The words carried no idea at all of pulpits, robes, sermons, pews, or even churches. Two Greek words are commonly translated "to preach" in English Bibles (*kērussō, euangelizōmai*). The first, *kērussō*, had a wide variety of meanings: 1) to be a herald or auctioneer, to proclaim a message as a herald; 2) to issue a summons by a herald, to proclaim an announcement or declaration; 3) proclaim or announce a message (such as a sale, a new colony, a crime), to declare or tell news, or to proclaim or announce publicly (Liddell, Scott, and Jones 1940). The main idea was the act of communicating a message by a herald (or representative). Both words are widely used in the culture and heritage of the Greco-Roman world, not isolated in the religious jargon of a separated religious community.

Notice that the third definition includes to declare or tell news. *Kērussō*, in other words, could refer to the work of a news reporter. Several Indian friends, upon hearing this, made an instant connection to their own cultural past. Before newspapers, radios, or television, they tell me, certain men would walk through the streets beating a special drum and reporting announcements and news. This was like a European "town crier" who carried a bell and performed the same reporting function. These cultural reporting models are both closer to the original idea of *kērussō*, than the religious specialization that Christians have defined as "preaching."

Christian tradition has taken a word with broad cultural meaning and limited it to religious, church-based speaking. To remove this barrier, Indian believers need to examine how the functions of *kērussō* might best be expressed and practiced in their own cultural setting.

WESTERN ASSUMPTIONS ABOUT PREACHING BEHAVIORS

The meaning of preaching is not the only source of barrier, though. Christian tradition has, for centuries, added layers of rules and expectations for how "good preaching" must be done. An entire field of study, *homiletics*, is dedicated to training preachers how to "preach properly." Often Indian Seminaries use Western homiletics texts to teach preaching, ensuring that old Western cultural forms will be perpetuated in a radically different cultural context.

Unfortunately, almost all these rules and expectations are rooted in Western, Greco-Roman, Euro-American cultural traditions of what constitutes good rhetoric and oratory and what comprises acceptable sermon creation and sermon delivery. These traditions were created over the centuries as believers "became all things to all people" in Greco-Roman, Euro-American contexts. They came from human culture, not from God or Scripture.

Sadly, some Christians in India feel they must adhere to these rules and expectations for preaching in Indian churches. These norms, developed in a very different rhetorical and oratorical context, are somehow assumed to be still essential for proclaiming the good news in India.

The cultural separatism of Christians can lead some to disregard and dismiss communication forms and styles they judge to be "not Christian." For example, Indian teachers usually deliver a spiritual message sitting down. Most Christian preachers ignore this and seem to assume that they must stand to deliver their messages. They ignore the fact that Jesus himself delivered his major messages sitting down (Matt 5, 13; Luke 5; John 8). How much more would Hindus listen to the good news, if believers simply followed Jesus' example and normally sat down to teach?

Such questions about preaching beg to be considered and explored in the Indian context. Numerous foreign layers of preaching can declare that Indian Christians are committed to foreign styles and assumptions in the way they communicate their message. When Indians see and hear this foreign proclamation, at times conducted in harsh and angry tones, they have little hope of learning of the love and salvation of Jesus. Foreign styles of preaching may shout too loudly for them to hear the good news.

So, when that student said, "We preach the gospel, but they don't listen," he answered his question. Sometimes "we" are the problem. How "we" preach. What "we" mean by gospel. How "we" view the people to whom we speak. "We" must, I believe, examine ourselves (take the log out of our own eye, Jesus said), before pointing a finger of blame at our audience.

Hindus may not be listening precisely because Christians are preaching in Western ways when Jesus wants to speak in Indian styles, Indian tones, and Indian postures, as well as Indian languages. Christians may need to stop "preaching" (Western word) and start heralding, announcing, proclaiming, and presenting in ways that are faithful to Scripture and to their own culture, rather than to the West's preaching culture.

ADDRESSING THE BARRIER OF EVANGELISM, GOSPEL, AND PREACHING

Given the potential barriers presented by Christian traditions about evangelism, gospel, and preaching, I close with two considerations.

The Good News of Cultural Freedom

We sometimes miss a key element of what made Jesus good news to Gentiles (non-Jews) in the New Testament. The God-fearers, like Cornelius or Lydia, attended Jewish worship and loved the God of Israel. They did not want to convert to Judaism, though. They seemed to know intuitively that they could remain within their culture, community, and society. They sensed that they did not have to extract and join the foreign, isolationist culture of the Jews.

When he sent Peter to Cornelius (Acts 10), God affirmed this Gentile desire to follow God within their own community, not within Jewish culture. The message that they did not have to accept the culture and religion of the Jews was itself good news. When Paul adapted his message to the

God-fearers in the synagogue at Antioch (Acts 13), they too recognized the good news that God wanted them to follow him directly, not through the Jewish culture and religion. They invited the whole city to come hear the same liberating good news. When the Jerusalem Council determined that Gentile believers did not have to become Jews to follow Jesus, Gentiles again received that good news with joy (Acts 15:31).

If our "gospel" is truly good news, it will, as in the New Testament, free believers to follow Jesus within their own culture, rather than adopt the foreign, alien ways of someone else's religious culture. We must "become all things to all people" so that this freedom to follow, worship, and share Jesus within one's own culture is an inherent and essential part of the good news of Jesus.

We have already observed that the barriers of separatism, Christian identity, and church can arise from unnecessary and unscriptural traditions. One application of the good news of Jesus in India is that Hindus should not have to identify with these foreign-created expressions of faith. They, like the first century God-fearers, should hear the good news that they can incarnate Jesus, and Jesus only, within their culture and community. If they face shame because of Jesus himself, they must be ready and willing to do so. They do not, though, ever need to adopt a "Christian" identity, or join a church. I am convinced that this is an essential implication of the good news in India today, at least for many segments of the population. My ministry now focuses on encouraging and advocating for those who desire to follow Jesus in incarnational ways.

Peter's Advice to Believers in Challenging Contexts

To hear many Christians today, especially those from America, it seems that evangelism requires believers to "Go loud, and go proud!" They tout a form of gospel boldness that is more a product of American cultural brashness and pushiness. Listen to Indian evangelists, watch Indian Christian TV, observe Indian Christian publicity videos, and you can see repeated examples of an evangelistic fervor and urgency intent on "giving them the gospel." Such presentations of Jesus do not resonate well with India's spiritual psyche. They can sound harsh, angry, and disrespectful.

In contrast to this Western din, Peter points believers in a different direction. Peter's first letter provided guidance to believers who faced a challenging context. Around the time of Nero's persecution of Christians

(AD 64), Peter wrote a letter of encouragement to believers who faced increasing opposition by the culture around them (Barclay 1965, 164–171; Robinson 1976, 140–169). The increased cultural skepticism and rejection led to questions about how believers should live in relation to the surrounding society.

While Peter addressed them as "aliens" in the beginning, this did not imply a separatist, extracted community (see Chapter 1—Cultural Separatism). His instructions implied continued connection with their community and culture.

Rather than calling people to a loud, proud, confrontational lifestyle, Peter advocates the opposite. He instructs them to pay attention to their own lifestyle, to *live lives of moral excellence* among the non-believers so that their accusers would have no real grounds to condemn them (1 Pet 2:11–20; 3:13–15). They were to *honor their government* (1 Pet 2:13–15), *honor their fellow citizens* (1 Pet 2:17), and *honor their ruler* (1 Pet 2:17). Notice that Peter wrote this specifically to people who were under Roman Imperial rule and under Nero as the emperor. They were to be known for their respect, not disrespect, no matter who the government or ruler was, so that they would not appear subversive or treasonous (1 Pet 2:16). They were told to *live their lives with mouths primarily shut*, not open. While this instruction was specifically addressed to women (1 Pet 3:1), its principle could apply equally to anyone under someone's authority (slaves, children, citizens). Their witness (testimony) was mostly by their example. Faced with rejection and insults, they were specifically instructed to follow Christ's example of quietness and *returning only blessing* (1 Pet 3:10).

All this instruction—*live quietly, work honestly, honor all men, set an example, not talk*—eventually led to questions by those around the believers. Then, and only then, Peter tells believers, "Set apart Christ as Lord in your hearts, always ready to answer everyone who asks you to give an account for the hope that is in you, yet with gentleness and respect" (1 Pet 3:15). The key phrase there is "everyone who asks you." Peter says, don't push, don't force, don't confront, don't even talk. Just live and incarnate the life of Jesus intentionally. But when they ask, be ready to explain the difference that he makes in you, the hope that he has given you.

The final words of his instruction are critical in addressing the Christian barrier to Jesus in India. I have heard so many tales of harshness and disrespect in the way that Christians "give the gospel" to Hindus.

All such presentations are a direct violation of Peter's clear instructions in a challenging context, to speak "*with gentleness and respect.*"

India today needs far more believers who follow Peter's quiet, gentle, respectful model, rather than the West's loud, proud, confrontational model. Peter's model of living, then sharing, the good news provides a powerful antidote to the Christian barrier to Jesus represented by too many models of evangelism and gospel in India today.

CHRISTIAN AND BHAKTA CONSIDERATIONS

Before Jesus ascended to heaven, his last words were, "You shall be my witnesses" (Acts 1:8). The New Testament clearly expects that those who follow Jesus will share his good news. So how will the good news of Jesus come to Hindus in incarnational, culturally natural ways?

Christians

From our discussion above, Christians must examine common assumptions about sharing the good news in light of Scripture. To "become all things to all people," they must consider how evangelism has often modeled Western cultural assumptions with too little concern for and adaptation to the Hindu contexts of India. The issues raised in this chapter are merely suggestive of the kinds of considerations Christians should make to help Hindus truly encounter the good news of Jesus.

Another Christian challenge arises from church scheduling. I recall many conversations with Christians who said, "Church keeps us so busy during our weekends that we have no time for relationships with non-believers." As I write, I'm looking in my journal at a conversation with one pastor who described long Sunday morning services, Sunday evening prayers, Tuesday evening prayers, Wednesday evening "cottage prayers," and Thursday evening "deliverance prayers for Hindus." This tendency to keep Christians occupied with gatherings and meetings poses a real barrier to the good news. It keeps believers primarily separated from the community around them, and less available for relationships and eventual conversation about Jesus. Wise congregations need to equip believers for more intentional relationships and reduce programming in order to free believers to be friends to those around them in meaningful ways.

ANSWERING THE STUDENT'S QUESTION

Let me return one more time to the student's question, "When we preach the gospel they do not listen. What can we do?" Based on the considerations in this chapter, here is how I answered. As I stood on the stage, I suggested they picture the stage as the Christian community. I asked them to consider the back of the chapel as a Hindu community.

Typical evangelism, I suggested, sees Christians standing in their community shouting and yelling to Hindus, "Come here! Leave your community and come to meet Jesus in ours!" Recently my wife saw a church sign in the US with a similar perspective: "If you want to meet Jesus, come to church." If that is our primary message, few will ever consider listening, much less coming to Jesus. If they have to come to church to come to Jesus, that isn't an option for them. When, in addition, Christians shout the "invitation" in condemning, accusing tones, they just compound the barrier.

"But," I continued, "if we were to leave our place [I jumped off the stage], and instead went to where they are culturally, what might happen? If we took Jesus there so that he could eat with them, stay with them, live among them, befriend them, what might happen?" Then they might see Jesus as a friend of Hindus, one who loves them, rather than as an enemy who despises and hates them. My questioner responded, "*We never thought of that!*"

He summarized the barrier of evangelism in five words. Why had they never thought of that? Christian traditions of cultural separatism taught them to disregard the culture, concerns, and sensitivities of the people to whom they preached the gospel. They thought that if they "preached" to Hindus they had fulfilled their responsibility.

My heart breaks for Christians who have been so enculturated to such models that they have not even considered Jesus' own model of gentle, respectful engagement. For believers who have never been taught that "becoming all things to all people" applies, as much as anything, to how they proclaim the good news of Jesus to others.

PROSELYTISM OR EVANGELISM?

In talking with Christians about this barrier, I have often encountered an understanding more in line with Stott's description of proselytism.

> Proselytism and evangelism are not the same thing. To proselytize is to convert somebody else to our opinions and culture, and to squeeze him into our mould; to evangelize [in the biblical sense] is to proclaim God's good news about Jesus Christ to the end that people will believe in Him, find life in Him and ultimately *be conformed to His image, not ours.* (Stott 1976, 173; emphasis mine)

I would add, based on our previous discussions, that when believers are conformed to the image and spirit of Jesus, they will incarnate that image within their cultural context (Phil 2), not extract from it. The good news is, at heart, a call to incarnation, not isolation or extraction.

Yesu Bhaktas

When believers stay within their Hindu communities of origin, some contend, they will be better able to relate the good news of Jesus to their family and fellow Hindus. In theory, this sounds good. In practice, this does not always happen.

The Hindu family is often sensitive both to the Christian separatist spirit and evangelism agendas. Yesu bhaktas, in trying to remove suspicion that they are hidden Christians, must carefully navigate their genuine identity among their family. This can lead to reticence in witnessing about Christ so that they do not appear to judge and condemn their family.

In addition, at least some Yesu bhaktas were originally in Christian churches for a time. They experienced and heard the Christian evangelism and conversion agenda. In reaction to overly pushy, and culturally insensitive versions of Christian evangelism, they can take a path of extreme caution that leads to little or no witness.

Since "Christianity" emphasizes overt evangelism and conversion as the common model, they rarely received training or awareness of less confrontational, more incarnational forms of witness in Scripture. Jesus is good news, and believers who have found that good news will want to share it with those around them. Alternative approaches must be developed and taught for doing that in culturally appropriate and sensitive ways, "with gentleness and respect" (1 Pet 3:15).

Bhaktas themselves will need to seek the Lord's direction and develop their own ways to tell the good news. They do need to find natural ways to explain their experience with Jesus that are not "triumphalistic" (a common concern I have heard), confrontational (common Christian model), or foreign (many current explanations).

CLOSING REFLECTIONS

F. F. Bruce rightly observed that "the disciples of Christ are his witnesses, called to spread to the ends of the earth the *joyful news* of God's salvation which they have received through their Master's death and resurrection" (Bruce 1987, 60–61; emphasis mine). At the same time,

> If the Good News of the Bible means anything to people, it should enter into their lives in such a way that its proclamation becomes a natural matter, rather than a foreigner's noisy propaganda. (Nida 1954, 14)

I offer this chapter in the hope that in India, Hindus will have greater opportunity to hear the good news of Jesus in just these ways, not as a "foreigner's noisy propaganda," but as a natural expression of his "joyful news."

CHAPTER 5

THE BARRIER OF CONVERSION

The late Bishop Azariah asserted, "We (i.e. many missionaries, Indian Christians, and myself) are convinced that Christianity has always stood for conversion, and for *changing people from one society to another. . . . This inevitably means breaking with the old fellowship and joining a new fellowship*" (cited in Kim 2013, 18; emphasis mine). With those words, he articulated a common understanding that cultural conversion is a Christian obligation.

Contrast that, though, with the following from Christian leader and thinker, Ralph Winter:

> First, let's be done with the word "conversion." In Standard English that word usually means merely an outward change, a change of culture, clothing, diet—it means to proselytize. Well the NT very clearly opposes any proselytizing as essential to salvation. Logically, then, if I were asked at the border of _____ "Are you here to convert _____?" the most accurate answer I could give would be, "The Bible instructs me not to proselytize anyone at any time" . . . Conversion is part of our Evangelical dialect, but we ought to lay it aside if we want to make sense to outsiders. (Winter 2008, 38)

How do we explain the stark discrepancy between these two Christian statements? Is one right and the other wrong? How would we decide? Or does India's complexity demand a both/and perspective, instead of either/or?

Let's start with a basic definition of what we are talking about. Since Azariah was an Indian church leader, I'll let his definition above provide the benchmark for what conversion means: "changing people from one society to another . . . breaking with the old fellowship and joining a new fellowship." Conversion, from this perspective, meant extracting people from one community and joining them to a different, separate one.

Pradip Ayer, in his contrast of conversion and regeneration adds a further perspective on common Christian practice, "'Conversion' is about outward conformity, whereas regeneration is about an inner change that begins a transformation process centered on the heart and attitudes" (Ayer 2001, 184).

Bringing those two together, we find that conversion, as commonly practiced in India today, first extracts new converts from their socioreligious community to a separate Christian community—the separatism of Chapter 1. It then requires conformity primarily to external church rules rather than inner conformity to Christ. The external rules are often markers that reject the former socioreligious community and demonstrate allegiance to the new. As such, this conversion practice has led to considerable debate in India for decades.

CONVERSION IS DEEPLY OFFENSIVE TO HINDUS

Hindus Attest to Its Offensiveness

The issue of conversion has historically antagonized many Hindus. It continues to rouse passionate opposition today. *Bridges and Barriers to Hindu-Christian Relations* notes, "Recent violence reacting to Christian strategies of conversion in India has emphasized the potential for intense conflict between Hindu and Christian communities globally. In many cases tensions are created within previously peaceful communities as their shared identity is fragmented by allegiance to these apparently conflicting groups" (Frazier 2011, 4). Here are some Hindu voices who have expressed concern about conversion.

SAVARKAR

An ardent opponent of conversion, V. D. Savarkar articulated the *"Essentials of Hindutva"* (Hindu-ness) in the early 1920s. His thinking on what it means to truly be Indian has laid the foundation for much of the Hindu nationalist movement. Savarkar reasoned that Christians and Muslims, who shared the Indian fatherland and Indian blood, could not be truly Indian because in "their adoption of the new cult they had ceased to own

Hindu civilization (*sanskriti*) as a whole. They belong, or feel they belong, to a *cultural unit altogether different from the Hindu one*" (Savarkar 1921–22, 37; emphasis mine). In other words, conversion made them disown Hindu culture, and in so doing, their Indian-ness. As Savarkar and those following his lead see it, to convert means to fundamentally deny the cultural heritage of India, and in so doing, to disown one's Indian-ness.

Gandhi

To the Christians who interacted with him, Gandhi repeatedly expressed concern about conversion. In an interview with the missionary statesman, John R. Mott, he said, "I disbelieve in the conversion of one person by another. My effort should never be to undermine another's faith but to make him a better follower of his own faith" (Gandhi 1929, 145).

In a 1931 interview, Gandhi was asked about foreign missionaries in India after independence. He responded, "If instead of confining themselves purely to humanitarian work and material service to the poor, they do proselytizing by means of medical aid, education, etc., then I would certainly ask them to withdraw. . . . We need no converting spiritually" (Gandhi 1931, 277).

Gandhi's concerns about conversion were as much political as spiritual. Kim observes, "As he opposed the British Raj so he opposed conversion because he saw it as another form of aggression against the rights of the Indian people" (Kim 2013, 19).

Niyogi Commission

In the 1950s the Niyogi Commission investigated and reported on conversion activity primarily in the state of Madhya Pradesh (Niyogi, et al. 1958). Their report highlighted numerous concerns about fraudulent and manipulative conversion practices. This report was partly responsible for the religion laws in certain states today aimed at curbing illicit conversion practices (see State Laws section, p. 120).

Frawley

The article "A Fraudulent Mission" provides one of the most concise and clearly articulated Hindu summaries of Christian missions and conversion activity (Frawley 2008). Anyone concerned about Hindu contexts can get a good synopsis of Hindu views of the issues and challenges, even though they will not agree with much of what he says. Christians have, he charges, "set aside billions of dollars to convert non-Christians to Christianity. . . . They have trained thousands of workers, formed various plans of evangelism and conversion, and targeted certain communities for this express purpose" (ibid., 35).

The entire article is permeated with deep feeling against mission activity and conversion, but toward the end Frawley issues a call to Hindus: "Let us expose and put an end to this missionary business, and let us not think that this missionary business is tolerant. The missionary business is not about freedom of religion. It is about the triumph of one religion. It is not about secularism. The missionary business is based on the idea that one religion is true. It is a religious war aimed at religious control" (ibid., 36). What is the missionary business? Conversion! What is its aim? Religious control!

These representative statements and perspectives help frame today's Hindu resentment. Given these deep Hindu sensitivities about conversion, just introducing a conversation about Jesus can immediately sound to some like a conversion attempt. In such a context, the reaction can be instantaneous and intense.

If believers ignore these concerns, and just push Jesus on people, pursuing Christian conquest or conversion agendas, they increase barriers and perpetuate Hindu stereotypes of Christians. On the other hand, if they stop and listen to the concerns of the other, Indian believers might find ways to faithfully represent Jesus (Chapter 4), while reducing negative perceptions of believers that unnecessarily feed Hindu animosity.

Conversion as Violence

Hindus sometimes characterize conversion as "violence" or as a denial of fundamental human rights. Any attempt at witness ("propagation") can be defined in this way, and then attacked as anti-Hindu violence and "force." The most eloquent articulation of this view was made in a 1999 speech by Swami Dayananda Saraswati. In his message, "Conversion is Violence," he asserted that when a person converts from his former religion and culture, he, his family, and his community are all hurt. Saraswati then elaborated, "I call it violence. It is not ordinary violence. It is violence to the deepest person, the core person, in the human being" (Saraswati 1999).

Saraswati concluded,

It is not that they preach their own religion. They preach against other religions. And I consider that kind of preaching is violence . . . I am hurt and many others like me are hurt. Millions are hurt. There are so many other issues to be discussed with reference to conversion. But I have only one to discuss here. *It is the violence that is allowed to be perpetrated against humanity, against cultures, against religions.* That is the only issue here; there is no other issue. (ibid.; emphasis mine)

Hindus regularly observe the negative, denigrating comments about Hinduism and Indian society on mission websites and reports. For example,

Grand Rapids-based [mission name withheld] argues that in India "superstition and idol worship have an iron grip—there is no forgiveness or joy." Such denigration of one's faith has a long-term impact on the psyche. It cuts families apart . . . Moreover, the claim is false—kshama (forgiveness) and ananda (joy) are alive and well in India. (Kuppa 2012)

I won't post links, but you do not have to look hard on Google or Facebook to find Indian mission sites with negative rhetoric about Hindu religious traditions, idolatry, caste system, persecution, and other items of their concern. Many of these are written by Indian Christians, which simply intensifies Indians' sense of betrayal and attack.

Conversion strategies that focus on attacking and tearing down other religions (Hinduism included) can alienate people before they even meet Jesus. Fronting such approaches and attitudes on public web sites and social media unnecessarily irritates and alienates Hindus as a form of violence. It drives them further away from Jesus before they have a chance to hear or consider the good news.

Unfortunately, that published information on conversion numbers and anti-Hindu sentiment attracts Western donors. The more Indian Christians can vilify Hindus, it seems, the more money they can make in certain circles, so ministries that say they want to reach Hindus publicly market themselves to donors in anti-Hindu ways. In the process, they offend and alienate many of the people they claim they want to reach. Would those who truly care about Hindus in the spirit of Jesus consider talking this way to or about them?

Conversion as Anti-Community Treachery

Concerned believers must also wrestle with the collective mindset of India, rather than assuming a Western, individualistic one. Craig Storti, consultant in cross-cultural business communication and interaction, maintains, "*The one aspect of culture* that accounts for more miscommunication between Indians and Westerners than any other is what is usually called the concept of identity. *Simply stated, Indians are more group-oriented (collectivist) and Westerners, especially Americans, are more individual-oriented (individualist)*" (Storti 2007, 19; emphasis mine).

In "Evangelization of Whole Families," Chua Wee Hian has also alluded to Western Christians' difficulty with collective thinking: "At times it is difficult for individualistic Westerners to realize that in many 'face-to-face' societies, religious decisions are made corporately. The individual in that particular society would be branded as a 'traitor' and treated as an outcast if he were to embrace a new religious belief" (Hian 1999, 614).

In his introductory case studies, Hian provides one example of two missionary women who ignored the communal and family orientation of Chinese society. They reported on the "hardness of heart" among the men and parental resistance when teenagers wanted to receive baptism. Much of the resistance these missionary women faced had nothing to do with Jesus. It instead resulted from their conversion strategies that bypassed communal and familial decision-making. Jesus was not the problem. Individualist and non-community assumptions made by these Western missionaries created an unnecessary barrier to Jesus. They were, in effect, asking people to become "traitors," an act of violence from the view of their family and community.

Donald McGavran expanded on this issue in his influential study, *The Bridges of God*. In "The Group Mind and Group Decision," he noted decades ago:

> To understand the psychology of the innumerable subsocieties which make up the non-Christians nations, it is essential that the leaders of the churches and missions

*strive to see life from the point of view of a people, to whom
individual action is treachery.* Among those who think
corporately, only a rebel would strike out alone, without
consultation and without companions. The individual
does not think of himself as a self-sufficient unit, but as a
part of the group. (McGavran 1961, 11; emphasis mine)

McGavran wrote this reflection out of his experience with the Indian context. Indian Christians are deeply aware that decision-making is
more collective in their society. Yet they may insist on following Western,
individualist conversion models because that is how Western Christianity does it, that is the methodology they are taught, or that is what the
donors expect. Too often, they seem intent on ignoring and violating this
fundamental feature of their own culture. In the process, countless families and communities end up hurt, shamed, alienated, and offended when
conversions are pursued in such culturally inconsiderate ways. This too
contributes to the barrier of conversion.

Hindus Track Conversion Practices

Another indicator of Hindu concern involves the detailed way in which
Hindus track and comment on Christian conversion practices. In its first
issue, *Tehelka* published an exposé entitled "Preparing for the Harvest." The
author, V. K. Shashikumar, described a "worldwide conversion movement"
that after its initiation as "AD 2000 and Beyond" transformed into the
Joshua Project. He described this evangelistic initiative as "a sledgeham-
mer—a breathtaking, decade-long steamroller of a campaign" to harvest
India. The AD 2000 "plan was based on a military model with the intent
to *invade, occupy, control, or subjugate its population*" (Shashikumar 2004,
1; emphasis mine). I am not saying that this article is factual or unbiased.
However, the writer read and referenced publicly posted evangelical plans
to evangelize India, plans that often used militaristic and triumphalistic
language. He may have misunderstood some of the statements. Overall,
he did not misunderstand Christian intentions to strategically go after
India with the gospel. He illustrates how much Hindus read and react
to Christian publicity about conversion plans and intentions for India.

Chad Bauman's insightful analysis of *Hindu-Christian Conflict in India*
concurs that such concerns were partly "a response to well-publicized—and,

to many, offensively strategic—Western, Christian evangelical efforts, such as AD2000 and Beyond, or the Joshua Project, which set ambitious goals to reach the whole world with the Christian message by the end of the millennium" (Bauman 2013, 635).

Hinduism Today at times publicizes Christian conversion activity (see Frawley 2008, for example). The following sites post regular reports on various Christian conversion activities and strategies:

- *Christian Aggression*
  (http://www.christianaggression.org)
- *Christian Watch India*
  (https://christianwatchindia.wordpress.com/)
- *Tracking Evangelism*
  (http://trackingevangelism.blogspot.com/)
- *Hindu Existence*
  This site has a section devoted to Christianity in India
  with exposés of conversion tactics and approaches
  (http://hinduexistence.org)
- *Christian Aggression* Facebook Page
  "Stop Converting Hindus to Christianity in India"
  (https://www.facebook.com/ChristianAggression)
- *Tracking Evangelism* (YouTube channel)
  (https://www.youtube.com/channel/
  UCfsFDP3OV-AZYx-_8k8Xnjw)

In "Predatory Proselytism" (even the title reflects Hindu sensitivities), Padma Kuppa addressed several Hindu critiques of common Christian conversion practices. She cited examples where missions used disasters and poverty to further their conversion agenda. As she put it, "This intimidation and exploitation of the most vulnerable segments of society is primarily rooted today in a surge of international conversion campaigns" (Kuppa 2012).

Stories of poverty and disaster provide powerful appeals for more mission funding in India (and elsewhere). Mission websites, Facebook groups, and other public communication provide abundant examples for Hindus of how Christians are targeting India for conversion. A significant amount of this material relates to benevolence outreaches as an avenue to "reach people" (see Chapter 9).

Recently a ministry in Chennai had its operations significantly curtailed after the government investigated its use of funds. Publicly in India they portrayed themselves as a social relief agency helping poor families and children. In the US, their material advertises their evangelistic, church-planting purpose. When Indian investigators examined the finances, they discovered that significant money was going to churches, even evangelists' salaries, rather than sponsoring children and helping families as declared. This did not constitute government persecution. The authorities can legitimately ask whether an organization is doing what it declares it is doing with its money.

Those who are working in India (and their supporters) should be aware that Hindus monitor their publicity materials, their public funding reports (Indian FCRA and US 990 filings)[15], and their websites. They should assume that what they write and report about India and Hindus will be monitored. If they want to "become all things to all people," believers should consider how even their reporting and fundraising messages can actively influence Hindus for or against Jesus.

Historical influences, legal rulings, community considerations, Christian anti-Hindu rhetoric, and even Christian marketing materials all interact in India's complex resistance to conversion. Instead of just coming in and "preaching the gospel," genuinely concerned believers should take a step back and assess how best to approach such a charged context. We should not obliviously or intentionally pour gasoline on the fire of resentment while claiming to serve Jesus in India. We just might be working against Jesus instead of for him.

Christians Confirm Hindu Concerns About Conversion

The issue is not a recent development, and Christians have demonstrated awareness of its pervasive concern among Hindus. Sharpe, in his biography

---

15. The Indian Foreign Contributions Regulation Act (FCRA), requires entities that receive foreign contributions to provide annual reports of funds received and how they were used. In the same way, the US IRS requires an annual 990 report for certain non-profit organizations to maintain their non-profit status. In both instances, the reports are a matter of public record and can be reviewed by anyone interested in the financial activities of entities in either India or the US.

of Sadhu Sundar Singh, describes the Hindu disquiet even in the early 1900s:

> To express respect and even admiration for Jesus Christ was common enough in India in the late nineteenth century; for a Hindu or a Sikh actually to announce a desire to become a Christian by baptism [see next chapter for Baptism concerns] was another matter altogether. *Conversion was a social and political, as well as a religious matter: a blow directed at the heart of the social unit.* This was something that Evangelical Christians could never fully understand, still less accept, since in their view, only "religious" motives counted as worth taking seriously. (Sharpe 2003, 36; comment and emphasis mine)

Sharpe's observation highlights not only the Indian concern about conversion, but also Christians' common disregard for its broader cultural implications. In addition, Christian conversion practices represent a tangible expression of the *cultural separatism* already discussed in Chapter 1. In *Christ's Way to India's Heart,* J. Waskom Pickett noted, "The process of extracting individuals from their setting in Hindu and Moslem communities does not build a Church. *On the contrary it rouses antagonism against Christianity and builds barriers against the spread of the Gospel*" (Pickett 1938, 27; emphasis mine).

Kim, in an analysis of relationships between *Hindutva*, secular India, and Christianity, remarks that Hindus in the 1950s considered conversion to "foreign" Christianity "not only as a *religious intrusion* . . . but also as a *political scandal*—the continuation of foreign influence and dominance even after independence" (Kim 2005, 109; emphasis mine). The same author later elaborates: "They regarded conversion as a *denial of Hindu identity* and therefore a *rejection of being Indian*, and the missionary as an instrument of *foreign oppression*" (ibid., 115; emphasis mine).

Christian anthropologist Eugene Nida, writing in the 1950s, summarizes the Hindu view of conversion in rather stark terms, "The crucial issue which Christian missions face in India today involves precisely this matter of exclusivism. In brief, Hinduism says that all religions are good and lead to the same God. Hence, [from their perspective] *it is immoral to convert a person from one religion to another*" (Nida 1954, 139).

Hindus, and at least some Christians, agree on one thing. Hindus are deeply troubled by Christian conversion and the cultural separatism that it represents.

INDIAN LAWS RELATED TO CONVERSION

The Constitution of India guarantees, "all persons are equally entitled to freedom of conscience and the right freely to profess, practice, and propagate religion" (Government of India 2007). The Constitution adds, though, that freedom of religion is subject to concerns for "public order." In general, Hindus usually have less problem with Christians who profess or practice their faith. They more often raise concerns about Christians propagating their beliefs in a way that overtly seeks conversion and creates communal disturbance (a public order issue to them).

Freedom of Propagation and Indian Law

The Indian Penal Code contains several sections intended to prevent or minimize conflict or tension between religious communities (Government of India 1860, 153a, 295, 295a, 298). Conversions can be construed as promoting enmity by advocating Christianity against Hinduism (Section 153a), insulting other religions (Section 295), or outraging the religious feelings of others (Sections 295a, 298). When Christians require converts to denounce Hinduism, reject family, break pictures or images, or to perform other overtly anti-Hindu acts, Hindus can perceive this as a violation of one or more of the above laws. Some preachers' attacks on Hinduism and its various traditions, could, from what I've heard, "wound the religious feelings" of Hindus (Section 298) or "insult other religions" (Section 295). In such instances, conversion certainly can become a barrier to Hindus.

When some Christians blatantly and intentionally demean, denigrate, and denounce Hindus in harsh, disrespectful ways, they directly disobey the laws of their own country. They also violate Peter's injunction to speak with gentleness and respect (1 Pet 3:15), instruction given during a time of intense persecution under Nero.

State Laws Regarding Conversion

In addition to the national laws, six states in India have enacted Religious Freedom laws (Orissa, Madhya Pradesh, Arunachal Pradesh, Chhattisgarh, Gujarat, and Himachal Pradesh). These seek to prevent conversions through "force, inducement (allurement), or fraudulent means" (T. Arora 2012, 5). Contrary to Christian assertions, these are not "Hindu" laws. Similar laws existed in some of these states under the "Christian" British Raj to prevent conversions through inappropriate means (see further details in Chapter 9, p. 209).

Furthermore, none of these laws are "anti-conversion laws" as often misrepresented by Christians to Western donors. No state prohibits conversion. The laws prohibit people from using dishonest means to pursue conversions (something Christians themselves should oppose). They do require some reporting mechanism to ensure that deception or manipulation was not used in a given case.

Some Christians adamantly attack the laws publicly, especially to Western audiences. For example, "These bills are *weapons* in the hands of the state governments, local officials to *browbeat* the Christian missionaries in particular" (Puniyani 2013, 29; emphasis mine). Or more recently, a national Christian spokesman asserted, "The situation for Christians has been aggravated because six Indian states have laws that criminalize evangelism and put extraordinary restrictions on conversions" (Ali 2016). This is a common Christian misrepresentation, but none of these laws "criminalize evangelism" or directly forbid conversion. As written, every state's law restricts predatory conversion practices (force, inducement, fraud).

We must acknowledge that antagonism toward conversion is deeply seated in certain Hindu communities. Any attempt to encourage Hindus to know and follow Jesus can be labeled as forceful, induced, or fraudulent "conversion." Believers indicate that sometimes local definitions of "force," "inducement," or "fraud" can be so narrowly applied that any witness or benevolence at all is reported as a violation of the law. Christians find that where this is the case, local officials may side with the community rather than fairly investigate the legitimacy of accusations. Believers must consider these concerns, while faithfully encouraging people to consider and follow Jesus.

In a discussion of these laws, though, Vishal Arora acknowledged an interesting fact. Even though some have existed since 1960, no Christian has ever been convicted under these laws in any state (V. Arora 2015). If these state laws were such a threat, one would expect multiple trials and convictions for violating them.

When Christians complain about "anti-conversion laws," this serves to confirm their conversion agenda to Hindus, and intensifies the resentment Hindus feel toward them. They also appear to misrepresent and disrespect India's laws to Christians overseas, confirming to Hindus their anti-national spirit as well.

I have heard of Christians who ignore or condemn the state laws as a violation of their Christian rights. Christians, though, have no right to convert people by "force, deception, or inducement." They should themselves reject and oppose such dishonest practices. In opposing these laws, they may appear to advocate for the very activities that Christians themselves should oppose. They should instead make it clear that their only concern lies in cases where the laws are used in restrictive ways that hinder legitimate Christian worship or witness.

These discussions of conversion law in India are an important touchstone as we examine the conversion issue. They reflect Hindu concerns about conversion and, at the same time, provide some of the language used to commonly condemn conversion. While national and state laws have some impact, local governments often provide more immediate response to conversion concerns.

Local Restrictions on Conversion

In July 2014, an order was passed by fifty *gram panchayats* (village administrative councils) in the Bastar district of Chhattisgarh. It banned all "non-Hindu religious propaganda, prayers and speeches in the villages." This prohibition of non-Hindu expression was enacted "to stop the forced conversion by some outsider religious campaigners and to prevent them from using derogatory language against Hindu deities and customs" (Dahat 2014).

Three issues are raised in this one sentence. We have an allegation of "forced conversion" which is a commonly cited Hindu concern—the article identifies economic inducement, guilt manipulation, even fear of hell as some of the force used. Secondly, they perceived that "outsider religious campaigners" were doing this work—missionaries or evangelists from elsewhere in the country were creating the conversion trouble. Finally, these campaigners for Jesus were "using derogatory language against Hindu deities and customs." Their evangelistic strategy was apparently one of attack and condemnation.

Each issue is deeply problematic for Hindus. Together, they represent a Christian campaign against the local community and culture. If Hindus target Christians for reconversion, Christians complain of a "Hindu campaign" against them. When Christians target Hindus, how is it any different, especially when Christians refer to such conversion outreaches as "campaigns" and even "crusades" in their own literature and meetings? Why is it wrong for Hindus, but desirable for Christians? Christians must deeply examine this inconsistency and address it, before they ask for respect and acceptance from Hindus. Neither "campaign" nor "crusade" is a scriptural term for Christian witness, and both carry serious negative, militaristic connotations.

Honestly, Hindu concerns in this Bastar district are difficult to understand from a numerical standpoint. An analysis of Joshua Project's district level data (Spring 2014 JP Dataset) indicates that only 1.4 percent of the district were identifiably Christian. Hindus, on the other hand, made up 97 percent of the district. Of 310 people groups in Bastar only thirty had any identified Christians at all. Only seven of those groups had over one hundred Christians. The Christian "threat," in other words, appeared more perceived than real. However, the strong response here indicated that a limited Christian presence had created substantial barriers in this district far beyond their numbers.

Several months after the ban, Supriya Sharma interviewed various participants in the Bastar events and reported on some of the contributing factors. From what Hindus and Christians told her, *two key issues* led to the current unrest. First, she noted, "Villagers are known to take unkindly to those who decline to participate in community festivals and ceremonies after they start going to church" (S. Sharma 2014). Later, though, she described how some Christians regularly made contributions to the festivals and participated in some community events as far as they could, while not worshiping idols or making sacrifices. Some believers, in other words, have found respectful ways to interact with their Hindu neighbors even though they follow Jesus. Others, coached at conversion to take more negative stands, have created communal tension.

Sharma's interviews also determined a second source of Hindu frustration. Some Christ-followers do not identify themselves as Christians, yet they go to church, follow Christian traditions, and separate from other community members (act in every way as Christians):

> It is true that those flocking to the churches in the villages have neither formally converted to Christianity, nor do they identify themselves as Christians. But they are keenly aware that *their change in faith sets them apart from other villagers.* (ibid.)

To the local and regional Hindus this represents dishonesty and illegal activity. The Chhattisgarh conversion law requires that a conversion be recorded with the district collector (chief district officer) within thirty days. The Bastar district collector said that neither he nor his two predecessors have received a single notice of conversion. As Sharma reported, local pastors told her that they do not file the affidavits because people who attend services do not usually stay very long (ibid.). This duplicity angers Hindus and contributes further to the conversion barrier to Jesus for many Hindus.

For the record, in October of 2014, the Chhattisgarh Christian Forum filed a court case to challenge the restrictions on constitutional grounds. The Bilaspur High Court struck down the panchayat restrictions on October 16th, 2015 as contrary to believers' constitutional freedom to preach and propagate (All India People's Forum 2016, 4). Evidence suggests, though, that the court ruling has not significantly resolved tensions in the area.

While the Hindu concerns in Bastar have been publicized, they illustrate common Hindu concerns across India regarding conversion. Knowing this is such an issue, believers should at least examine what the Bible says about conversion and how they might faithfully follow and represent Jesus in contexts where Hindus are deeply suspicious.

When Christians push a conversion agenda with conversion language, they can drive Hindus away from Jesus before they ever have a chance to meet him.

Considering this deep resistance to conversion, let's examine some Christian conversion traditions, practices commonly assumed essential to become a follower of Jesus. We will then be able to examine both Hindu perceptions and Christian traditions regarding conversion in light of Scripture.

CHRISTIAN CONVERSION TRADITIONS

When Christians teach converts to reject their family, change names, change dress, eat forbidden foods, avoid community activities, and numerous other demands, these external requirements force them to change community. These and numerous other Christian conversion traditions raise barriers to Hindu society often through non-biblical requirements. When converts are taught to reject all aspects of their culture and to become demeaning, condemning, and disrespectful to Hindu communities, these enculturated attitudes add further barriers that we have already demonstrated are not biblical.

Troubling Conversion Practices

Dayanand Bharati's *Living Water and Indian Bowl* details many Christian conversion practices that alienate Hindus and present obstacles to Jesus (Bharati 2004). The following is a list of some of the issues he explores, many of which I have seen, heard of, or personally experienced in various Indian settings:

- Teach special Christian language no one else understands, or Bible study in English or trade languages, that separates them from their own heart language (ibid., 82–92)
- Utilize Western theological constructs and explanations that do not help Indians understand God and his word in relation to Hindu contexts (92–102)
- Coach believers to ignore or misuse Hindu scriptures in talking with Hindus (102–110)
- Invent Western or foreign birth, marriage, and death ceremonies that Christians now perpetuate, with maybe some Indianization (110–111)
- Require or encourage women to remove the *bindi/pottu* (dot on forehead), *sindur* (red paste at hair part of married woman), and *thali/mangalsutra* (wedding chain around neck) (111–116, 167–168)

- Inculcate a very negative, condemning view of Hindu worship practices and images, instead of helping people respectfully and politely to consider Jesus and his worship (116–119). This sometimes includes coaching converts to reject the *prasad* (food offered at temple) in an offensive, insulting way, rather than a polite, respectful way (119–123).
- Impose legalistic rules regarding marriage partners and funeral participation (123–130)
- Require believers to take a new "Christian" name upon conversion (see Renaming Converts next, p. 126) to clearly indicate their rejection of their old culture and adoption of a new one (130–132)
- Impart anti-Indian attitudes, including not honoring the country, not singing the national anthem, not saluting the flag, and other negative views toward India (132–143)

Imposing Personal Convictions on All Believers

Many of the issues on this list are matters of divergent convictions by different believers. Paul teaches in Romans 14:5–6 that people can hold opposite views of how they honor the Lord, whether in celebrating days, eating foods, or other choices. They are to find and follow what they believe is the Lord's will for themselves. They are not, however, supposed to bind their conviction on others or judge them for different conclusions. Christian conversion practice does exactly the opposite. Christians often pre-determine how converts should see many surface aspects of their culture and bind legalistic expectations on them, some explicitly, others by implication over time. New believers never know they are free in Christ and may never learn how to live and walk in that freedom (Gal 5).

This freedom to hold differing convictions highlights an essential element of how we disciple people to follow Jesus. The common Christian approach mandates certain external behaviors and customs that separate people from their culture and community in the name of Jesus, even though they are matters of opinion, not direct biblical teaching.

The fundamental attitude of many Christians has been the "cultural separatism" we identified in Chapter 1. As a result, these choices Christians made about the above issues all tended to be highly separatist. Converts were coached in all these areas to "come out from among them and be separate," to adopt a suspicious view of their former culture and community. In order to resolve these issues, we cannot just do Bible studies on them. We first must remove the separatist root that creates the barriers. Then believers can explore incarnational and bridge-building alternatives to the barriers Christians have created in each of these areas.

Renaming Converts as a Sign of Conversion

Some churches require Hindu converts to reject their old Hindu name and take a new name upon conversion. One day I was talking about this practice with some Indians. I made a comment about new believers being given Bible names when they adopted Christianity. My Christian friend laughed and replied, "Not Bible names. Christian names! George and Vincent are very popular."

A light went on at that moment. The new believers were not being asked to identify with biblical characters in their new walk with Jesus. They were being asked to identify with English culture, "Christian" culture, colonial culture. The naming had nothing to do with the Bible or Jesus, but with separating them from their own culture into a foreign, Christian one. Even those who adopt "Bible" names, are made to do so out of an anti-cultural bias that rejects their own name for a foreign one.

Renaming Creates Barriers to Jesus

Dayanand Bharati shares his own experience of the damage renaming did to his own family and community relationships when Christians renamed him.

> When I received a letter addressed to S. Christopher Kumar (my previous name, wrongly given to me by Christians), c/o Sambamurthy Iyer, my parents faced several problems in the locality in which they lived. They were mocked and joked at by the other Brahmins, which finally forced them to move their residence. I know that some might jump and shout, "Praise the Lord for such a witness for Christ." *On the contrary, this is not a witness as it never gave any opportunity to share the gospel to anyone there.* (ibid., 119; emphasis mine)

Later he adds, "My parents faced a lot of problems because of my 'Christian' name of Christopher. Do not say that it was a witness for Christ when in fact it was a stumbling block to my parents, who began to hate even the word 'Christian' because of that" (ibid., 132).

Making converts take a new Christian name can, in other words, create incredible relational barriers that effectively keep their family and community from Jesus. Why do Christians do it, if the practice can be so problematic? I'm glad you asked. The answer may surprise you.

BIBLICAL JUSTIFICATIONS FOR RENAMING

Christians who practice renaming typically assert, "The Bible says . . ." to justify this practice. Two reasons are often given for requiring the name change. As a new person in Christ, you should take a new name like Abraham, Peter, or Paul. The other common reason is anti-Hindu. If your name is a Hindu god-name or sometimes any Hindu name, they assert, you must change it so that you don't have a god-name, or a "Hindu" name.

WHAT THE BIBLE SAYS ABOUT RENAMING

Do people change their names in the Bible? Yes. Do they change to a culturally foreign name that separates them from the society around them? Never. Of thirteen key name changes in the Bible none of them changed away from their cultural name to a foreign, separatist name. In fact, in the cases of Joseph (Gen 41), Gideon (Judg 6), Daniel, Hananiah, Mishael, Azariah (Dan 1), Hadassah (Esther), Simon (Peter), and Saul (Paul) their new names connected them to the broader culture around them, rather than separated them from the culture.

Even more telling, Joseph, Gideon, Daniel, Azariah, and likely Esther all took foreign god-names by which they were known in their host cultures. In addition, some New Testament believers had names that originated with Greco-Roman religion or mythology: Apollos, Phoebe, Aquila, Narcissus, Hermes, Hermas, Olympas, Jason, and Nympha. None of these believers changed their god-name to a "Christian" name. The Bible did not teach this and the early believers did not practice or require this.

What About Peter and Paul's Renaming?

Since Peter and Paul are most commonly used to enforce this teaching, let me briefly address their situations. Both contradict common Christian teaching about renaming.

Simon was Greek for the Jewish name Simeon (indicated in Acts 15:14). He had a Bible name already. When Jesus changed his name to Stone (*Cephas* in Hebrew, *Petros* in Greek), he gave him a name no one else ever had in Scripture. Peter's name change is not from a cultural name to a Bible name. It's the other way around.

What about Paul then? His original name, Saul, was also a Bible name, that of the first king of Israel. Robert Priest, in his discussion of Christian renaming in other contexts, addresses this misapplication of Scripture:

> When asked to justify the requirement of a name change at conversion, nineteenth-century missionaries pointed to the switch from Saul to Paul in the New Testament. But while missionaries sometimes claimed that this name change marked Saul's conversion, *the narrative of Acts continues to refer to 'Saul' for years after his conversion* and only switches from Saul to Paul in the middle of Paul's first missionary journey. (Priest 2012, 179)

The change to Paul, in other words, was a switch from his Bible name, his Jewish name. That was a foreign name to the Gentile world in which he now served. Paul, on the other hand was already his cultural name as a Roman citizen from birth. It identified him as part of the Greco-Roman world, rather than separating him from it. Paul was not renamed; he simply switched his birth names in appropriate contexts.

When scriptural evidence is examined, then, we have no evidence for a name change that separated believers from their culture, not even when the name had a god component. Not a single example!

Is it wrong to take a different name? Maybe not. But if you want to follow the Bible, choose a cultural name that builds a bridge *to* the culture, not a barrier *against* it. Every instance of renaming in Scripture involved engagement with culture, not extraction from it.

So, we see that the Christian practice of renaming converts, even though it claims scriptural warrant, is contradicted by Scripture. This conversion practice, then, creates an unnecessary and unscriptural barrier to Hindus.

Urgency and Success Syndrome Fuel Conversion Concerns

Hindu concerns about conversion are intensified because of the success mentality of some Christians. Ramachandran, himself a Christian, asserts that this has clearly happened since the 1990s. The overt Hindu reconversion program, he argues, was sparked by "the 'numbers game' of Christian mission agencies" (Ramachandran 2013, 41). He elaborates several features of this "numbers game" that fueled Hindu skepticism and resentment. Churches and missions sometimes used "biblically unethical methods" to reach desired numbers. Donor-driven concerns led to a mentality of "more numbers = more dollars." To get these dollars, ministries would present "unnecessary and unwise propaganda" of their work for "donor expansion" (ibid.).[16] This would, at times, include anti-Hindu rhetoric, manipulated and mislabeled photographs, and other communications designed to elicit additional funding.

Ramachandran further asserts that the "numbers game" encouraged what he calls "instant church growth" which caused Indian ministries to "focus on conversion at the cost of disciple making." The resulting "shallow adherents" were particularly susceptible to reconversion efforts (ibid.). In my earlier Bastar discussion ("Troubling Conversion Practices," p. 124), pastors never filed the required conversion affidavits because people did not stay long enough in their churches to warrant the effort. The quicker they "converted," the quicker they "reconverted" or faded away.

My own conversations with Christians in India corroborate Ramachandran's sense that Western desire for numbers and success have contributed substantially to India's resistance to conversion since 1990. Hindus have discussed the AD 2000 India targets and they exhibit awareness of Joshua Project's and other agencies' ongoing India advocacy. To them, these numbers and targets confirm that Christianity intends to "convert" (= "conquer"?) all of India.

---

16. Chapters 9 and 10 of this book will elaborate on why these financial concerns are troubling to Hindus.

We have seen both from Hindu and Christian perspectives that conversion is troubling to the Hindu community. We turn now to examine what Scripture says. We need to at least ask whether conversion is an essential element of following Jesus as Azariah indicated at the start? Or is it, in fact, a problematic tradition that, like Winter, we would be well advised to abandon? Our study will clearly provide needed guidance for these questions, and some surprising answers.

WHAT DOES THE BIBLE SAY ABOUT CONVERSION?

For all the concern about conversion among Hindus and Christians, you would expect to find it everywhere in Scripture. You would anticipate numerous commands, instructions, and examples. Open the Bible, though, and we find a very different story. The following chart summarizes where different English versions have "convert" or "conversion."

Table 5. Convert and Conversion

Reference	KJV	ESV (2001)	NIV (2011)
Verb—Convert			
Isa 6:10 (quotations in Matt 13:15; Mark 4:12; John 12:40; Acts 28:27)	Convert, converted	Turn	Turn
Matt 18:3	"be converted and become as little children"	Turn	Change
Luke 22:32 (Jesus' prayer for Peter)	" . . . when thou art converted, strengthen thy brethren"	Turned again	Turned back
Acts 3:19	Repent ye, therefore, and be converted . . .	Turn back	Turn to God
Jas 5:19f.	Convert (a wandering brother back to the way) x 2	Brings him back	Bring that person back

Reference	KJV	ESV (2001)	NIV (2011)
Noun—Convert			
Matt 23:15	Proselyte	Proselyte	Convert
Acts 2:10 or 11	Proselytes (2:10)	Proselytes (2:11)	Converts to Judaism (2:11)
Acts 6:5	Proselyte	Proselyte	Convert to Judaism
Acts 13:43	Proselytes	Converts to Judaism	Converts to Judaism
Rom 16:5	Epaenetus, the "first fruits" of Asia	First convert	First convert
1 Cor 16:15	"First fruits" of Achaia	First converts	First converts
1 Tim 3:6	Not a novice	Not a recent convert	Not a recent convert

"Turning"

Where King James uses "convert" as a verb, it renders common Hebrew or Greek words for "turn." There is no specific verb for "convert" in either language. The more modern versions give the accurate sense of turn or turn back. Isaiah 6 and the citations based on it refer to the Jewish people who were already God's people. They were being called to return to God, to "turn back" to him. Both Luke 22 and James 5 refer to believers who needed to be restored in their faith. None of these verses support any sense of cultural, communal conversion as Christians commonly assert.

The Greek verb, *epistrephō* occurs thirty-five times in the New Testament. It is rarely translated "convert" because that is not what it meant. It meant to turn, to return, or turn attention to or from something (Liddell, Scott, and Jones 1940; Bauer, et al. 1979, 301).

In the New Testament, it often means physical turning and returning. Occasionally, it has a figurative sense of *turning away* from God or *turning toward* God. In this last sense, for instance, believers *turned* to God from idols (1 Thess 1:9). They turned to God, though, within their culture, not entirely away from their culture.

Proselyte—Never Used for New Believers in Jesus

The noun usage is even more challenging. Both King James and ESV properly render the original Greek word as *proselyte* (Matt 23:15; Acts 2:10; 6:5; 13:43). Why ESV breaks from this in Acts 13:43 is not clear.

These verses show that the writers of the New Testament had a Greek word available for "convert." The Jews used it for centuries to describe those who left their Gentile culture to join the culture and religion of Judaism. This term for Jewish "converts" was proselyte (*prosēlutos*), and was only used in this sense. It occurs nowhere else in Greek literature. Among the Jews it referred to "the relatively few" Gentiles "who fully accept Judaism and are circumcised" (Kuhn 1985, 944). The *proselytes* gave up their own culture and fully identified with the Jewish beliefs, culture, and community (Neill 1990, 25). They were religious and cultural "converts" in line with Azariah's understanding at the start of this chapter.

To become a *proselyte* meant to reject one's own culture, community, and religion to take on the Jewish one (the cultural separatism of Chapter 1). This is, in fact, what some Jewish believers were asking Gentile believers to do (Acts 15:1,5)—to become, in effect "Christian proselytes," cultural converts. The Jerusalem Council (Acts 15) said, "Absolutely not!"

Proselyte only occurs four times in the entire New Testament and is never used of Christian "converts." If "conversion" to Jesus required the radical cultural rejection and extraction practiced by Jewish proselytes, then it would have been a natural term to use for such Christian cultural separatism, but the New Testament never uses the term for believers. Instead it indicates that new believers remained within their own cultural communities.

Jesus, in fact, strongly denounced proselytizing (cultural converting): "Woe to you, scribes and Pharisees, hypocrites! For you travel across sea and land to make a single proselyte [convert], and when he becomes a proselyte [convert], you make him twice as much a child of hell as yourselves" (Matt 23:15). Proselytizing (converting) operationalizes the extractionist, separatist spirit of the Old Covenant. Jesus rejected this aspect of that spirit along with all the others. This is diametrically opposed to the incarnational spirit of Jesus in the New Covenant. Jesus' condemnation should give pause to all Christians who pursue proselytizing, converting agendas. They might find themselves on the wrong end of Jesus' denunciation.

New Testament believers avoided *proselyte* as a term for new believers in Jesus. They knew they were not called to extract and isolate as Jewish *proselytes* (converts) were expected to do. Neither are believers today.

No "Convert"

What about the remaining three verses? Some English translations insert "convert" in Romans 16:5, 1 Corinthians 16:15, and 1 Timothy 3:6. The original Greek has no word for convert in any of these verses. If your version has "convert" there, the translators added it, it's not in the text. Romans and Corinthians speak of "first fruits" and 1 Timothy of a new believer.

What does the New Testament say about "convert"? The noun "convert" (a person who has converted to Christianity) does not exist anywhere in the New Testament for the followers of Jesus. The verb "to convert" in the sense of evangelists converting people to Jesus never occurs in the New Testament. All the talk about converting and converts is not found in the Bible itself. It's human tradition, not Bible teaching.

"Conversion" Once, but Not Azariah's

What about "conversion" then? As much as that is used, surely the Bible has a great deal to say about it! Wrong again! "Conversion" only occurs in some versions in Acts 15:3, where Paul and Barnabas described the "*conversion* of the Gentiles" (ESV, KJV, NASB). The Greek word, *epistrophē*, only occurs here in the entire New Testament (Moulton, Geden, and Moulton 1978, 372). This is rather strange, because it was commonly used in secular Greek with a wide range of meanings related to its root idea from *epistrepho* of "turning" or "turning around" (Liddell, Scott, and Jones 1940). In other words, Paul and Barnabas reported the "turning" of the Gentiles. This is the only time, though, that "conversion" occurs in some translations of the New Testament.

That one use of "conversion" in Acts 15:3 is very instructive. It immediately argues against Azariah's definition of conversion, which is a common model for India (and elsewhere). In reporting the "conversion" of the Gentiles, what were Barnabas and Paul reporting? Did the Gentiles convert from their Gentile people and join a separate Christian people and society? No! They remained Gentiles. Some Jewish believers demanded that the new believers leave their Gentile culture and community and "convert" to the Jewish way of following Jesus. The Jerusalem Council specifically rejected this separatist "conversion" requirement. They established the decree that Gentiles did *not* have to "convert" to a foreign form of faith in Jesus. Gentiles (Greeks, Romans, and others) were to remain within their Gentile cultures and follow Jesus incarnationally within their culture.

As with "Christian," we must then ask, "Why does the church today talk so much about 'conversion' with all of its traditional assumptions and accumulations?" That noun only occurs once in the entire New Testament. Today's "conversion" tradition does not originate from Scripture, because Scripture says nothing about it. The prevalent use of "conversion," as we saw with "Christian," originates from human tradition not clear scriptural teaching.

CHRISTIAN AND BHAKTA REFLECTIONS

Christians

We have examined India's deep concern about conversion, the problems with Christian conversion traditions, and the paucity of scriptural support. The choice between Azariah's path and Winter's becomes clear. Why would the followers of Jesus insist on requirements and practices that are scripturally unfounded and that are guaranteed to offend much of India?

Let's be done not only with the word "conversion," but with the numerous offensive, separatist practices with which Christians have encrusted it. This chapter only scratches the surface of much deeper problems with conversion.

Believers who care about Hindus and want to "become all things to all people" among them, must take the time, dig deeply into Scripture, and reexamine conversion traditions in light of God's word. In doing so, they will find new freedom in Jesus, instead of a yoke of slavery to Christian conversion.

Yesu Bhaktas

The choice to not become Christians, to not separate from their community, to not follow the "conversion" path, is supported by Scripture.

Bhaktas do not need to change people, change community, or change society to follow Jesus.

This chapter, though, has illustrated Hindu concerns about followers of Jesus who say they are not Christians, but who are actually pseudo- or crypto-Christians. The choice to not identify as a Christian raises questions even among some Hindus. Some of them may portray the *bhakta* choice as the same duplicity. Yesu bhaktas must ensure they have solid, practical answers to these questions about their identity and place within the Hindu community. Why is it appropriate to follow Mukti-nath (Jesus) without converting to Christianity? How is their choice not the same as these secretive Christians? Most importantly, how can they be genuine bhaktas of Muktinath, and stay fully in their Hindu family, culture, and community?

Only bhaktas can address and answer these questions appropriately, but answer them they must. The community of bhaktas I know has developed solid scriptural answers to address these questions when they arise.

CLOSING REFLECTIONS

If we want to represent Jesus faithfully, Winter's advice provides the resolution. Stop defending conversion. Stop pursuing conversion. Stop talking conversion language. For some Christians that will sound like heresy, but we just read every specific reference to conversion in the New Testament. There aren't that many.

What if believers could honestly say to Hindus, "We don't want to change anyone from a Hindu community to a Christian one. The Bible doesn't ask anyone to become Christians. The Bible doesn't ask anyone to change their community. The Bible doesn't ask anyone to convert. The Bible doesn't demand the conversion markers that Christians have made up. We will not demand them either."

If "the NT very clearly opposes any proselytizing [converting] as essential to salvation" (Winter 2008, 38), we should follow Scripture and oppose it too. Taking conversion traditions out of the way would remove one of the biggest hindrances Hindus face in considering Jesus. Scripture sides with Winter here. Let's get conversion out of the way!

CHAPTER 6

THE BARRIER OF BAPTISM

Recently, some Indian friends recounted several baptism stories. In each instance a couple was getting married and one was a Hindu. The church required the Hindu spouse to be baptized in order for the wedding to take place. In these three instances the churches did no teaching about Jesus or about the meaning of baptism. The ministers simply insisted that the Hindu be baptized to "become a Christian" and fulfill church membership and marriage requirements. From the church's perspective, their baptism signified that they had "converted."

In one instance, the baptized woman said, "I did not know what it meant, they just told me I must do it. Now I attend church with my husband, but I understand nothing. I look around and many other people seem to sleep or not know what is happening."

For some Hindus, baptism itself is not a barrier. They may submit to baptism so they can marry someone they love, but it can simply be a meaningless church requirement that they never understand. These Hindus still don't really know Jesus and may only learn from their experience that Christianity is a hollow, empty religion devoid of real meaning. If that's their only experience, then the church's ritual use of baptism can keep Hindus from truly knowing and following Jesus, even if they "convert" and join a church.

While some Hindus don't react negatively to baptism, this is not always the case. Another couple we know faced the similar situation. In their case the husband was Hindu and the church required that he get baptized. This time, though, his family was offended by the choice. He and his wife faced years of family estrangement and misunderstanding.[17]

---

17. I tell the story of their eventual reconciliation with their family in 'Christian Encouragement to Follow Jesus in Non-Christian Ways' (Pennington 2015).

You do not have to dig far to discover that baptism can be troubling for portions of Hindu society. Out of their survey of Hindu Christ-followers in Chennai, one couple observed,

> *Baptism is often a point of offense to Hindu families. . . .*
> Baptism is seen not only as an initiation ceremony relat-ed to religious faith, but also as initiation to enter a new community, leaving one's birth religion and community behind. A baptized person is thus not fully accepted in the Hindu community and they sometimes have been excommunicated from society and are not allowed to par-ticipate in important events or functions. (Kannan and Kannan 2001, 166)

As commonly practiced, baptism represents the visible point at which a convert adopts the barriers we have discussed so far: cultural extraction, Christian identity, church membership, and numerous conversion tradi-tions and rules. Hindu concerns about baptism raise legitimate questions that believers need to address. These questions challenge some fundamen-tal assumptions about the meaning and purpose of baptism. They require us to carefully reexamine what Scripture says about this spiritual experi-ence, and in the process, could help address some of the confusion around baptism in both Christian and Hindu circles.

IS BAPTISM A BARRIER TO HINDUS?

So how do Hindus view baptism? Is it a problem for them, and if so why? Let's survey the evidence for the barrier that baptism can present.

Unnecessary Social Offense and Displacement

Several decades ago, Herbert Hoefer became aware of how deeply trou-bling Christian baptism could be for Hindus. He began to meet and interview people he eventually described as "non-baptized believers in Christ" (NBBCs). His book, *Churchless Christianity*, described his re-search and findings (Hoefer 2001b, 5).

The people he interviewed and studied believed in and followed Christ, a few for generations. Yet for various reasons, they had not taken the socially stigmatizing step of baptism:

In our survey of the rural non-baptised believers in Christ we found that baptism was a problem not because of a lack of faith-commitment but because of consequent social and cultural implications. *Baptism for these non-baptised believers did not mean the uplifting, freeing Gospel. . . .* It meant a self-removal from social, family and cultural ties about which they are justly proud and happy. (ibid., 151–152; emphasis mine)

Several respondents avoided baptism because of family challenges, spouse resistance, or concerns about marrying their children to appropriate spouses (ibid., 10, 13). The family tensions, however, represent a challenging issue. Baptism can provide a visible marker of the new believer's rejection of prior social relationships and entry into a separate Christian community.

Petersen, for instance, describes the sociological disruption that baptism presents to the broader culture: "From the perspective of Hindu attitudes in general and that of Indian civil law, baptism, in whatever particular form it is practiced by the churches, primarily signifies birth community change. It is not merely the usually public profession of a believer in declaring his spiritual allegiance to Jesus Christ. It is indeed more sociological than merely spiritual" (Petersen 2007, 93). Baptism, in other words, primarily entails not a faith commitment, but radical social extraction.

Similarly, the Kannans reported,

Though the high-caste people often have a high regard for Christ and the Bible they do not want to identify with Christianity. Some people still feel that an Indian who is patriotic should be a Hindu. *These things contribute to the offense of baptism to the family members.* (Kannan and Kannan 2001, 166; emphasis mine)

The Kannan's survey of upper caste believers in Chennai found that all but four were baptized Christians and church members. Only seven of the fifty-one had introduced any family members to Jesus. Why such little influence? "Rather than the gospel spreading as a leaven in Hindu society, the common pattern is the extraction of disciples and the negating of any hope for positive influence in the family and community." (ibid., 169).

Furthermore, most of these baptized believers were so separated from their Hindu family and community by the church that they eventually had no more Hindu associates. Their entire life revolved around Christians and church, effectively sealing them off from those they could most likely have introduced to Jesus without the cultural extraction (ibid.).

Baptism, then, initiates believers into a Christian identity that alienates them from their own family and community. The emotional pain of that extraction and the resulting social isolation keeps millions of Hindus away from Jesus by isolating them from the very family members who could have been their bridge to Jesus.

Christians don't always consider how their conversion and baptism traditions affect the abandoned families. H. L. Richard describes the conversion of an early Christian contextual leader, N. V. Tilak. That account provides two windows into the emotional feeling that baptism and conversion can raise among those left behind. "Hindu society, and especially Tilak's own family, reacted with anguish and outrage on learning of his baptism. Lakshmibai [his wife] especially suffered immensely and was near suicide a few times" (Richard 2001a, 192). In fact, they remained separated for four and a half years due to his baptism. During that time, Christians tried to convince Tilak to find a Christian woman and remarry (directly contradicting Paul's instructions about such situations in 1 Cor 7:12–16, I would add).

Richard, in his biography of Tilak, quotes a particularly painful scene recorded by Lakshmibai. Two of her relatives went to visit her husband to learn the truth about his baptism and conversion. "As he left," she wrote, "Keshav saw that the sacred lock of hair on Tilak's head had been cut, and he sobbed aloud. However angry he had tried to appear, his eyes had been brimming over from the beginning; now the very last tear was drained out of his heart" (Richard 1998, 26).

Based on these considerations, Richard rightly asks:

> Is it not time for evangelicals to seriously listen to and empathize with the honest expressions of pain from Hindu society at the conversion of one of their friends? Are the true roots and reasons for such distress properly

understood and accounted for? Does not the love of Christ demand that strong steps be taken to mitigate this anguish that is inevitably felt when a Hindu confesses faith in Christ? (Richard 2001a, 192).

Much of this pain could be avoided were Christians to stop using baptism to simply enforce their separatist community and spirit (Chapter 1). A Yesu bhakta leader recently demonstrated an alternative way to present "baptism" respectfully and incarnationally. He called it *guru diksha*. It's the water bath their fellowship uses to initiate a believer into Guru Yesu. The new believer is first helped to discuss their decision with the family politely and respectfully. The bhaktas explain that the person is *not* being asked to leave family, culture, or society. She is and will remain a sociocultural Hindu. She is, however, publicly declaring that Yesu is now her *ishta devata* (chosen God), the only God she will worship. If possible, the *diksha* ceremony is conducted at the family home, not in a "religious" setting, so that the family witnesses the commitment in their environment. Presenting baptism in such a way addresses layers of family conflict, separation, and extraction.

DEEPER HINDU CONCERNS ABOUT BAPTISM

A deeper exploration of Hindu resistance to baptism, though, uncovers an ironic reality. Some of the confusion surrounding baptism practices exposes how far Christian traditions depart from New Testament teaching. If they listened to Hindu concerns and addressed them, Christians could simultaneously find themselves closer to New Testament teaching and able to build bridges rather than barriers through appropriate baptism practices. Three additional questions expose these possibilities.

Why Baptism?

Indians commonly use online matrimonial sites to find prospective spouses, whether parents arranging marriages for their offspring or adults seeking "love marriages." A Hindu girl asked one Indian matrimonial site (InterfaithShaadi.org) whether she should accept the church's requirement to get baptized in order to marry a Christian man. The administrator replied, *"Baptism is not as much about Jesus but for the church"* (InterFaithShaadi Admin 2014b; emphasis mine).

That succinct reply from a non-Christian articulates the heart of baptism's barrier to Hindus in India. Much Christian tradition identifies baptism with church membership, conversion, and separatist Christian identity. Hindus perceive that baptism is primarily "for the church" because Christians seem to believe and practice this.

The administrator provided several examples of Christian traditions around baptism to support her opening assertion. Even if couples want to marry between denominations (both "Christ-followers"), churches may require them to be rebaptized. They also named Indian churches that require rebaptism if a believer transferred from another congregation. To the extent that different Christian groups require rebaptism to even change Christian communities, this confirms to Hindu minds that baptism is not about Jesus (common faith), but about denominational or institutional association (church affiliation).

The administrator further pointed out that baptism is not just about church membership. As we already saw, it also entails a change of community. In fact, they noted, it changes one's legal identity in India: "Baptism is not a hollow ritual devoid of meaning. We recommend not to 'fake-convert.' . . . After the Baptism dip and marriage in their church, you are legally a Christian" (ibid.). They correctly mention that when a person officially adopts Christianity, she even changes from being under Hindu personal law to Christian personal law (Petersen 2007, 91–92). India has different personal laws for different religious groups (Government of India 2011).

Conversion or Regeneration (Christian Reflection)

Pradip Ayer, in his discussion of "Conversion or Regeneration," demonstrates the extent to which Christians link baptism to church, not Jesus. In two family situations, non-believing spouses were pressured to accept baptism just to satisfy church rules. In neither instance was any attempt made to introduce the person to Jesus, only to baptize them. The one spouse was baptized with no change of heart or commitment to Jesus (Ayer 2001, 183). In the other case, the pastor told the Christian spouse, "Just let your husband be baptized and become a member of the church and then let him follow whatever he likes afterwards" (ibid., 184).

These representative reflections, one Hindu and one Christian, expose how baptism is too often presented and practiced by Christians. Jesus may be mentioned, but ultimately, baptism is mostly about church. Sometimes it can be a meaningless ritual that just keeps Hindus from understanding Jesus. For others, baptism can symbolize deeper connotations that create confusion or conflict, and these often have nothing to do with its scriptural significance.

Whose Baptism?

Christian disagreement over baptism, for instance, can contribute to the barrier of baptism for Hindus. How can Hindus have any idea what baptism entails, when churches are so divided themselves? Hoefer summarizes the confusion:

> [An] issue about which everybody is unclear is the relationship of Baptism to conversion. As mentioned above, some say Baptism is the very act of conversion. Others say Baptism is a public testimony of one's conversion decision. Others say "Baptism in the Spirit" is the only baptism that matters. Some say Baptism in water is essential for salvation; others say it's necessary but not essential; others say it's not even necessary. *In the debate about conversion and Baptism in India, what are we Christians going to say that we can all agree on and others can understand?* (Hoefer 2001a, 47; emphasis mine)

The barrier that this division creates was referenced in the InterFaith Shaadi comments about baptism. They noted that even some churches require rebaptism because one church's baptism is not recognized by another church. Such division within Christianity increases confusion and misunderstanding on the part of Hindus. Even if one wanted to become a follower of Jesus, this fundamental difference about initiation presents a barrier. Which church should I join and whose baptism should I receive?

Forms of baptism are also confusing. Is it sprinkling, pouring, immersion? If immersion, should it be forward, backward, or straight down and up? Is it done once or three times? Christians have created multiple traditions to answer these questions, but how is a Hindu to decide which tradition is the right one?

Hoefer's ending question above is critical to this conversation. How should we resolve baptism differences? One way to remove the barrier of baptism would be to find expressions and forms that are most in line with Scripture and most appropriate for the Hindu culture. Instead of assuming that baptism is a "Christian" possession to enforce Christian identity and tradition, is it possible to liberate it from centuries of Western encrustation and division?

We need to "become all things to all people," even in how we understand, explain, and practice baptism. If we do, we might find that baptism isn't such a barrier to Hindus after all. In fact, it's just possible that it could present a significant bridge to Hindus instead.

Is Baptism Really a Barrier to Hindus?

My third consideration may appear to unravel all the preceding discussion. Hindus may react strongly when a member of their family or community receives baptism. The reaction, though, may not be directed at the act of baptism itself. They are angered at what that baptism represents: the cultural separatism, Christian and church communal identity, and conversion.

B. V. Subbamma, a Kamma woman who became a Christian, testifies, "It is often said that in discipling Hindus the crux of the problem lies in baptism. *But this is not true for the rite of baptism itself.* The water, the complete dedication to a special deity, the words—*all of these are common in Hinduism.* The crux of the problem lies in one significant detail only—that baptism is believed to entail leaving one community and joining another" (Subbamma 2011, 116; emphasis mine).

Baptism, in other words, could be a familiar bridge to Hindus, if we eliminated the extracting, extreme separatism of Christian church tradition. Can we do this? We will examine Scripture shortly to explore just this question.

Subbamma, though, provides a tantalizing hint of the possibilities. Some of her Kamma family had long been interested in Jesus, but would not begin to consider following him because they assumed they had to get baptized and join a church. "This is the case," she says, "with thousands of Hindus. In view of the supposed necessity of becoming a Christian by way of joining the church [through baptism], they deny themselves the privilege of knowing the gospel at all" (ibid., 117).

Through careful, respectful bridge-building, she demonstrated to her family that she had not abandoned or forsaken them, that she was one of them. In time, many of her family came to faith in Jesus and, through them, hundreds more followed Christ from their Kamma community (ibid.). Baptism presented no barrier to Hindus following Jesus . . . when separatism and conversion were removed and Jesus lived incarnationally through her with her people.

In *Churchless Christianity*, Hoefer describes a discussion group with Yesu bhaktas where they articulated "twenty reservations and objections to structured churches." They did not mention baptism. Hoefer concluded,

> *Once again, the issue is not baptism. Baptism within cultural forms would be quite acceptable.* In fact, the group discussed the pros and cons of adapting baptism into a family ritual as most of the Hindu religious customs of initiation are traditionally practiced" (Hoefer 2001b, 218; emphasis mine).

So, is baptism really a barrier? Only when it imposes communal separation or denominational division, when it's more about church than about Jesus. Our way forward is best expressed at this point by Hoefer's summary of his findings: "These believers in Christ are convinced that *baptism is obscuring, not conveying, the Gospel* in the way it [baptism] is now popularly understood and used by the church" (ibid., 157; emphasis mine).

ADDRESSING THE BARRIER OF BAPTISM

If, however, baptism is obscuring the good news currently, how can we address this barrier? Based on what we have seen, five challenges require our attention. If we could address these, much of the barrier of baptism could be removed. Let's summarize the key challenges.

- *We need to find common ground to reduce baptism divisions and questions.* The only common ground we have is what Scripture says. If we start from denominational traditions, we face a hopeless quagmire. Assuming inspired Scripture as our source of authority, decisions about baptism should derive from what Jesus and his apostles taught and practiced. If that sounds too simplistic or naïve, I have nothing else to offer. Maintaining human baptism traditions will only perpetuate the barrier. Solution: Start with Scripture only. Seek common ground from there.

- *Current baptism traditions seem to obscure or even ignore Jesus and the gospel* (the good news). In contrast, the New Testament makes baptism all about Jesus and his good news, not church or communal identity. A return to those scriptural emphases could build significant bridges to Hindus. Solution: Restore NT emphasis on Jesus and the core of the good news.

- *Baptism is primarily associated with separation, conversion, becoming a Christian, and often joining a particular church.* It has been encrusted with all the separationist barriers addressed in Chapters 1–3 and 5. To recover New Testament baptism, we must disassociate it from these unscriptural and unnecessary Christian traditions and restore the emphasis on embodying the good news of Jesus. Solution: Remove conversion, Christianity, and church as the focus of baptism.

- *Hindus are not turned off by the rite or form of baptism.* Careful attention to Scriptural forms and culturally appropriate expressions of those forms could build powerful bridges instead of current barriers. Scripture gives little detail about how baptism was performed, except that it was by immersion. Hindu-background believers should develop their own forms that emphasize the New Testament focus on Jesus, and that represent the good news clearly to their own culture. Solution: Restore NT forms using culturally appropriate expressions.

- Since baptism presents such a barrier, should we treat it, as Hoefer suggests, as an adiaphoron, a non-essential practice (ibid., 154–163)? Hoefer is careful to suggest this as a possibility, not to advocate it as a final solution. We must ask whether to minimize baptism is advisable, desirable, or scriptural just to remove the barrier that it might present for Hindus. If we can address the first four challenges, the "adiaphora principle" might become unnecessary.

Solution: Baptism is not an adiaphoron in Scripture, but addressing the other four challenges makes this choice unnecessary.

SCRIPTURAL ANSWERS TO THE BAPTISM CHALLENGES

Before I proceed, I am keenly aware that Christians and churches approach baptism from widely disparate perspectives and traditions. I cannot adequately address all the challenges and questions regarding baptism in the limited space of this chapter.

Let's begin, then, with Hoefer's call for "common ground." How we deal with that determines whether we might find workable solutions to the other four challenges.

Challenge 1: Finding Common Ground Regarding Baptism

I cannot think of a better starting point in addressing these challenges than Paul's appeal for unity among believers (Eph 4:1–6). If we cannot find common ground here, we have no hope of resolving the baptism barrier and the issues that surround it.

ONE BAPTISM (EPHESIANS 4:3–6)

When he enumerated the foundational elements of the "unity of the Spirit" (Eph 4:4–6) Paul included "one baptism" in his list. Christians generally agree with the other six items (one body, one Spirit, one hope, one Lord, one faith, one God and Father), although they differ in the details.

Baptism on the other hand, presents a divisive challenge for Christians, as we noted earlier (see p. 141). Some traditions accept that it should be there as an identifying and unifying mark of those who belong to Jesus. Other groups, who see baptism as non-essential or optional, ignore or gloss over its presence in the list.

If baptism was not an essential element for unity, Paul should not have included it. Since all the other elements are essential, Paul implies that the "one baptism" (whatever he understands by that), is equally essential. By including baptism in this list, Paul is telling us something about its significance in relation to the other elements of unity.

This, I suggest, is where we should begin in our search after "common ground" regarding baptism and the barriers it poses. Baptism's presence in this list, along with its placement, actually provides a starting point for addressing the other four challenges.

Challenge 2: Baptism's Relationship to Jesus and the Good News

As we noted earlier, common Christian baptism practice can hide Jesus and the good news behind layers of Christian traditions about conversion, social extraction, Christian identity, and church membership. These institutional customs and purposes obscure the essential meaning of New Testament baptism, the "one baptism" to which Paul refers.

BAPTISM IS ABOUT JESUS

Who is baptism for? Paul directly links the "one baptism" with "one Lord" and "one faith" (Eph 4:5). This is not accidental. It reflects consistent New Testament teaching and practice. Baptism is commonly modified by "in the name of Jesus" or "into Christ Jesus" (Matt 28:19; Acts 2:38; 8:16; 10:48; 19:3–5; Rom 6:1–5; Gal 3:27).

David Bosch reflects this understanding:

> The unity that prevails among believers has its basis in the fact that they are all, through baptism, incorporated into Christ. I have indicated that Paul's preaching, indeed his entire theology, centers in the death and resurrection of Christ. This also explains his understanding of baptism. The believers—not as so many individuals but as a corporate body—are baptized into the death of Christ and are likewise raised from the dead; they are crucified with Christ, have died with him, but now live with him and are alive to God (Rom 6:3–11). They have "put on" Christ, crucified and risen, and have been adopted as children of God (Gal 3:26f; cf Col 3:10). (Bosch 1996, 167)

Leon Morris, likewise, in his commentary on Romans, emphasizes this Jesus-centered view of baptism:

> Paul goes on to characterize baptism as *into Christ Jesus* ("into union with Christ Jesus", GNB, NEB) . . . Baptism, so to speak, incorporates the baptized into Christ; they are baptized "into one body" (1 Cor. 12:13), made

part of that body which is the body of Christ . . . The act of baptism was an act of *incorporation* into Christ. (Morris 1988, 247)

Beasley-Murray also articulates this connection from Paul's own testimony:

From Acts 22:16 it would seem that the name of Jesus was invoked by the baptismal candidate ["calling on his name"]; it is also likely that the name of Jesus was also called over the candidate by the baptizer ["in the name of Jesus"]. Leenhardt not unreasonably concluded from this that we have to do with a rite which *draws its whole meaning from the person of Christ and the relationship established with Him.* (Beasley-Murray 1962, 100; emphasis mine)

Baptism is supposed to be about Jesus. In fact, the New Testament focuses it almost entirely on his person and work and believers' identification with him.

BAPTISM IS ABOUT THE GOOD NEWS

Paul, in Ephesians 4:5, also links the "one baptism" to "one faith." The faith to which Paul refers here is "the faith of the gospel" (Phil 1:27) or what Jude terms "the faith once for all delivered to the saints" (Jude 3). That faith is the good news of Jesus, described by Paul in 1 Corinthians 15:1–4: "That Christ died for our sins according to the Scriptures, and that he was buried, and that he was raised on the third day according to the Scriptures."

The one faith, the good news, is, at its core, the death, burial, and resurrection of Jesus. As the above quotes by Bosch and Morris illustrate, the New Testament clearly links baptism to Christ's death, burial, and resurrection (Rom 6:3–11; Gal 3:26f; 1 Pet 3:21). New Testament baptism somehow symbolized and connected believers to the core of the good news of Jesus. It had no power in itself.

So, when Paul places "one baptism" next to "one Lord" and "one faith," he addresses the second challenge presented by the baptism barrier. When this New Testament emphasis is correctly recognized, it enables believers to clearly answer Hoefer's concern, "Where ninety-seven percent of the population is looking at baptism from the outside, we must be sure that baptism clearly presents the Gospel-gift of God's uplifting, freeing, redeeming love in Christ" (Hoefer 2001b, 158).

Challenge 3: Baptism and Conversion, Community, Christianity, or Church

Then what about our third baptism challenge? All the conversion, community, and church baggage Christians have attached to baptism? What does the New Testament say about that?

Nothing! Absolutely nothing.

Look at all the New Testament says about baptism and you will find little basis for common Christian teaching and practice regarding baptism. Conversion, as we already observed, is not a New Testament word. Early believers did not identify themselves as Christians, so baptism had nothing to do with conversion or Christian identity.

Hoefer's research with non-baptized believers led him to ask, "Should they be uprooted from their home society in order to be baptized and thus cut off totally from all they know and love—and from those to whom they might naturally witness?" (ibid., 49). This far into the book, I hope the reader can readily answer that question. Hoefer himself, in reviewing the scriptural significance of baptism, rightly concluded, "Baptism was clearly not intended by Paul to separate people from their homes and societies" (ibid., 148–149). Believers should refrain from using baptism in ways that are incongruent with the teaching of Scripture.

One verse might suggest church-centered baptism: "For by one Spirit we were all *baptized into one body*, whether Jews or Greeks, whether slaves or free; and we were all made to drink of one Spirit" (1 Cor 12:13; emphasis mine). This refers to one element of the Spirit's role in baptism in passages like John 3:5, Acts 2:38, and Titus 3:5. It does indicate, though, that *you don't get to Jesus through the church, you get into the ekklēsia when his Spirit adds you at baptism.*

Having addressed the first three baptism challenges, we find that the Hindu marriage site administrator (InterFaithShaadi Admin 2014b) correctly identified the discrepancy between common Christian practice ("for the church") and the true focus of baptism ("about Jesus"). Interestingly, an earlier post on the same site advised, "Follow Jesus, not the Church" (InterFaithShaadi Admin 2014a).

If we want to "become all things to all people," regarding baptism, then we must wrestle scripturally with these first three challenges. Correctly address these challenges, and we would significantly reduce the baptism barriers in Hindus' eyes.

Challenge 4: Hindus Not Offended by the Rite of Baptism

Earlier, we observed that Hindus are not necessarily offended by the rite of baptism itself, only by the unscriptural associations Christians have attached to it. Having dealt with those, let me briefly suggest at least three possible connecting points between New Testament baptism and Hindu practice.

IMMERSION IN WATER IS FAMILIAR

Hindus are familiar with immersion in water as a religious practice. I have watched them immerse themselves at the bathing *ghats* (steps) of the Ganges River in the holy city of Varanasi. I have also often seen them do so at the bathing tanks near or within temples. Devout Hindus, in fact, bathe every morning before their time of worship.

These regular acts of washing, bathing, or immersing, are not unlike the repeated cleansing practices of the Jews. They too were required to regularly bathe themselves when ceremonially unclean or on certain special occasions. John's baptism, Edersheim suggests, may well have reflected the same preparatory cleansing that Moses commanded before the giving of the first covenant at Sinai (Edersheim 1980, 273–274).

In both Hindu and Jewish practice, then, there are both initiatory and repeated immersions with spiritual significance.

Christians have certainly developed various forms of baptism. Most believers acknowledge, however, that *baptizō* originally meant immerse or submerge, and that New Testament baptism was originally performed by immersion. This is reflected in Acts 8:28f. where Philip goes down into the pool with the treasurer, immerses him, and then they both come back up out of the water.

Original New Testament practice, then, could provide a familiar bridge to Hindus, if believers were to use immersion. In Romans 6, in fact, Paul indicates that immersion portrayed a believer's identification with the death, burial, and resurrection of Jesus (the good news). Immersion is, in fact, the only form of baptism that does so. As such it addresses our second challenge above by visibly tying immersion to Jesus and his work.

Water Initiation (Jal Diksha) Is Familiar

Local believers would also need to be encouraged to develop culturally appropriate specifics for what this immersion rite might be called and how it might be performed. For example, Petersen has described practices of Yesu bhaktas in North India who call it "*jal sanskar* (water ritual or sacrament) and *guru diksha* (initiation into the absolute authority of a master and teacher)." In addition, he is "aware of many Hindus who have taken this form of *jal sanskar* (called *guru diksha*) by means of immersion in a nearby river. The possibilities of linking the biblical meanings to this event have appeared to be intact, in addition to the disassociation from the negative meaning of 'community change' that is inherent in Christian baptism in India" (Petersen 2007, 94).

Hoefer earlier noted that Indian believers want to and should develop appropriate cultural expressions of baptism. Since the New Testament provides little specific detail about how the immersions were carried out (forward, backward, up, and down), local believers should develop natural forms for their culture, rather than adopting those cultural forms imposed by Western Christianity and church tradition, along the lines of Petersen's observations.

Even the words used—"in the name of the Father, Son, and Holy Spirit" (Matt 28) or "in the name of Jesus" (Acts)—will need to be selectively chosen for local appropriateness. Acts uses the shorter phrasing instead of the fuller Matthean triune formula. Based on Acts, the apostles do not seem to have been as insistent on the triune formula as modern Christians can be. We should not impose one tradition on believers where the New Testament reflects a variety. Local believers should be made aware and then allowed to choose the best expression for their situation.

Removing Sins and Seeking God is Familiar

Hindus also see immersion as a means of removing sins, as a contributing means of salvation and reconciliation with their god. These concepts provide a potential starting point for conversation about the meaning of New Testament baptism into Jesus.

Some Christians are uncomfortable with New Testament language about baptism's connection to forgiveness and salvation. They find numerous ways to avoid or explain away this language. But if what we observed about Jesus and the good news is true, then this language is not so surprising.

"Christ died for our sins according to the Scriptures," asserts Paul (1 Cor 15:3). He also teaches that baptism somehow connects us to Christ's death (Rom 6:1–5; Col 2:12). Given these two realities, Peter's assertion that baptism in the name of Jesus leads to forgiveness of sins and the gift of the Spirit (Acts 2:38) is not so difficult. The water is not magical. Jesus simply ordained it as the place (Matt 28:19; Mark 16:15f.) where believers demonstrate their faith in and connection to him and his good news. That expression of faith is certainly more scriptural than praying a "sinner's prayer" (found nowhere in the New Testament).

Paul himself connected his own baptism with "washing away your sins, calling on his name" (Acts 22:16). He made this statement in Jerusalem only three to four months after penning his letter to the Romans from Corinth (Acts 20:1–6; Rom 16). In fact, Paul's own testimony here should tell us how he understood Romans 10:13, which he wrote so recently. Rather than excluding baptism from any role in salvation, Paul says that he called on the name of the Lord at his baptism. Beasley-Murray is correct, I believe, when he says, "Here is an aspect of baptism to which justice has not been done in the Church since its early days: baptism as a means of prayer for acceptance with God and for full salvation from God . . ." (Beasley-Murray 1962, 102). This is exactly what Peter means when he asserts, "It is baptism that now saves you, not the putting off of the filth of the flesh, but an appeal to God for a good conscience, through the resurrection of Jesus Christ" (1 Pet 3:21). Peter and Paul are both describing the same baptismal experience as an appeal to the Lord or a prayer to him ("calling on his name").

Wayne Meeks, in his insightful analysis of *The First Urban Christians*, clearly relates Romans 10:9–13 with the baptism experience:

> Baptism is the most likely setting for the simple confession mentioned by Paul in Rom. 10:9, "The Lord is Jesus!" (*kyrios Iēsous*). . . . Such a declaration was at least one referent of early Christian interpretation of the Joel passage, "Everyone who calls on the name of the Lord will be saved" (as, for example, in Rom. 10:13). Paul's biographer still associates this with baptism in his description of Paul's conversion (Acts 22:16). (Meeks 1983, 152)

New Testament baptism, then, as far as Peter and Paul were concerned, connected believers to the Lord Jesus, and was the place where they called on his name (sought salvation). It was also the place where, by faith and the Spirit, their sins were forgiven and washed away. Christian tradition, as Beasley-Murray noted, has obscured or denied these truths.

These New Testament views of baptism (immersion in water and spirit, forgiveness), when properly explained and taught, could provide a powerful bridge between Hindu longing for forgiveness of sin and the forgiveness provided by Christ. Rather than having to bathe repeatedly to remove sin, we can introduce them to a once-for-all identification with Jesus. That relationship permanently connects us with both his forgiveness and his indwelling presence by his Spirit to overcome sin.

Challenge 5: Does the Adiaphora Principle Apply to Baptism?

Having considered the other four challenges, we are now able to examine Hoefer's suggestion that baptism be considered an *adiaphoron* (optional or non-essential practice). My starting point is again Ephesians 4:5 and the "one baptism" there (see One Baptism, p. 147).

Table 6 summarizes the essential elements for unity that Paul described there. We must consider why baptism was included in the list and the significance of that inclusion.

Table 6. Essential Elements of Unity

	Essential	Peripheral Optional Adiaphora
One Body	✓	✗
One Spirit	✓	✗
One Hope (heaven)	✓	✗
One Lord (Jesus)	✓	✗
One Faith (the good news)	✓	✗
One Baptism	✓	✗
One God and Father	✓	✗

First, since Paul included it in the list, we must assume it is as essential as the other elements in that list. Whatever our church tradition or doctrine says about baptism, it was important enough for Paul to include it in the seven (not six) essentials for "the unity of the Spirit." None of the other items in that list is optional.

While an intriguing proposal, Hoefer's suggestion of the *adiaphora* possibility (Hoefer 2001b, 154–163), cannot be the way forward in resolving the barrier of baptism. Paul's placement of baptism precludes it being dispensable any more than Jesus or faith could be. We would not consider removing any other item from that list. I don't see, then, how we can be faithful to Scripture and do so with the "one baptism" either.

If, however, we adopted the solutions to the prior four challenges, the baptism barrier could be primarily resolved. We know that some Hindus are interested in Jesus, just not Christianity and church. Addressing Challenges 1 and 2 opens a scriptural door for them. We also know that the Christian communal and conversion baggage around baptism keeps Hindus from Jesus, and we have also addressed those through Challenges 1–3. Remove those barriers, and Hindus are open to a rite that signifies forgiveness and identification with God, connections already familiar to them. Indian solutions to Challenge 4 can provide scriptural and culturally meaningful bridges to Hindus in place of the numerous current barriers.

If we take care of the first four, we do not need to remove or avoid baptism. Instead, it could present a powerful witness and bridge to Hindu communities about the love, grace, and forgiveness of Christ. It becomes, in fact, a perfect entry point for Christians or Yesu bhaktas to dedicate themselves to love, worship, and serve Jesus.

CHRISTIAN AND BHAKTA CONSIDERATIONS

Christians

There is no way around this. Christians who care about these issues will need to carefully consider what the New Testament actually says about baptism. When they do, they, like me, will likely discover that a great deal of what their church or denomination says is nowhere to be found in Scripture. We are only obligated to obey Jesus and his word, not the traditions of men.

If we care about Hindus, and want to "become all things to all men" to help them meet Jesus, then we must carefully reexamine our baptism traditions. We must ensure that the baptism we teach and practice is clearly Jesus-centered and good news-centered, not church- or conversion-centered.

Yesu Bhaktas

Bhaktas know that they should not convert to separatist Christian identity or church, as we have already observed. When they avoid Christian baptism practices with church-centered associations, they have made the right choice.

The New Testament, though, does portray an immersion in water and the Spirit (John 3:3–5; Acts 10:44–48) that significantly connects believers to Jesus and his good news. To the extent that Christians have hidden that reality behind church-centered traditions, I apologize for those unscriptural barriers that have pushed some bhaktas away from this significant experience.

I pray that Yesu bhaktas, through the reflections in this chapter, will find freedom to develop and use forms of *jal sanskar* (*guru diksha*) that are faithful to Scripture, clearly reflect Jesus and the good news, and communicate Jesus to their fellow Hindus. May the Lord lead them to develop forms and expressions of this experience in their culture just as Western Christians have developed their own cultural versions for centuries. They are under no obligation to follow someone else's models, only to follow Scripture and "become all things to all people" among their own communities, even with this *sanskar*.

CLOSING REFLECTIONS

Sadly, a scriptural experience that was intended to symbolize the freeing good news of Jesus, has become a symbol of many of the barriers we have already encountered. Centuries of Christian tradition have encumbered baptism with practices and beliefs that come, not from Jesus or his word, but from human opinion, tradition, and invention. An item of New Testament faith and practice intended to unify believers (Eph 4:6) has instead become a source of incredible disagreement and even division.

These baptism issues are not an academic, theological family disagreement between Christians. If the evidence in this chapter is at all reflective of Indian reality, baptism traditions can serve to keep millions of Hindus from meeting or considering Jesus.

I am under no illusion that we have addressed all the issues, much less resolved all the challenges in this brief space. We have skimmed the surface of issues that each deserve much fuller treatment. I do pray, however, that the suggestions presented here will challenge Christians and Yesu bhaktas alike to reexamine their own practices regarding baptism and *diksha* in light of Scripture and the Hindu concerns about current baptism practices.

Just possibly, if we address these challenges, we might see a day when many Hindus see *diksha* into Jesus as a positive, culturally natural witness to his good news. May that *diksha* help many find a genuine relationship with him.

CHAPTER 7

THE BARRIER OF WORSHIP

Some Indian church leaders once initiated an interesting discussion. They had recently been visited by some ethnomusicology students who expressed interest in learning about their culture's traditional music. A university professor taught the students some of the local instruments and music. Then, with his help and accompaniment, these students composed and sang a worship song using local language, instruments, and music.

That recent affirmation of their local cultural music, though, had raised questions for these leaders. They had appreciated what they heard. Was their local music really the "devil's music," as they had been taught for so long? Could they worship the Lord with their own culture's music? Did they even want to do so?

Generations of Christian tradition had taught that their local music was "the devil's music," something evil they should reject in preference for good "Christian" music. In their situation, the missionaries had translated hymns and choruses from the West, sung to slightly adapted Western tunes. They used "Christian" instruments to accompany this music.

More recently, some had moved from hymns to the most current Western worship songs. They began to sing Hillsong or Chris Tomlin songs nearly as soon as they were released. Some of the worship leaders even sang the English lyrics with the American or Australian accents of the original singers, further highlighting the foreign nature of the songs in their context. This Western music, translated into their own language, was their heartfelt music of worship. They sang deeply and passionately to the Lord in these Western forms.

This conversation made me keenly aware of one critical dimension of the barrier of worship. Christian worship can present a significant obstacle to people when it emphasizes foreign forms over indigenous forms. I will focus primarily on music in this chapter, but foreign worship forms also include the buildings used for worship (architecture), the visual arts used to accompany or foster worship (painting, sculpture, photography, symbolism), the clothing and accessories associated with worship, and what kind of body movement (dance, rhythm) may be permitted.

EMPHASIZES FOREIGN FORMS OVER LOCAL FORMS

As a guitar player myself, I know first-hand that music forms, genres, and styles can represent a minefield for believers. Churches have divided over their convictions about what music is the "Lord's music" and what is the "Devil's music," even in the West. Different Western denominations follow diverse liturgies, musical preferences, and worship settings. Numerous American congregations have different services that cater to more traditional tastes or more contemporary ones. Try mixing the music between those services and you will quickly discover how deeply people feel about what form of music honors the Lord.

Western Forms over Indian Forms

Believers will likely never all agree on what music or worship forms are preferable. They should not have to. We should be concerned, however, when Western forms are privileged as "Christian" by default over Indian forms.

DEMANDING WESTERN FORMS

Jacob Joseph observed, "Today most mainline denominations in India still follow a completely Westernized liturgy and use Western music in worship" (Joseph 2013, 137). I have worshiped in Indian churches where I did not know the language, but could sing along to every song in English, because the tune and rhythm were well-known Western church hymns or choruses. In others, the songs weren't familiar, but the worship band up front used only the accoutrements of Western worship, and imitated Western-style Hallelujahs, Amens, and "Check, Check, Check" (mic check before each song).

Indian believers were originally taught to sing the songs of Western Christianity either in the Euro-American languages, or translated into the local vernacular. The tunes, rhythms, and lyrics, however, still bore the stamp of the Western Christian culture of origin. This "Christian music" was the only acceptable expression of worship to the Lord. In other instances, they translated lyrics into local languages, then used more local music to accompany the songs. The wording and phrasing, though, could be unnatural to local ears, even when music sounded somewhat familiar.

The following missionary account from the nineteenth century was rather telling:

> The missionaries of the American Board at an early day prepared translations of standard hymns, with the Psalms in paraphrase, to be sung to our good old tunes. With the native Christians, Western song was heavy work, but undertaken as a Christian duty. (Hauser 1884)

Western missions, all too often, assumed that whatever the preferred style was at home, that should be the preferred style for Indian believers also. They or their initial converts condemned the local music as the "devil's music," thus ensuring that their "Christian music" was adopted. Where this happened, it fostered varying levels of disregard among local believers toward their own culture's music.

DISDAINING LOCAL FORMS

The music barrier does not stop at choosing and preferring foreign music. Generations of Christians, raised only with "Christian music" specifically or Western cultural music in general, can sometimes disdain or dislike traditional forms of Indian music.

Some conversations with Christians about worship have paralleled Bharati's testimony: "When I ask the Christians why we should use hymns with Western music rather than compose and use *bhajans*, their reaction generally is, 'Oh, we don't want to sing *bhajans* like the Hindus, we want to have our own Christian music.' For them, Western music itself is Christian music, and they do not even know that the so-called Christian (Western) music has heathen ancestry" (Bharati 2004, 76).

If, as occasionally happens, they ignore or denigrate India's rich musical heritage in preference for Western music (even if translated or Indianized), this too can offend some Hindus. Bharati elaborates,

> Music is an integral part of worship in the Hindu community. Several times they have *naadopasana* (music worship) alone. But even living in this country with

> rich classical music (both Carnatic and Hindustani), the
> churches have sadly preferred to adopt Western music for
> their worship. By saying this, I am not degrading West-
> ern music. Let the Westerners have their own music, but
> *why should we abandon God's rich gift to us in Indian music?*
> (ibid., 75; emphasis mine)

Bharati's question, I believe, requires a considered answer in today's India. With 95 percent of India alienated in various ways from Jesus, it is vital that we ask how our music choices might contribute to this barrier.

Susan Harper has detailed ways in which significant portions of Indian communities have moved to Jesus wholeheartedly and embraced Western forms and expressions in doing so (Harper 2000). Western music and worship forms have become their heart music and their worship expressions of choice. I have dear Christian friends for whom Western music—varying styles from country to rock—touch their soul deeply and resonate with them. For generations, that music has become *their* cultural music.

Fusions of Indian and Western are an ongoing musical reality in India today as evidenced by numerous music channels broadcasting incredibly diverse musical mixes on television. Some younger people may not resonate at all with Indian traditional music, while others are dedicating themselves to master classical art forms.

When, however, Christians specifically demand that Western forms of music or lyric are the only acceptable "Christian" music, this can create a cultural barrier. The lyrics, the music, or both combined can communicate to the surrounding culture that this is a foreign religion that worships with foreign music.

Chris Hale, a trained sitar player and advocate for using Hindu music, provides an insightful analysis of the many different cultural music influences in India (Hale 2011). He notes, though, despite their many musical preferences, Hindus, especially in the North, resonate with bhajans. Hale's explanation of this music form might be helpful at this point:

> These songs have Indian lyrics, Indian tunes, and an In-
> dian worship format. Historically, they are taken from
> Hindu devotional practice, but there is nothing un-
> scriptural about these forms. The forms are conducive to

biblical meditation. First, there is the exposition of the passage by the preacher which enlightens the understanding through the Holy Spirit. Then there is the repetition of the biblical thought through the singing of the bhajan and the thought goes from the mind into the heart and touches the emotions and the will. (Hale 2011, 121)

Several Christian friends of mine came to Jesus directly from Hindu backgrounds. They have shared at times that the Christian music does not resonate at all with them, even after years of church worship. They sing the songs because Christians do so, but their hearts are not really touched in worship. To this day, though, certain bhajans (Hindu worship songs) still stir their souls deeply; they wish there was a way to worship Jesus in that style, but their Christian communities say, "Bhajans are only for Hindus; and many Hindus don't even like them anymore." Christian disregard can be a barrier to genuine heart worship even for Hindu-background Christians. If they feel this disconnect years after following Jesus, they find it difficult to invite others from their family and community to experience the same disconnect.

Just to illustrate how complicated these issues can be, let me recount another story. A man came to Christ from a Hindu shaman's family. They separated from everything they had known and embraced Christianity. Later, this man was introduced to some bhajans written to worship Jesus. Initially he completely rejected this music because it reminded him of his Hindu past that he had renounced and abandoned for Jesus; it made him too uncomfortable. Over time, however, he has come to realize that this music can help Hindu-background believers express their love and worship for Jesus in more natural ways. The music wasn't the problem; it was more the cultural separatism that controlled his mind. When he found a more scriptural balance, he reconsidered his rejection and instead affirmed his culture's musical heritage more freely.

When Christians are taught to disdain or demonize local music forms, they reject and condemn the culture that produces and uses that art. This reflects the "cultural separatism" spirit of believers and ensures that they will not utilize local music to build a bridge to the community around them. Where this spirit is strongest, it prevents believers from "becoming all things to all people," from incarnating the life and way of Jesus within the musical forms of their own people who need to meet Jesus.

DISREGARDING LOCAL FORMS

One day some Indian seminary students treated my wife and me to a song accompanied by *tabla* (type of Indian drum) and tambourine. When they had finished, my wife asked what the song was about. It was a traditional love song. She then asked, "Do you ever use such music to worship Jesus?" They responded, "Oh, no! This is traditional, not Christian music. We don't use this music in church."

They did not use the "devil's music" argument, maybe they had never heard it. They were aware, however, that their church did not use local instruments or music forms for "worship." I find Christians who don't know why this is the case, it's just clear that Christians don't utilize traditional music for some reason—that's the church tradition.

The global export of Christian music seems to assume that one form of music is universal. Robin Harris has rightly observed, "music is *not* a universal language" (Harris 2013, 83; emphasis mine). The same music can convey different senses and feelings across cultures, in subgroups within one culture, and even within the same congregation. Western missionaries, though, followed the false assumption of "universal music," branding local music as "primitive and heathen" and "encouraging the translation of Western Christian songs into indigenous languages. . . ." (ibid., 85). "Even today," Harris adds, "one can find cross-cultural workers who fail miserably at valuing the God-given musical and artistic resources of the host cultures in which they minister" (ibid.).

Some Christians may not demonize local arts. For one reason or another, though, they may have learned to simply disregard them as inferior, undesirable, or "unchristian" in some way. They are not always sure why or what the rationale is. It's just not done.

I attended an intensive ethnoarts seminar in India a while back. The leaders divided us into groups and asked us to list a variety of musical forms from the group's dominant culture. They then asked each group to take those forms and classify them under three headings: Can Use in Church, Can't Use in Church, Can be Redeemed. The ensuing discussion was intriguing. Initially, each group identified many forms that have been used or could be used in church worship. Each group also listed several that were not used, but that could be redeemed and used. Several groups had one or two items in the Can't Use category.

The leaders explored those Can't Use items carefully. Why could they not be used? Were they demonic? Were they offensive to people? Did they hinder worship? As the groups discussed their reasons for rejecting these forms, it became apparent that we had primarily disallowed them out of personal taste more than objective reasons. In every instance, the groups ended up shifting these items to the Could Be Redeemed category.

Where Christians disregard the local musical culture in preference for a more Western Christian music this can present a barrier that needs to be addressed. I must not leave this section, though, giving the impression that all Christians do so. Many have, in fact, sought to address these challenges in a variety of ways.

I have worshiped in gatherings where the only instruments were Indian drums (*dholak, mridangam, tabla*) and hand cymbals (*karatalas*). The people sang, clapped, and even danced to songs of their own composition in words and tunes that resonated with their own culture. In some urban churches, believers sing songs with their own lyrics and tunes accompanied by a fusion of Indian instruments and Western keyboard, guitar, and drums. Some congregations, in urban or mixed culture environments, create a blend of cultural forms and expressions so that believers from different communities learn to worship in and appreciate a variety of styles.

Believers must consider whether their music of preference might provide a barrier to Jesus or a musical bridge. In some settings, where Christian music has been traditionally foreign for generations, some believers will likely need to "become all things to all people" musically. They will need to step out of their musical comfort zone and learn to appreciate, affirm, and adopt the music of the cultural community around them as a new music of choice. Instead of disregarding or disdaining that music, they will need to intentionally and actively embrace local arts that are initially strange and unfamiliar, until these actually touch their heart and become a new part of their life. They don't have to reject their formerly favorite music. They will need to honestly expand their musical love to entirely new genres.

Recently this came home to me at a speaking engagement in the US. Just before my presentation, the music team led a bhajan called *Bhaj Pavanatam Yesu Naam* (Praise the Holy Name of Jesus). Just three years earlier, that song and its Indian musical genre were completely unknown to me. That night I sang to the Lord from my heart through a song Indian believers have made dear to me. We can learn to appreciate, understand, and affirm new musical styles. I believe Jesus is calling his people to do so in India today.

In the West, Christians do not just listen to "Christian" music or attend "Christian" concerts. Many Christians attend classical music concerts, operas, and ballets. They also attend country music concerts, rap concerts, rock concerts, concerts of all styles and genres. I know there are some Christians in the West who assert that believers should only listen to "Christian" music, but they are in a small minority. Most Christians have an eclectic taste of some Christian and much cultural music also. If more Indian believers honored, patronized, and enjoyed the music of their own culture, they might find fewer Hindus criticizing them for being anti-cultural and anti-national. They would also find that Jesus is not nearly so offended at the local culture's music and its beauty as some Christians have portrayed him.

"CHRISTIAN" MUSIC IS CULTURAL MUSIC

Remember those leaders at the start of the chapter and their struggle over using their culture's music for worship? As we discussed these questions, the Lord drew my attention to the platform behind me. Sitting in plain view were two of their Christian instruments of choice: an electric guitar and a Western drum kit. The irony of the conversation hit me, and I started to laugh. I turned back to my friends and asked, "Do you see those two instruments on the platform? Did you know that they were both called 'the devil's music' by churches in the West just sixty years ago?"

That came as a surprise to these leaders. I went through a little Christian musical history, not only about guitars and drums, but earlier debates over pianos, choruses, hymns, and chants. Unfortunately, the Western Christians only gave them the forms. They were not taught the principles of cultural adaptation (incarnation) that had led to those forms. My Indian friends felt compelled to adopt every new Western expression as "Christian" music, and the West never divulged its secret. All "Christian" music was first cultural music.

In every instance, Western believers "became all things to all people" musically, and adapted cultural musical forms to help different cultures

meet and worship Jesus, even though some of those forms had been initially labeled "devil's music" by Christians in the West. They rarely taught
this fundamental Christian practice to believers in India. Indian believers
were taught that their local music was the "devil's music," that it should
never be used under any circumstances. Had Western Christians followed
this same "devil's music" spirit in their own churches, Indian Christians
would have little of the "Christian" music they sing so dearly today.

If they wanted their culture to meet and follow Jesus, I suggested,
Indian believers should be free to do with their own cultural music what
Western Christians have been doing for centuries. It's time to let Jesus do
the same in India that he has done in the West for generations. Believers
need greater freedom to "become all things to all people" musically in
their own culture and context.

Indian Forms from One Culture over Indian Forms in Another

Several years ago, an evangelist worked to help a new tribal group meet
Jesus. He did not know their language, and they knew some of the local
Telugu state language, so he preached in Telugu and taught them to sing
and pray in Telugu. They worshiped for some time using the trade language, but it never felt completely natural and few people were drawn to
their fellowship.

This evangelist, to be fair, had never taught them that they could only
use Telugu. He actually knew better himself. However, a subtle cultural
disregard led him to not even consider how to help them worship and
pray in their own tongue. As a result, they assumed they should just use
Telugu. Since he was the evangelist, the teacher, cultural precedent determined that he should not be questioned, so no one asked about the
language issue, they simply assumed they should use the language he did.

I share this to illustrate that cultural forms sometimes are not overtly,
explicitly imposed on other believers. They are sometimes simply caught
by a cultural osmosis. Unless the teachers are aware of this dynamic, and
specifically address it, they can unintentionally foster traditions that disregard local culture.

One day a Bible translator spent some time with these believers. He
asked what led them to not worship and pray in their tribal, heart language. They replied that they had only been taught in Telugu, so that was
all they knew. He explained that they could use their heart language and

that God hears and understands regardless of language. I'll let the translator tell what happened in his own words:

> Shortly after that, the oldest believer surprised me by praying in her own language at church. Her daughter and niece sang a song in their language. This church is usually a noisy place. But on that day, as the sound of their language filled the room, everyone else was so moved that they fell silent. It was absolutely amazing.
>
> Afterwards my heart nearly broke when the woman who had prayed came to me and said, "I wish we had known that we could talk to God and sing in our own language. So many more of us would be here if we had known." (Anonymous 2013)

The barrier of foreign worship culture, then, is not just an issue of Western music, styles, or forms. My Indian colleagues have talked about the Malayalization and Tamilization of churches in the North. They detail ways that Christians from Kerala and Tamil Nadu in the south take their worship forms and styles to the Hindi states in the North and impose them on new believers there.

A Hindi-speaking Indian missionary told an ethnoarts workshop about preaching to a tribal group for ten years. Early in his work a tribal man came and asked if he could sing a song he had written in his own music and language. The missionary recounted, "I told him he could not. We only use Hindi in church." A decade later, at the ethnoarts training, he had learned that you could affirm and value local cultural arts to help people meet and worship Jesus in their heart language and music. He told the group, "[My rejection] was a big blunder. If I had known and given permission, we could now have many cultural songs to the Lord" (Soundaraj 2016).

Let me close this section with a vision of the alternative. A friend of mine, a Christian dentist, worked for several years at a hospital in a highly resistant area of the North. For a century, they had tried to evangelize the people around them with no tangible results. The medical staff and the evangelists were all Indians, but the approaches they used and the music they used communicated that their religion was foreign.

One of the evangelists felt led to "become all things to all people" in this context instead of perpetuating the cultural disregard that had driven so much work. He dedicated himself to mastering a local instrument and music of the people. He learned their own songs and learned to sing them well. They had a tradition of telling stories through music, so he learned to tell their stories in their musical style. Eventually, when he became proficient enough at their forms, he created a few stories of his own from the Old Testament. Then he added a few more, still in their style, but now about Jesus.

Having prepared himself over considerable time, he went to a village and began playing and singing their own story songs. The villagers were intrigued by an Indian from another place who honored their own musical tradition this way. A number gathered to listen, and they invited more to come and hear. After several familiar songs to open the door, he then introduced one of his new songs from the Old Testament. The villagers were intrigued by a story they had not heard that used their own musical form to tell it. They invited more people to hear and asked if he had more songs. He sang a few more and the crowd continued to grow. He would always stop before singing too many songs, and they would ask him for more. He made sure to sing at their invitation, not his imposition.

When he had an active, interested audience, eventually he moved to the new songs about Jesus. For the first time in their lives, these people heard of Jesus in tones, words, and rhythms that incarnated him within their culture and context. Over time these musical gatherings touched numerous people's hearts and they began to consider Jesus as their friend, not an alien, foreign god. In early 2014, the chief of this group decided he wanted to follow Jesus. Since then, hundreds have joined him in that decision.

What removed the barrier to Jesus for these people? One man who decided to abandon cultural separatism and its disregard for the musical culture of the people. One man who "became all things to all people" by taking the time to learn their music and instruments proficiently. One man who affirmed and adapted that cultural music to tell the story of Jesus in a way that was natural for those people to hear. One man who forsook the barrier of foreign music and built a bridge to Jesus using their own musical forms and styles.

India needs a generation of believers who will catch a similar vision. Believers who will step away from cultural separatism and embrace, learn, and use local musical forms to honor and share Jesus in creative ways. In a country that is far more diverse than the US, this will require openness to widely varied expressions, styles, and forms.

Seeking Appropriate Forms

Ultimately, when a new culture is first introduced to Jesus, we should not impose external traditions, derived from our human choices, for how to conduct various aspects of worship. We should, rather, introduce them to the appropriate scriptures and encourage them to determine what local expressions would be best. We should encourage them to

- Search the Scriptures (Acts 17:11),
- Ask the Lord for wisdom (Jas 1:5),
- Discuss the options together (Acts 15), then
- Follow what seems good to the body and the Holy Spirit (Acts 15:28).

This process can take time initially. It will, however, lead to more authentic, incarnational expressions of worship, music, prayer, Lord's Supper, baptism, proclamation, and other aspects of life and practice. Believers from one culture are too ready to interject and model their own familiar tradition as "the way" to express these aspects of following the Lord, but when they do, they shortcut the process of allowing Jesus to incarnate within the culture as he wants so that as many as possible can meet and follow him. Cultural short cuts can create long-term barriers.

Cultural forms can contribute to worship barriers and must be addressed. We must, however, consider a deeper worship issue that presents another barrier. Western Christianity has often taught believers to prioritize public worship over personal life and worship. My Indian conversations suggest that the issues arising from this assumption can contribute to serious misunderstanding and disconnect.

EMPHASIZES PUBLIC WORSHIP OVER PERSONAL DEVOTION

On several occasions, Indian Christians have asserted to me, "Hindus do not really participate in corporate worship." This initially confused me, since I have observed Hindus engaged in group worship in various settings.

One evening, I stood on the *ghats* (bathing steps) on the banks of the Ganges River in the ancient city of Varanasi. Thousands of people were gathered to watch the *Ganga Aarti* (evening fire ceremony). Some sat on the stone steps leading down from the city to the ceremony platform. Others sat on the bathing steps and the docks by the water. Many more sat in numerous boats pulled up to the water's edge. For most of the service everyone just watched the rituals as the *pujaris* (priests) performed them, not unlike some Christians who mainly observe the more formal rituals of certain liturgical church services.

Late in the ceremony, though, a certain drumbeat and tune began to play. Spontaneously, almost as if choreographed, everyone began to sing loudly and passionately. Some sang with hands folded and eyes closed, apparently immersed in the words. Others clapped and sang with joy on their faces. It clearly appeared to be a corporate worship experience for those who participated.

Our local temple has a video of a large group of Hindus jointly reciting the *Hanuman Chalisa*. Different participants took turns singing the verses of this popular forty-verse hymn, not once but 108 times, to show their devotion to the god Hanuman. This participatory experience demonstrated another expression of Hindu corporate worship.

We visited a Brahmin family one evening at their apartment. As we sat down, the man apologized for the *veena* (large stringed instrument) on the floor in the middle of the living room. It was still there from the previous night's family *puja* (worship service).

From what I understand, much Hindu worship can be individual and more personal. Yet for many Hindus, their spiritual experience does involve corporate elements. Satsangs, festivals, *melas* (large events), and other gatherings provide regular opportunity for shared, corporate expressions of their faith. These corporate experiences just don't resemble a church service.

Christian Concerns About Hindu Corporate Worship

Christian descriptions of Hindu worship provide hints at what they perceive as essential.

MINIMAL INTERACTION

Richard, in his book *Hinduism*, observed "While the *Hindu home must be counted more significant than the temple*, temple worship is nevertheless a vital aspect of Hindu life. It has often been pointed out that temple worship is not usually congregational in the way that Christian worship is, but rather individual in a central location" (Richard 2007b, 40).

Some Christians have criticized Hindu temple worship to me because it is "individualistic" and lacks fellowship. Is this only a Hindu phenomenon, though? A while back, an Indian Christian woman told me of going to her home church in another Indian state. She was deeply disappointed because all the Christians came, went through the service, then returned home without fellowship or interaction. She had hoped to visit with people, but no one stayed to even chat. Christians in other words can sometimes display spiritual individualism themselves, even when they "attend church."

Recently, a friend and I attended a megachurch service in Chicago. Apart from the obligatory handshake and nervous smile during the "greeting" time, no one interacted or expressed any interest in us at all. We were anonymous attendees, not active, fellowshipping participants. Churches too can foster a disconnected, individualistic "worship," even when hundreds gather in the building at one time.

When Christians criticize Hindus for individualistic, "disconnected" worship, they must consider how this comes across to Hindus. Before leveling such criticism, they must be sure that their own fellowship and interaction is more tangible and compelling.

MEANINGLESS REPETITION

Some Indian friends of mine have been asking Hindus about their use of the well-known Gayatri Mantra in daily life and worship. Hindus have commonly reported that they may recite this and similar mantras in the original Sanskrit without knowing what the words mean. From their perspective, the original language recited in the proper way produces the needed spiritual effect.

A Brahmin friend of mine recounted an experience from his childhood. Every day, after he alighted from the school bus, he had to pass a cemetery to reach his home. As he passed that frightening spot, he would recite the Gayatri Mantra. Picture a ten-year-old running down the road as he repeats *"Tat Savitr varenyam, bhargo devasya dhimahi, dhiyo yo nah prachodayat"*[18] as fast as possible. Why? For protection from danger. This ancient Hindu prayer can be used, I've been told, in just this way—to ward off evil, to prevent or remove sickness, or to bring some blessing or favor the person desires.

I have heard and read Christians who decry Hindus for mindlessly repeating mantras and *slokas* (verses). Those features of Hindu meditation and worship can be private or corporate. But before being overly judgmental, let's stop and consider Christian practice for a moment.

Is this that different from many recitations that Christians use (*Our Father, Ave Maria,* etc.), also in rote fashion? Some Christians seem to recite them for the same superstitious, protective purposes that Hindus repeat their mantras. Believers once recited creeds and verses in Latin with little idea of what they meant. My Christian readers have likely attended at least some church services where believers sang hymns or choruses mindlessly without thinking about the words.

When Christians repeat "Hallelujah, Hallelujah, Hallelujah" or *"Stotram, Stotram, Stotram"* (roughly Praise, Praise, Praise) or anything else, is that qualitatively different from Hindu practice? The sounds are different, but the mindless repetition in both instances can disobey Jesus' specific command in Matthew 6:7 to avoid meaningless repetition in prayer and worship. If that meaningless repetition confuses and alienates Hindus, makes them say "you are mad" (1 Cor 14:23), it's doubly disobedient to the teaching of Scripture.

Some Christians have characterized Hindu worship, public and private, as primarily concerned with gaining social or material benefits. From their perspective, Hindus go through the motions of worship, but are more concerned about themselves and their interests, not actually interacting with god.

I suspect that these same Christians, though, could recognize church worship gatherings where members and believers attended the public worship, but mostly went through the motions and then returned home. Isaiah and Jesus speak of people who draw near to God "with their lips,

---

18. Rough translation: That most excellent Savitr (Giver and Sustainer of Life), may we attain your divine glory, may he guide our thoughts. From Rig Veda 3.62.10.

but their hearts are far from me" (Isa 29:13; Matt 15:8). Isaiah 58 provides a detailed criticism of people who fast for their own benefit, not out of submission to God or compassion for others.

In some churches, believers may go through the standard rituals, kneeling, standing, sitting, and saying the appropriate words at the right time. While this can be a meaningful experience for some, others simply perform the rites without thinking about them or engaging their hearts. I have even known pastors who admitted to sometimes leading services without really engaging with what they were saying.

We must be sure that we do not condemn Hindus with excessive harshness for practices of which Christians themselves are guilty. We must first clean our own house before presuming to clean someone else's. These Christian concerns about Hindu worship, though, do raise questions about corporate worship and the barriers it presents.

Hindu Concerns About Christian Corporate Worship

Hindus, at the same time, express concerns about Christians and their worship. These reveal other corporate worship tendencies among Christians that can represent obstacles to Hindus.

DISCONNECT BETWEEN PUBLIC WORSHIP AND PRIVATE LIFESTYLE

One of the greatest criticisms that Hindus have leveled against Christians concerns their devotion to public proclamation and worship of Jesus while their lives may reflect too little of the character and teaching of Jesus. Gandhi has been incorrectly credited with the commonly cited quote, "I like your Christ. I do not like your Christians" (Snopes 2010). The quote appears to be someone else's summary of several statements in *The Christ of the Indian Road*.

Gandhi replied to Jones' request for advice, "I would suggest, first, that all of you Christians . . . must begin to live more like Jesus Christ" (Jones 1926, 126). According to Jones, Bara Dada (brother of the poet Rabindranath Tagore) remarked, "Jesus is ideal and wonderful, but you Christians—you are not like him" (ibid., 121).

When the day-to-day life of Christians reflects little of the character and teaching of the Jesus they claim to worship on Sunday, this worship disconnect can create skepticism among Hindus who are looking for spirituality among Christians. The New Testament actually says a great deal about how believers live out worship in everyday life. Jesus questions those who perform their righteousness "to be seen by men" (Matt 6:1–18) and who say, "Lord, Lord" but do not do what he says (Matt 7:21–23).

In light of this commonly asserted disconnect between Christian worship and everyday behavior, I must raise the biggest concern regarding Christian corporate worship and its potential barrier to Hindus. Christian tradition seems to have developed an unhealthy emphasis on believers' corporate worship over their private worship and personal lifestyle. Part of India's resistance to Jesus may arise from unfortunate Christian assumptions about corporate worship that must be reexamined and adjusted.

The Big Issue—Imbalance Between Corporate and Personal Worship

If we are not careful, churches can tend to emphasize the corporate, public worship event over a personal lifestyle of worship for believers. Philip Schaff, in his work on church history, describes early worship as "the *public* adoration of God in the name of Christ; the celebration of *the communion of believers as a congregation* with their heavenly head, for the promotion of the glory of the Lord, and for the growth and enjoyment of spiritual life" (Schaff 1870, 118). Look back also to the English definitions of "church" (Chapter 3) and the first thing that comes to people's minds is a building or location for "*public* Christian worship."

This same assumption is reflected in the old, but at one time widely popular, *Halley's Bible Handbook*. Near the back, Halley says, in poetic form,

> The Churches are
> The Most Important institutions
> In any community.
> The Sunday Services are
> The church's Principal Way of doing its work;
> It is THE EVENT of the community life.
>
> Nothing ever happens in any community
> As important to the life of the community
> As the regular Sunday Worship Services.
> Every community ought to love its churches,
> And, at this appointed time, turn out, en masse,

To honor HIM in whose name the church exists.
(Halley 1965, 819; emphasis in original)

Later he refers to this worship attendance as "one Fundamental Christian Duty" (ibid., 820). Schaff and Halley reflect Western assumptions about church-based worship. However, they are cultural assumptions, not New Testament teaching about how the early ekklēsia viewed public and personal worship.

We must ask, though, "If 'church' is a *location* for *public* Christian worship, what is the ekklēsia (Chapter 3) doing when it is not at 'church'?" This assumption of meeting-based worship compartmentalizes "worship" into an activity that believers attend occasionally ("go to worship"). When believers overemphasize corporate worship, it contributes to the barrier Hindus feel toward Jesus.

FOSTERING SPIRITUAL IMMATURITY

A Yesu bhakta leader observed, "I never understood how Christians can limit worship to one or two hours a week" (Bharati, 2015). From an Indian bhakta perspective, one should worship and love the Lord all the time, in every aspect of life. True believers in Jesus would share this desire for a lifestyle of worship, rather than just occasional worship events.

I know many Christians who do practice daily personal worship— their lifestyle is one of devotion to Jesus. My comments here are not meant to question their genuine faith in any way. Yet on my travels and observations in India I have encountered many situations where the missions and ministers seemed to define spirituality and maturity by attendance at church services and prayer meetings. They gave the impression that one's spiritual health was primarily determined by the meetings attended to keep you "stirred up." Believers were made permanently dependent on meetings, rather than equipped to develop and express their personal worship within their family, occupation, and community.

Believers seem to depend on the services and programs for their primary nurture and relationship with God. Rather than equip believers for authentic personal worship, churches create and multiply events to artificially prop up spiritual life. Believers who are dependent on corporate worship events for their spiritual feeding and experience can remain spiritual infants, always in need of someone else to spoon feed and lead them in worship.

KEPT BUSY WITH CHURCH SERVICES

Some of my earliest exposure in India to the Christian barriers to Jesus, in fact, revolved around a second issue related to this overemphasis on corporate worship. Christian friends described a church schedule that kept them so occupied all weekend they had no time for relationships with family, neighbors, friends, or coworkers who did not know Jesus. Every moment was taken up with Christian activities and meetings.

Frankly, Hindus will never meet Jesus or want to meet him, if churches keep Christians so busy they have no time for interaction, friendship, and relationships. I can't imagine a more effective way to keep people from Jesus in India than the packed church schedules Christians have described and evidenced in different parts of the country. India needs much less "going to church" and much more of the ekklēsia (the people of Jesus) being involved regularly and meaningfully, incarnationally in fact, with family, coworkers, and neighbors.

Many Indians, particularly in India's cities (over 50 percent of population) work long hours six and a half days a week. They then face long commutes on both ends of the workday. Their only time for interaction and relationships can sometimes be half of Saturday and all Sunday, so when churches teach that you must attend every service and devote all free weekend time to the church and "worship," they embody the "cultural separatism" that is keeping India from Jesus.

I know that Hebrews 10:25 says that believers should not forsake gathering together. I'm not sure that means attending hours of worship and meetings on Sunday plus other meetings to take up all of one's available time during the week. Such a schedule intentionally or unintentionally keeps believers from Hindus. It thus keeps Hindus from the only Jesus they might ever meet, his followers. Those gatherings in Hebrews 10:25 were, more often than not, informal house gatherings. We know from many Indian conversations that non-believers are far more likely to come to homes than to church gatherings. Excessive church meetings ensure that they won't come.

RESTORING NEW TESTAMENT BALANCE

The New Testament, in contrast, expected the ekklēsia, the people of Jesus (*not* a location), to always worship Jesus, at home, at work, and when gathered. Their public worship was not the focus of their lives. The public gathering was instead their mutual expression of the worship they lived all week. The epistles say much more about the private lifestyle and personal worship of believers than they do about public worship gatherings.

Hindu ideas of worship, in this regard, may be more in line with the New Testament in some areas than Christians understand. As Bharati has noted, "Worship is the pivot on which the *entire spiritual life* revolves, particularly for Hindus. They never worship just three hours in a week plus . . . one house prayer meeting" (Bharati 2004, 74). When believers live a life of personal worship, this would resonate more with Hindus who, at least in this regard, can be deeply devout in their own practice, trying to incorporate god into all of life.

The early ekklēsia, according to Paul, was more participatory (1 Cor 14:26; Eph 5:19; Col 3:16). Believers encouraged and admonished one another with their singing and worship. They most likely looked at and talked with each other in a circle, rather than staring at a screen or leader at the front of the room.

Public worship that is not grounded in private, personal worship can become superficial. Public gatherings of believers should focus first on equipping believers to live lives of worship and obedience all week long. They should also allow believers to celebrate and share what God has been doing during the week in participatory ways. The more that the body of Christ focuses on personal worship, the more like the New Testament ekklēsia it will be. When and where that happens, Hindus will more likely see Jesus incarnated in believers' lives and be drawn to him.

DON'T MISAPPROPRIATE WORSHIP FOR CONVERSION

One danger I see involves a common misappropriation of worship for evangelism and conversion (see Chapters 4 and 5). For some Christians, adapting worship to the culture is a means to their evangelistic end.

In adapting worship to Indian forms, we must not assume that all Hindus will immediately be pleased. Some Hindus actually are offended by any efforts toward cultural adaptation by believers. Sita Ram Goel, an ardent critic of Christian attempts to subjugate India, expressed deep concern about what he called, "Indigenisation: A Predatory Enterprise." As he saw it, Christians first changed their tune from attacking Hinduism to appreciation and respect. From his and others' views, this amounted to a ruse with ultimately sinister, anti-Hindu intent:

> It should not be a matter of surprise, therefore, that the mission has started singing hymns of praise to Hindu culture. That is the mission casting covetous glances before mounting a marauding expedition. What causes concern is the future of Hindu culture once it falls into the hands of the Church. The fate of Greek culture after it was taken over by the Church is a grim reminder. (Goel 1989)

Rajiv Malhotra, more picturesquely, uses the metaphor of a tiger (Western Christianity) digesting a deer (Hinduism):

> Just as the tiger, a predator, would, the West, a dominant and aggressive culture dismembers the weaker one—the deer—into parts from which it picks and chooses pieces that it wants to appropriate; the appropriated elements get mapped onto the language and social structures of the dominant civilization's own history and paradigms, leaving little if any trace of the links to the source tradition. (Malhotra 2012)

Hindus who are deeply sensitive to conversion agendas will be skeptical of Christians who co-opt Hindu culture for the primary purpose of converting Hindus. Their concerns are not completely unwarranted. I have observed sessions where Christians, both Indian and Western, were trained to use *satsangs* and Indian worship forms to evangelize Hindus. Indian friends of mine, who once used this methodology, have expressed concern to me about how artificial and forced these attempts could be.

When "worship" (even *satsang* style) becomes a cover or scheme for "evangelism" (Chapter 4) or "conversion" (Chapter 5), most Hindus will quickly see through it. This will not be indigenous worship. Those leading may say words of worship, but the "worship" experience, however "indigenized," can represent a manipulative attempt by the leader(s) to hook Hindus.

When "worship" of any kind (Western-style service or Indian-style *satsang*) is conducted primarily for proselytizing purposes, Hindus will recognize the attempts. They may be turned off by such overt abuse of worship, with the primary motivation being conversion (our aggrandizement), not God's glory (His adoration).

There is a fine line here that I find incredibly difficult to articulate. It's likely different for different churches and different contexts. Our worship, though, should be focused on Jesus, not conversions. We should be worshiping and lifting him up for who he is, not with an eye for how many converts we might make.

Contextualizing worship should not be a strategy for converting more Hindus. That agenda will only do more damage and drive more Hindus away from Christ. If that is the Christian motive, then Goel's and Malhotra's criticism is an accurate portrayal of Christian intentions.

Contextualizing worship should only be about one thing: Indians' right to worship Jesus in culturally appropriate ways, not in foreign ways. Setting Indian believers free from foreign shackles so that their Indian hearts can rise in worship to Jesus in Indian forms, Indian accompaniment, Indian rhythms, and Indian expressions. Jesus wants to incarnate within the worship forms of India, not reside as an alien in the forms of a foreign religion.

Do I want Hindus to meet and consider Jesus? Absolutely! Should believers co-opt and manipulate worship to do so? Absolutely not!

CHRISTIAN AND BHAKTA CONSIDERATIONS

So how do we address the worship barriers? India needs believers whose personal life exudes personal devotion and love for the Lord (*bhakti*) not just public worship attendance. This applies equally to Christians or Yesu bhaktas, so I will address both as we conclude. The following verses clearly call all believers to a personal lifestyle of worship, not primarily to corporate worship events.

Let your light shine before men in such a way that they may see your good works, and glorify your Father who is in heaven. (Matt 5:16)

Therefore I urge you, brethren, by the mercies of God, to present your bodies a living and holy sacrifice, pleasing to God, *which is* your spiritual service of worship. (Rom 12:1)

Whether, then, you eat or drink or whatever you do, do all to the glory of God. (1 Cor 10:31)

Whatever you do in word or deed, do all in the name of the Lord Jesus, giving thanks through him to God the Father. (Col 3:17)

Whatever you do, do your work heartily, as for the Lord rather than for men, knowing that from the Lord you will receive the reward of the inheritance. It is the Lord Christ whom you serve. (Col 3:23–24)

Rejoice always; pray without ceasing; in everything give thanks; for this is God's will for you in Christ Jesus.
(1 Thess 5:16–18) (NASB)

Believers should mainly worship the Lord like this in their homes, in their neighborhoods, in their occupations, and in their broader communities, not just in church services or satsangs. As they live lives of worship in these locations, they will "display the sweet aroma of knowing him in every place" (2 Cor 2:14). When they do this, Hindus will be either drawn to or repelled by Jesus in them, not by foreign, artificial worship practices.

When believers, whether Christians or Yesu bhaktas, have developed a deeply personal relationship with Jesus, this will reflect in the way they live their lives. Their prayers, devotions, and private service (*seva*) for Jesus, together with their love and integrity, are all parts of their personal worship to the Lord. Hindus see their quiet, gentle lives and are often impressed. Hindus have expressed to me their respect for such believers, even if they do not agree with their faith. My Christian and Yesu bhakta friends have recounted similar examples.

Hindus seem drawn when they see personal devotion in the life of believers. They long for connection with the divine and they are attracted when someone has truly found this in Jesus. Private and personal worship of Jesus, rather than presenting an obstacle to Jesus, can overcome the worship barriers and open doors for the good news of Jesus.

CLOSING REFLECTIONS

I sat on the stage of a Bible college chapel in the US along with some instrumentalists. We had rehearsed three Indian-style bhajans and used a mix of Indian and Western instruments to play them. When students came in that morning for worship, the chairs had been moved to the back of the room, and participants were encouraged to sit on the floor as Indians would at a satsang.

The songs were on the screen in Hindi with a transcription and the meaning translated. We sang in Hindi to expose the students to the different language and sounds of worship in another culture. The call and response format of bhajans lends itself to such an experience.

After the songs, I briefly commented that their discomfort at the unfamiliar words and tunes was not unlike what many Hindus experience with Christian worship in India. When Christians only use Western music (whether words, tunes, instruments) it can feel as uncomfortable for many Indians as Hindi bhajans feel for Westerners.

When the singing was finished, I sat down, Indian-style, on a carpet at the front of the stage and placed my Bible in a wooden book stand on the floor (not on a pulpit). I began with an ancient Hindu prayer recited daily by millions of Hindus. I then showed how that prayer provides several powerful bridges to understand and appreciate what Scripture says about the uniqueness of Jesus, but through Indian eyes.

We worshiped Jesus. I proclaimed the word of God and the uniqueness of Jesus. But the service was done using more Hindu cultural forms rather than traditional Western Christian forms. When the president and faculty of the college joined the students on the floor and sang bhajans along with them, it conveyed a powerful message. We can learn to "become all things to all people" even in worship, to get out of our comfort zone and embrace the unfamiliar, so that people in different cultures can naturally love and worship Jesus.

When we all gather around the throne in worship (Rev 7:9), God will be just as pleased and honored by the bhajans of the Yesu bhaktas as by the choruses or hymns of the Christians.

CHAPTER 8
THE BARRIER OF FINANCIAL DEPENDENCY

We were traveling with some Indian friends who were encouraging a new church plant. They wanted to examine a property the congregation was purchasing with its own resources. At lunch, the leader politely asked, "Could we go without you and leave you here in town? If you go to the property with us, the surrounding people will assume that we have donors from the West. Hindus will increase their scrutiny and possibly make things difficult for the church. Believers will also stop taking responsibility for the church, assuming Westerners will donate the needed funds for the building."

Our host recognized and articulated a dual challenge that foreign funding presents in the Indian context. He understood that Western resources raise Hindu concerns about foreign subversion and interference in independent India. Those external funds may also suggest to some Hindu minds that Christianity is a foreign religion dependent for its survival on foreign resources.

He also recognized that the mere possibility of foreign resources could cripple a congregation that was growing in responsibility. Just the appearance of Western funds could exert subtle influences in Indian believers to keep them dependent on Western donations rather than responsible for their own congregations.

FINANCIAL DEPENDENCY—A BRIEF DEFINITION AND SOME QUALIFICATIONS

The issues around finances in Christianity can present a highly sensitive topic. I am deeply aware that some Christians will find what follows a welcome exploration of issues that often remain undiscussed. For others, this discussion may sound like direct confrontation. Glenn Schwartz has been speaking and writing on dependency issues for decades. Near the beginning of *When Charity Destroys Dignity*, he articulates what I would say to my readers:

> There is no intention to cause hurt or do harm to anyone in the Christian movement. However, it is clear that if progress is to be made regarding the dependency syndrome, serious attention will need to be given to root causes. Otherwise the problem will be perpetuated into future generations. *The author apologizes in advance for any statement that should have been made in a more helpful and less disconcerting way.* (Schwartz 2007, xxxvii; emphasis mine)

What do I mean by financial dependency? Let me begin with what I do not mean. Receiving resources from the West does not in itself constitute "financial dependency." I know of healthy, respectful partnerships where Indians are fully responsible for their own ministry, but funding from the West enables them to serve in ways they might not otherwise be able. Receiving outside funds does not automatically and necessarily imply financial dependency.

Financial dependency, as I use it, occurs when believers in one context feel obligated to follow the expectations, the agendas, the priorities, sometimes the explicit directions of donors, even when those might not be appropriate for their context. Financial dependency also occurs where local believers, in order to maintain or increase foreign funding, shade the truth, misrepresent what is happening, or market their activities in ways that contradict Scripture or reality.

Financial dependency can also occur when foreign funding prevents local believers from exploring local funding options by God's provision. When believers think that God can only provide for ministry from Western sources, this can stifle local creativity and generosity, and can tempt them to put their trust in donors, rather than God.

Financial dependency is not an isolated, separate issue. It is deeply enmeshed with the barriers of cultural separatism, Christian identity, church, evangelism and preaching, conversion, and worship. At times, donors contribute in ways that ensure that their agendas, targets, and expectations are met regarding these barrier-producing features of Christianity. When this happens, foreign funding contributes to India's significant resistance to Jesus, even when given to "reach India."

Hindus are deeply aware of this foreign funding, and believers need to consider the negative effect it can produce.

FINANCIAL DEPENDENCY FROM A HINDU PERSPECTIVE

Christian funding certainly seems to antagonize many Hindus and turn them away from Jesus. So how do Hindus view Christianity's dependency on foreign funds? Let me provide a brief overview of three common themes in Hindu critiques. Christians are often tempted to dismiss these perspectives as persecution or misrepresentation. But it is important that we at least consider their viewpoint.

Subversion

Rajiv Malhotra, in a *Huffington Post Religion* blog, for instance, asserts: "Most liberal Americans are simply unaware of the international political machinations of evangelicals. *Funded and supported by the American Christian right*, they promote a literal and extreme version of Christianity abroad and *attempt to further a fundamentalist Christian political agenda using unscrupulous methods*" (Malhotra 2011c; emphasis mine). From this Hindu perspective, there is "a huge enterprise—a 'network' of organizations, individuals, and churches—that seems intensely devoted to the task of creating a separate identity, history and even religion for the vulnerable sections of India" (Malhotra 2011a).

Sandhya Jain has called attention to the "backing by Western-Christian governments for this imperialist project and its special focus on India" (Jain 2007). She cites several instances of missions, non-governmental organizations (NGOs), and governmental agencies collaborating on projects that seem to target India. This conflation of evangelical and governmental involvement may be overstated, but is not an uncommon Hindu perception of Christian intentions.

Some websites and social media sites specifically monitor and follow Christian funding models. *Crusadewatch* has posted articles exposing Christian funding of "conversion" efforts. More radically, they claim that Christian funds are aiding separatist movements in several Indian states ("Christian Terrorism" section). Bharata Bharati gathered articles from News Bharati reporting on foreign finances and their influence in India. In their view, foreign funding supports activities "against the nation's interest," including conversion (Bharata Bharati Admin 2013). They also call attention to the large sums of money received from foreign sources by Indian non-governmental organizations (NGOs). Their conclusion: These large sums all fund activities counter to India's national interests.

One repeated critique involves a common Christian practice. When ministries file for government permission to receive foreign currency, they typically list their purposes as economic, social, or educational. Hindus look at these filings and see what they have reported to the government. They then look at the publicity such ministries provide to their Western donors (see *Tracking Evangelism* footnote, next section). There they find clearly articulated fundraising for evangelism and conversion. Christians have had to rationalize this double speak in order to function in India, but they cannot avoid the Hindu perception that they are misrepresenting their intentions to the government and Indian society at large.

One Hindu perspective, then, entails the concern that Western funds are actively being used to fund separatist, anti-national movements within the country. They perceive from many online and social media posts that the West is targeting India for un-Indian goals and agendas. This is not the only theme that raises Hindu concerns, though.

Soul Harvesting Business

Because of the incredible amounts of money involved, Hindus also use a metaphor of the "Christian enterprise" as *missionary or conversion business*. To them much Christian presence in India could not survive if not for Western funding. They assume, with some justification, that Western-ers continue investing to perpetuate their interests and activities in India. These charges against Christian mission practice may trouble you, but it is again important to see how they are viewed by those outside looking in.

In "A Fraudulent Mission," David Frawley, a convert to Hindu faith, frames his critique in business terms. First, he observes, "The global missionary business is huge, perhaps the largest business in the world" (Frawley 2008, 35). Further, "The conversion business is especially big in India, because India is the largest non-Christian country in the world where missionaries have the freedom to act and proselytize" (ibid.). Frawley seeks to expose the anti-cultural and destructive purposes of this Western-funded "business." To the Hindu mind, this business is about tearing down all their culture and heritage and replacing it with a purely Christian (Western) one.

Sites such as *Hinduism Today*, *Christianaggression.org*, *Crusadewatch. org* and YouTube channels like *Save India from Missionaries* and *Tracking Evangelism* post exposés on Western funding and the agendas that drive much of this Indian "conversion business."

One exposé of evangelistic methods calls it the "Onsite-Offshore Model of Soul-Harvesting Business" (Tracking Evangelism 2014b). After reviewing the outsourcing model for IT services, they summarize their understanding of the Christian version of this model:

> Christian missionaries also have a similar onsite-offshore model. The clients are countless Churches, Ministries and evangelistic Christian communities in the US, UK, Germany, etc. The vendors are evangelical NGOs in India. . . . The "saved" souls are the profit of the collective efforts of the clients and their offshore vendors/counterparts. (ibid.)

They call attention to the money flow (where it comes from), the amounts contributed, and the ultimate "profit" or purpose of the "business." Having developed this framework, they then examine the business model ("funding model") by detailing a specific ministry. View the links in the footnote[19] and observe how carefully these Hindus peruse a variety of information sources. For each ministry, they examine annual foreign contribution filings submitted to the Indian government. They glean details and claims from mission websites, YouTube channels, and social media accounts. They are familiar with Joshua Project statistics and how ministries use this data to support their "subversive" business agendas in India.

The level of scrutiny and the rhetoric used on these research sites is evidence that Hindus are deeply concerned about foreign financing of Christian work in India—financial dependency. I do not want to imply

---

19. See the Tracking Evangelism site at http://trackingevangelism.blogspot .com/2014/08/onsite-offshore-model-of-soul.html to view the level of detail they have gathered in their analysis. And see https://www.youtube.com/watch ?v=10oDS09GP24 for their analysis of another Indian client/donor relationship.

that all the above claims are accurate representations of Christian attitude or practice. They often are not. The reports and exposés, however, express the perceptions and understanding at least some Hindus feel toward the foreign funding of Christianity in their country. Christians should at least be aware of and consider how these issues can be perceived.

An additional, unmistakable assumption permeates the conversion outsourcing metaphor. Indians are the outsourcing vendors, providing their evangelistic services to the foreign clients who hire them to further their Western goals and purposes. From Hindu perspective, Indians who participate in this model are subservient to Western interests and control. The clients set the values, standards, schedules, and goals for the business. They hire Indians to do their bidding and to conduct their subversive activity. No matter how much local autonomy Indians may have, Hindus assume they answer to those who pay the bills. Sadly, that assumption may not always be groundless. It is possible, like it or not, that those who accept Western funds will be suspected of being under foreign control.

Perceptions of Pastors

Before I proceed, I do not want to appear to attack or condemn Indian ministers themselves. I have dear friends in India who are dedicated ministers, who love the Lord, and who serve their people as faithful servants of Jesus Christ. I do not mean to question their devotion to Jesus, their calling, or their ministry. In fact, some of what follows comes from their own reports of how Hindus sometimes perceive their ministries.

The disturbing reality remains, though, and some of them attest to it. Hindus seem deeply suspicious of professional pastors and ministers (proselytizers, they sometimes call them).

PAID PASTORS AS THE FRONT LINE

One common feature of the traditional funding model involves the widespread practice of paying pastors or "indigenous missionaries" through missions and Western sourced funds. To Hindus, paid pastors are the West's front line in the conversion business. That's because Western Christian tradition insists that a "real church" (see Chapter 3) must have *a pastor*, preferably a paid one. Western funds have been raised and donated for generations to artificially supply this "essential" that some Indian Christian communities can't afford.

Some missions have reasoned, "Why send a Western missionary, when you could send multiple local missionaries for the same amount each year?" This sounds good theoretically, but the reality in India can be highly problematic. These "missionaries," as they have been termed, mostly serve as "pastors" over one or more churches. Foreign support, then can simply mask perpetual funding for the colonial model of churches run by individual pastors (Schwartz 2007, xvi). Jesus sent his disciples out two-by-two, but Western missions long ago abandoned that accountability model for a more monarchical leadership style that creates problems in many parts of the world.

Other ministries solicit funds for "barefoot pastors" since this image capitalizes on Western sympathies for "poor natives." How many of these pastors were "barefoot" before this funding? Few if any! Indians have ready access to shoes, when they want to wear them. The only time pastors are typically barefoot is when they take off their shoes to enter a church building (a common cultural practice). Such appeals serve to perpetuate unhealthy paternalism and dependency associated with colonial-era missions, not necessarily respect for local believers and their real situation.

Glenn Schwartz highlights another popular form of dependency:

> There is a significant move away from self-supporting in-
> digenous churches toward what are called "international
> partnerships." I usually refrain from using the term "part-
> nership" because of the current usage. I feel that it is often
> used when the term sponsorship would be better. (ibid.)

These appeals use new terminology, but it's the same colonial dependency model packaged under different names (ibid.). Foreigners sponsor local pastors' salaries and livelihoods, regardless of the marketing label. Hindus recognize this system when they see it, no matter what Christians call it.

If Christians don't solicit salaries for ministers they may request funds for bicycles, motorcycles, or other "essential" pastoral paraphernalia. Or they request funding for trainers at another level of organization who will then "equip" local leaders to serve. Typically, this "equipping" ensures that Western donors' expectations around church, evangelism, preaching, and worship are maintained. In other words, the training may guarantee that

Christians will continue the practices that have already presented barriers to Hindus. The funding ensures it.

How Do Hindus See Paid Pastors?

Why should we care about how Hindus view this system? Because Scripture indicates that we ought to. I will shortly examine how Paul radically changed his own funding model because of the way outsiders would have viewed that model (1 Cor 9:22). Given that scriptural example, India's resistance suggests that Christians—Indian and Western alike—consider how Indian society at large views ministers and the Western funding models that sponsor them.

One Indian mission organization (unnamed to protect privacy) states on their website, "In the eyes of the people, national missionaries do not represent a foreign country or a strange religion." Abundant evidence from Christian and Hindu sources indicates that this claim is not entirely accurate. The mission that funds them receives its funds from foreign donors, and as much of this book has illustrated, Christianity and church, all too often, are clearly perceived as foreign.

So, how do Hindus see paid ministers in India? The *Niyogi Committee Report* on mission activity in Madhya Pradesh called them "a class of professional proselytisers" (Niyogi, et al. 1958, 103). Sita Ram Goel, a critic of Christianity, noted the widely unequal salary scales for missionaries compared to "their native mercenaries" (Goel 1996, Ch. 17). These are representative examples of the derogatory terms one can find in conversation and Hindu literature regarding professional ministers.

Indians commonly tell me that paid ministers can be viewed as "professional proselytizers"—attacking Hindu culture and heritage in the name of their God and dividing families and communities. Their funding from foreign sources ties into the issues already raised about "foreign subversion" and "soul harvesting." They are perceived as foreign agents, "native mercenaries" actively complicit in the West's subversion plans. To some extent, this can also make them appear as traitors (sellouts) because of their Western allegiance and funding—after all, Christianity is the religion of the West.

Not too long ago I sat in a seminary faculty meeting in India. Two of the faculty described conversations they recently had with rural Indians. These people asked them why Christian pastors mostly come to rural areas to do their work among uneducated people. They asked, "Why don't the pastors go to the urban professionals? They are educated and informed. Instead they only go to villages for easy converts." Some pastors have developed a reputation of going to the gullible and uneducated who cannot or will not check or question what they say or do.

Hindus are also aware of preachers who shift from mission to mission for the sake of better pay, or who secretly work for three or four separate agencies to make more money. Some, I'm told, even file false reports of non-existent or inflated ministry activities to keep mission income flowing.

When funds run out from one mission, pastors have been known to jump to other missions who have money, taking the believers and churches with them. Their allegiance to a particular ministry or denomination was only as strong as the funding they received.

Other ministers openly charge for every service they perform to enhance their income. At the end of a prayer to dedicate a new house or baby, for instance, some will hold out their opened Bible, like an offering plate, a recognized request for compensation. When the gift is given, they close the Bible and the transaction is complete.

Dalal

As a result of perceived and real dishonesty among paid ministers, Hindus in North India sometimes call them *dalal*. The word refers to someone who exploits or profits from someone else. The term is commonly used for touts, brokers, pimps, panderers, or carnival barkers (Hinkhoj 2015). The word can include pushy and disreputable practices along with ill-gotten gain. English equivalents to *dalal* might include shyster, or huckster.

Indians are not as hesitant as Westerners to ask about someone's occupation and income. Minister friends have been directly asked (without it being considered rude, I must add), "How do you manage your funding?" Another common question is, "What do you get from this?" After reading this material one Indian friend added, "When [the Hindus] come to know that ministers are paid workers, then their respect for them completely goes away." Hindus, then, seem to have an innate problem with professional religious practitioners who serve their God for hire, especially when the funding originates from the West.

Sadly, believers who seek to represent Jesus may keep Hindus from meeting him simply because of how they are funded. Those who serve the

Lord in areas where this perception is prevalent should be sensitive to how they go about their life and service. Some are careful to follow culturally appropriate ways to ensure they live above reproach while still receiving funds. Others develop livelihoods in order to not take money for ministry and to also live above reproach.

From a Hindu perspective, then, financial dependency becomes a barrier when Western funding appears to sponsor cultural subversion and soul harvesting, and when it seems to hire Indian agents who conduct these activities, sometimes in questionable ways.

Ultimately, Hindus seem concerned that Western funding can exert levels of control over local believers. Indian Christians may, at times, be directed and managed by foreign donors' expectations. In too many instances, this foreign control looks like colonial influence decades after Indian independence. Hindus may resent Indians who seem to maintain religious subservience to foreign masters.

Some Christians, on the other hand, seem relatively unconcerned with the significant barrier that financial dependency can present to Hindus. Unlike my wise friend at the start of this chapter, some don't even consider the barrier that foreign funding may present. Indian and Western believers alike may perpetuate foreign funding models with little regard for how much they might keep Hindus from Jesus.

FINANCIAL DEPENDENCY FROM A CHRISTIAN PERSPECTIVE

A few Christians have been concerned by this financial dependency for some time. Call it what you like, dependency (R. Reese 2010) or financial paternalism (Kornfeld 1997), foreign funding can create barriers that Christians themselves identify.

Financial Dependency Can Impede Local Responsibility

Our friend at the start of this chapter certainly knew this. Just our presence at the church site could have easily led the fledgling congregation to stop giving, to wait instead for Western largesse. Other Indians have described the same phenomenon elsewhere in the country.

I have been told of occasions where foreign donors told Indian ministries that they needed a certain service—a school, hospital, or development scheme of some kind. Sometimes these foreign initiatives, intended to "bless" the Indian ministry, had a detrimental effect instead. They took attention, personnel, and finances away from more effective ministry, to serve the project the foreigners wanted to fund.

Some Western churches demand that their Indian recipients provide "bang for their (US) buck" (actually heard from Western leaders). Common measures for this "bang" include churches, buildings, pastors, converts (Christians), rescues, handouts, or other quantifiable measures.

A friend from the North lives in a town with a substantial Christian population. A significant number of Christian orphanages have been established there. Recently, she said, someone conducted a survey of these "orphanages" and discovered that few, if any, of the children were orphans. Almost all had parents (usually both). In most instances, they lived within an hour of the orphanage. Parents were sending their three- to five-year-old and older children to these orphanages to give them opportunities they could not give at home. As my friend put it, "Why are Christians in the West funding this pervasive breakup of families, just to make Western donors feel good about themselves?" No one seems to have investigated the deeper issues and bothered to explore local solutions that might keep families together. Western donors feel good about helping children in "need" and the "orphanages" will gladly take their money to provide the opportunity.

I know of situations where Indian missions, funded by the West, rule over local congregations and ministers through perpetual funding. These funds exert overt control over believers to ensure that they remain tied to the mission and maintain allegiance to mission and denominational affiliation. Mission leaders have told me as much on different occasions. Some foreign donors would not dream of telling Indian missions what to do directly, yet they willingly fund missions that usurp local congregational responsibility in the name of supporting pastors and churches.

Financial Dependency Can Perpetuate the Christian Barriers

Financial dependency, once in place, can perpetuate the foreign traditions and barriers, even when Indians know that these offend and alienate Hindus around them. They don't feel free to creatively and innovatively seek the Lord's leading for how he wants to engage with and incarnate within Indian society. In fact, they don't always feel free to explore what God's word says about the foreign expressions and the barriers these create.

Dependency can bind them to traditions and practices long after those should have been discarded.

Imposing Church on Indian Believers

Let me take the barrier of church as an example. Mark Johnson, in "Church in a Box," describes how a well-meaning Christian couple on a visit to Nepal decided that local, indigenous believers needed a church building. They told the local minister where to buy land, provided a quarter million dollars for the building, and sent the church a "pop-up cardboard model of the church building they were to build. Church in a box" (M. Johnson 2002).

Not all donors provide a physical model, yet mental models (assumptions) can be just as powerfully imposed on those who receive Western "generosity." The believers know that what they build or plant must meet donor expectations. Sometimes foreigners even come and build it for them to make sure it is done "right." Such expectations exhibit a colonial assumption that Western church models and expectations are superior to local ones.

Why do Indians keep planting churches that perpetuate church traditions instead of scriptural ekklēsias? Often because Western donors expect this. Why do Indian churches so often look like the churches that sponsor them? Follow the money. Donor assumptions influence Indians to meet those expectations (spoken or unspoken). In *Church Multiplication Guide*, Patterson and Scoggins identify some of these fundamental assumptions and their ultimate source:

> A common Western assumption is that the lack of a lot of people in one building means failure. This is not from Scripture. The early church in Jerusalem, like that of Ephesus and other cities, was a cluster of tiny house churches. So where do the assumptions come from, that we must have a *building*, a *large crowd* in one place, that we must pay *at least one professional pastor* full time or that he must be *trained in an institution* outside the church? *These are culturally based traditions.* The assumption that the Spirit of God needs these things is contrary to faith; it often damages the Church and frequently stifles growth

and reproduction in Christ's body. (Patterson and Scoggins 2002, 167; emphasis mine)

Let me first note that Patterson and Scoggins, in identifying "Western assumptions," do not address the most fundamental assumption of all. Their "church" terminology reflects the Western assumption that church is *the* normative expression of Christ's ekklēsia. Based on our considerations in Chapter 3, we must, I believe, reconsider those assumptions.

I know of many US churches that would not consider supporting an Indian ministry unless "church-planting" was part of its objective. Their funds will ensure that the entities planted meet those Western expectations articulated by Patterson and Scoggins (emphasized above), even when few, if any, of them originate from Scripture.

Imposing Other Barriers

I contend that these foreign assumptions—both about the nature of church and its cultural expressions—are significantly imposed on Indian believers through the funding that foreign donors provide. Funding that obligates Indians to follow foreign Christian traditions, rather than the Lord's leading for their own context, can exert a subtle colonial control over their decisions and choices. Sometimes they are not free to address the barriers we have identified in this book. Financial dependency obligates them to observe Christian traditions and practices, even when they recognize that these keep millions of Hindus from meeting Jesus.

Why do Indian Christians evangelize and preach using foreign forms and explanations? Because the donors need to see that they are "evangelizing" and "preaching" so that they will continue to support the work. Why do churches so often follow Western worship models and avoid forms connected with the local culture? Because Western Christians fund worship that looks familiar enough to them. If Indians were to adopt too many local worship expressions, donors might label them "syncretistic." That is, all too often, Western Christian code for "uncomfortable to us" and, ultimately, "unworthy of support."

Ultimately every foreign, unscriptural barrier we have explored in this book was or is partly enforced by the funds of Western donors. Indian believers will only be free to address these barriers when one of two things happen: either donors will realize the issues and free Indians to address these concerns appropriately, or Indian believers will free themselves from Western dependency so that they can follow the Lord's solutions to these barriers without Western restriction.

Financial Dependency Can Foster Deception

One uncomfortable aspect of financial dependency also poses a significant barrier to Jesus in India. Foreign financing has led to a substantial amount of misrepresentation and misappropriation of donated funds.

Every trip to India, Christians tell me new stories about the dishonesty that foreign funding breeds. If even a portion of what I have heard is true, Western donors must seriously examine the damaging effect their funds have had on Indian believers and the good news in India.

Indians are not the only ones aware of and concerned about the ethical barriers Western funds have created in India. I know of major donors and churches that have ceased supporting Indian ministries due to identified misrepresentation—after they poured substantial sums into what they initially believed were reputable ministries. An acquaintance of mine investigates ministries that receive major US funding. His exposure of disreputable practices has led to foundations and donors cutting off millions of dollars from ministries they discovered had misled them.

Two dynamics lead to this "discovery" of dishonesty. Sometimes the ministry starts out honestly, but over time, Indian friends tell me, ministries may shade the truth to maintain and increase support for their work. As they add ministry areas to satisfy donor demands, this adds pressure to report success, to present a positive "spin" on the ministry, and to raise funding levels for the growing system and staff that develops. At some point, honest reporting can begin to shade into exaggeration, then into misrepresentation for the sake of the dollars needed to maintain the enterprise. Donors want success, "bang for their buck," and the recipients don't want to disappoint them.

Others, my Indian friends tell me, were disreputable all along, but convinced Western donors to trust them. If the Western donors had done more careful homework, had asked other Indians, had learned to read cultural cues, they would have seen the telltale signs. Unfortunately, their desire to engage the Indian "market," to make an evangelistic "splash," led them to be less thorough than they should have been. The dishonesty was there all along in these cases; they just didn't recognize it until it was too late.

A friend of mine met a man who told of a fantastic house church movement. In three years, he said, he had a network of twenty cells across and ten down in places. My friend kept asking how he had done this, what was his secret, could he come visit and learn? Finally, when pressed, the man confided, "America has unlimited funds if you can document success." He put a chart on the wall some ten feet across with his cell church map and said, "This is my documentation." The entire system was simply a fabrication. That was his secret to success, not "church-planting" or "disciple-making" success, but money-making success.

Some of these schemes siphon significant Western funds from legitimate ministries to ones that may be more underhanded. Precious resources are thus wasted on corruption, mismanagement, and misuse. This is unfortunate, because India represents a place where wise, careful investment could genuinely meet significant needs. Diversion of funds keeps help from reaching people who desperately need assistance.

When financial dependency breeds misrepresentation and misappropriation, then, it can further dissuade Hindus from considering Jesus. It can also divert and dry up resources that might have provided a witness for Jesus if used in honest, culturally appropriate ways.

Western funds, appropriately given and utilized, could alleviate incredible suffering and build positive bridges to Jesus in India. This can only be done, though, in respectful, collaborative ways that significantly address the barrier issues related to financial dependency.

The Funding Models Themselves Can Be Foreign, Colonial Models

Many funding models for Christian missions today are not derived from scriptural teaching or practice. Western Christians invented them to artificially initiate and maintain "growth" in places where spontaneous expansion and growth did not happen naturally (Allen 1962, 107). Webster describes an early Indian church leader who "saw foreign support and control as 'narcotics' checking 'the spontaneous development of Indian Christianity'" (Webster 2007, 259). Several leaders, he adds, called for a "Swadeshi Church" (self-supporting and self-governing) as far back as the 1910s and 20s (ibid.). These calls, though, primarily went unheeded.

Early mission leaders like Rufus Anderson, Henry Venn, John Nevius, and Roland Allen repeatedly urged more scriptural funding models (Anderson 1869, 109–11; Allen 1962; Allen 1972; Nevius 1899; Knight 1880, 305–21). Their analyses of the financial concerns a century or more ago describe situations that can still be found within Indian churches and missions today.

More recent calls to better address the issues of "financial paternalism" (Kornfeld 1997) or dependency (R. Reese 2010; Schwartz 2007; Fikkert and Mask 2015) indicate that these problems are still widespread. Moves toward more sustainable and holistic funding models (Corbett and Fikkert 2012) seek to address the problems of traditional funding, a tacit acknowledgment that the problems are still too prevalent.

Despite these voices, traditional funding models continue to dominate. Why do Indians have to fund ministry this way? Because that is how Western Christians set up the system and Indian Christians are obligated to play along if they desire funding!

What is so wrong with the prevalent models of Western subsidy for so much Christianity in India? Ironically, Hindus may again be more correct than we'd like to admit. They allege that without Western funding Christianity would not survive.

Despite Christian denials, we simply need to ask one question to uncover the "irony of apparent success" as an Indian colleague terms it. What would happen if Western funds were not given? We do not have to guess, because recent economic events provided the answer.

A friend of mine from South India worked for a church-planting ministry in the North for a time. During the economic downturn after 2008, he told me, hundreds of churches shut down because the funds dried up to support them. They desperately tried to find other funding sources, but could not, leading to closure of numerous churches. Another Indian missionary described how a financial downturn had forced them to stop paying pastors and to shut several churches that were as old as thirty years.

Similar stories are troublingly common in India. Without Western funds, the apparent growth proves to be ephemeral, at least for the agency that loses funds. Some of these churches, as I observed earlier, might shift to another mission or denomination that takes up funding. Many actually close—sad testimony to the weakness of the colonial model to truly make lasting, genuine disciples and ekklēsias.

I hope, after this review of financial dependency, you have a better idea of some of my host's concerns at the beginning of this chapter. Just the possibility of Western funds could have presented challenges to the good news of Jesus both among Hindus and Christians alike in his area. Why? Because considerations of financial dependency are a very present reality in India.

Western Christian funding models have created substantial barriers to Jesus in India. These negative perceptions are deeply rooted and we cannot ignore them or argue them away. If we want to "become all things to all people" in Hindu contexts, we must honestly face and address this barrier of financial dependency and its foreign funding model.

The Apostle Paul, interestingly enough, faced a culture that was skeptical about his own traditional funding model. He provides an instructive example for how we might respond when local perceptions of our financing present a barrier to Jesus.

SCRIPTURAL PERSPECTIVES ON FINANCIAL DEPENDENCY

When Funding Models Create a Barrier

In 1 Corinthians 9:1–18, Paul discussed his funding model choices with the Corinthians. He first articulated the traditional model—preachers accepting financial support from those to whom they preached. In verses 3–11 he provided a series of scriptural and practical supports for this model. He concluded this section by asking, "If we sowed spiritual things among you, is it too much if we reap material things from you?" (v. 11).

At this point in his argument, we expect Paul to tell the Corinthians, "So please pay me what you owe me." But he does not! Instead, Paul completely changes direction in verse 12: "Nevertheless, we did not use this right, but we endure all things so that we will cause no hindrance to the gospel of Christ." He adds in verse 15, "But I have used none of these things [support rights]. And I am not writing these things so that it will be done in my case" (NASB). In verse 18 he again reiterates that he did not use the model of taking money from his hearers.

In verse 12, Paul indicated that if he had followed the traditional funding model—to take money or support from his hearers—this would have presented a "hindrance" to the good news of Jesus. Rather than allow that to happen, Paul intentionally adopted a different funding model to remove the potential barrier.

ANALYZE FUNDING MODELS FROM OUTSIDERS' PERSPECTIVE

Why was the traditional funding model a hindrance to the gospel? In verses 3–11 Paul makes it clear that the model of receiving support from those who were taught had scriptural and practical justification. That model was a legitimate, scriptural model under the right circumstances.

Paul, though, looked at the traditional funding model through the eyes of those he wanted to reach. He considered their view of the funding model, rather than his own rights or convenience.

When Paul considered the perspective of his hearers, what did he find? "It was not uncommon for itinerant lecturers to enjoy an evil reputation" (Barnett 1993, 926). Plato had expressed disdain for philosophers and teachers who made a living "selling their teaching" (*Euthydemus* 304 b,c; *Hippias Major* 282 b–e). He accused them of "trafficking and merchandising knowledge," "soul-merchandising" (trading in souls), and "trading in virtue" (*Sophist* 222d–224e). Socrates compared a traveling philosopher or teacher to "an itinerant huckster who touts his wares regardless of their value" (Wolfsdorf 2015). Philostratus later asserted that Apollonius had a bad reputation because of "doing everything for money," for "his love of filthy lucre" (i.e., sordid gain), and for "huckstering his wisdom." He commonly sold his teaching to the highest paying client (Philostratus 1912). Notice how many of these ideas are related to the Hindi term *dalal*: huckster, tout, soul harvesting, etc.

Can our funding models affect those we want to reach? Paul clearly thought so. Roland Allen understood this principle nearly a century ago:

> The primary importance of missionary finance lies in the fact that financial arrangements [funding models] very seriously affect the relations between the missionary and those whom he approaches. . . . what is of supreme importance is how these arrangements, whatever they may be, affect the minds of the people, and so promote, or hinder, the spread of the Gospel. (Allen 1972, 49)

Adopt an Alternative Funding Model
that Removes the Barrier

Paul considered the traditional funding model in light of these Greco-Roman concerns. From the non-believers' cultural perspective, financing his ministry in the traditional way would be deeply suspect.

Paul could have defended his right to receive funding from his hearers. He could have argued that he was not dishonest or greedy like those other teachers. He could have ignored the common cultural perceptions and just asked for local contributions anyway. Instead, he took their concerns so seriously that he radically changed his funding model. He "became all things to all people" financially (1 Corinthians 9:22) to address their concerns.

Ruth Siemens suggests, "Self-support was Paul's deliberate policy, part of his well-designed strategy" (Siemens 1999, 737). Rather than occasionally working with his hands, the New Testament evidence indicates that Paul made this his practice on all three of his missionary journeys (ibid.). He also called other believers to follow this example of working with his own hands (1 Thess 2:5f.; 2 Thess 3:7–9; Acts 20:33–35).

Applying the Scriptural Perspective

So, Paul analyzed the traditional funding model from the perspective of his potential hearers. If he took money from his hearers, the Greeks and Romans would view that as disreputable—greedy and dishonest (a *dalal* in Indian terms). Because of this consideration, Paul adopted a different funding model, one that would not allow them to accuse him of peddling the word of God for gain (1 Thess 2:3,5; 2 Cor 2:17).

I believe Paul would take the same approach in India today. He would first analyze the traditional funding models (Western funding, paid pastors, church dependency, benevolence) for how the Hindu majority views them. In conversations with Christians or Hindus, or in reading Indian media and Christian reports, he would observe the barrier-inducing concerns we have articulated in this chapter: Western subversion, professional proselytizers as disreputable *dalals* (peddlers, hucksters), Christian misrepresentation and misappropriation, along with benevolence as material inducement to conversion (see next chapter).

How would he respond to these concerns? He could argue for each one, providing examples where Christians did not warrant the perceptions, then justify the continued use of traditional funding models. He could use Scriptures and common sense to defend traditional funding models. He could ignore or disregard the perceptions entirely, and persist in following traditional funding models regardless of the barriers they present. All these approaches, though, would likely perpetuate, even intensify, the majority culture's skepticism.

Paul knew that the traditional model was defensible from Scripture and common sense (1 Cor 9:3–11). That did not make it appropriate for the challenging context in which he found himself. When it came to finances, perception was and still is reality.

Paul's approach is equally valid for India today. The traditional funding model seems to present obstacles to Jesus. India desperately needs believers who will courageously follow Paul's example instead of perpetuating the colonial models of a bygone era. Until they do, Hindus will remain distanced from the good news of Jesus because of Western money and funding models. We can't afford to keep following those models.

ADDRESSING THE BARRIER OF FINANCIAL DEPENDENCY

Adopting Viable Funding Alternatives

Given the deep-seated concerns about Western funding for Christian activity, how should Indian believers respond? Paul chose a rather drastic, inconvenient alternative to the traditional funding model. He worked with his own hands to remove the barrier in his hearers' minds. In many Indian contexts, Indian believers will need to do the same. They will develop viable, sustainable livelihoods for their own situations, rather than perpetuate the colonial funding model that keeps so many from Jesus.

Unfortunately, some Indian Christians reject this solution out of hand. Missionaries taught them that it was unspiritual for a "pastor" to do secular work, to dirty his hands, or to engage in any kind of business. This patently false teaching is clearly contradicted by Paul's own example. I'm not sure any human could claim to be a more spiritual, godly man than he was, or a more devoted servant of Jesus, yet he worked with his own hands to support himself on all three journeys as noted above.

He also encouraged other believers to follow his example (p. 199). Anyone who teaches otherwise ignores both Paul's example and his inspired instruction to Christ's followers. Such teaching is rooted more in the unscriptural clergy-laity traditions of Western churches, than in the teaching of God's word.

Rather than seeking Western funding, believers might seek support from Indians themselves who have been blessed with lucrative jobs in various parts of the world. They could provide both Indian accountability and Indian support that might foster more India-friendly solutions to the barriers in India today.

I heard of a situation in India where a minister led two business men to Jesus. They wanted to see him devote his time to helping others also meet and grow in Jesus, so they started a business and used some of their proceeds to support his full-time efforts at witnessing and disciple-making. No foreign funds were needed for this Indian solution.

A friend recently told me of a group of Brahmin men who came to Christ a few years ago in the North. They too are business people. Together they now use their business to provide funds to help people in need and to support some of their number who are gifted in teaching and making disciples. They are committed to take no foreign funds; they want everyone to know that they are Indian followers of Jesus, not followers of a Western religion.

It would be beneficial to remember early Western congregations two hundred years ago. Most American churches then did not have a resident "pastor" or a fancy building. They used what they had to provide an adequate shelter (sometimes with open walls). The believers themselves organized and ran the services because an evangelist only came once every few weeks or months. Lay people preached, led worship, witnessed, even administered the ordinances in less hierarchical churches. Such models required little to no resources to start or sustain, instead of the millions of dollars invested in "church-planting" and "disciple-making" movements today.

This book cannot fully explore the options Indian believers might pursue to remove the barrier of financial dependency. Let me briefly suggest a few possibilities concerned believers in the West and India are pursuing.

Equip Employed Believers, Not Professional Ministers

Instead of pulling believers from their occupations to make them artificial proselytizers (*dalals*), we might encourage them to stay in their workplaces and occupations. Training would shift from full-time mission workers, to equipping believers to live and share their faith in the workplace and community. They are already employed, so they do not need salaries. They have a natural presence in their work and community. They interact every day with people from various walks of life and communities. Their placement allows them to live and share their faith in natural ways rather than as professional evangelistic agents (see Chapter 4). India's future relationship with Jesus might depend on whether his people shift to Paul's model from the colonial model.

One seminary I know has, for several years, offered an extension master's program for urban professionals who work in IT, medicine, education, and other fields. They learn Bible, theology, and ministry, not to become professional "ministers," but so that they can serve the Lord competently and faithfully from their own occupation. By doing this, they are intentionally challenging the unscriptural assumption that only ordained clergy are qualified to serve the Lord and that ministry only takes place in church-related vocations and settings (practicing Eph 4:11f.).

Livelihood and Entrepreneurship Training

Some believers do not have jobs or livelihoods, or they need to develop new skills. Believers first need to be taught that employment, business, and economics are not inherently opposed to faith and spirituality. Paul ran a profitable business that let him meet his needs, meet colleagues' needs, and share with the needy around him, as did Priscilla and Aquila and Lydia. India needs more believers in Jesus who use their gifts in business and management to help meet needs around them. India is an amazingly entrepreneurial country with incredibly creative people. Through these human resources, Jesus wants to bless those who live there without requiring Western donations that keep them subject to Euro-American standards and expectations.

Such believers can also provide livelihoods and entrepreneurial opportunities for others. This helps alleviate generational poverty and debt.

It also sets people free, giving them meaningful employment and a responsible, sustainable lifestyle.

CHRISTIAN AND BHAKTA CONSIDERATIONS

Christians

Christians in India and those who fund them in the West face an incredibly complex challenge if they want to truly address the barrier of financial dependency. Those who ignore the issues will continue to face the same skepticism and criticism from Hindus.

Those who, like Paul, want to reduce the barriers, will develop creative alternatives that simultaneously remove the traditional funding model barrier and build respectful bridges instead. The workplace is and will increasingly be one of the most important places where they make this transition.

Western Christians must more deeply consider the cultural and relational implications of this chapter and the barriers their money can create. This entire book has been written to encourage Christians to step away from traditions and models that keep Hindus from Jesus. My Indian colleagues and I fully recognize that while Westerners keep funding the barriers, those barriers will continue to keep most Hindus away from Jesus. Our prayer is for a growing number of Christians in India and in the West to wrestle with these questions and resolve to follow and encourage more scriptural alternatives.

Yesu Bhaktas

For Yesu bhaktas, their incarnational ways of following Jesus do not require extensive funding or institutions. They reject Western traditions and forms for what they are—foreign cultural inventions that are not binding on believers in other parts of the world. By incarnating the way and life of Jesus within their culture, they remove the accusation of Western subversion and dependency. They are as much opposed to those Christian features as religious Hindus are.

As one Yesu bhakta friend told me, "We do not want any Western funds for what we do. That way we avoid the corruption those funds seem to bring to Indian hearts." Yesu bhaktas represent a scriptural and cultural solution to the issues raised both in this chapter and in those that precede it.

However, I know parts of India where Yesu bhaktas have sometimes been connected in unhealthy ways to missions or Western funding. In several cases, this has eventually compromised their desire to be followers of Jesus within their Hindu communities. Eventually, at least in appearance, they can become tools to further Christians' agendas. Their close association with Christians and Christian funding also leads Hindus to see them as "Christians in Hindus' clothing." Their witness for Jesus may be compromised by their apparent duplicity.

CLOSING REFLECTIONS

Why has this chapter focused on the negative perceptions of Western funding? On Hindu concerns about Western subversion, dependency, *dalals*, and dishonesty? Because these widespread concerns represent prevailing perceptions about traditional Western funding models. Christians may do incredible good in some areas of society, but they recognize that the issues I have raised make Hindus skeptical of Christian funding and benevolence (next chapter).

A Christian friend of mine works at a hospital in India that is predominantly Hindu. He has donated his time and energy for years to meet various medical needs in different parts of India. His medical supervisor, a Hindu, has repeatedly asked him, "What are you getting from this?" He sought to find any remuneration or material gain my friend receives for these labors. Only recently, after long skepticism, this Hindu man finally accepted that my friend offers his *seva* (service) for no charge and no remuneration. He is seeing a Christian who selflessly serves Jesus alone. If Western Christians began to contribute to his work to "help" him, his testimony would be finished immediately.

Believers face this incredible skepticism daily because of centuries of Western funding models. My friend is living out the alternative, working at his job in a gentle, quiet way. He finds ways to use the gifts and resources God has given him to bless others in Jesus' name. When Hindus meet such believers, followers who serve without Western funding baggage, only then will the financial barriers begin to come down and allow Hindus to see Jesus instead of Western money and the dependency it fosters.

CHAPTER 9

THE BARRIER OF BENEVOLENCE

In early 2015 a leader of the RSS (Hindu nationalist group) declared in a speech, "Mother Teresa's service would have been good. But it used to have one objective, to convert the person who was being served into a Christian" (Dhar 2015 Feb 24). What might appear to be an innocuous comment outside India led to an eruption of public debate within the country. Parliament had to be temporarily adjourned when confrontation over this statement became too heated (National Bureau 2015). Both the comment and the ensuing public controversy highlighted the level of scrutiny and skepticism some Indians feel toward Christian charitable and social work (Singh 2015; Staff Reporter 2015).

HINDUS AND INDUCEMENT—A LONG-STANDING CONCERN

Hindus respect those who give and serve selflessly. From the Rig Veda (earliest Hindu scripture) forward, Hindus have been encouraged to pursue charity and generosity (e.g., Rig Veda, Book 10, Hymn 117). According to Klostermaier, one early Hindu scholar asserted that "righteousness [*dharma*] connected with the body consists in *dana* (charity), *paritrana* (succor of the distressed), and *paricarana* (rendering service)" (Klostermaier 1989, 49)—all three clearly aspects of benevolence.

Hindu concerns about benevolence, then, do not arise from Christian service itself. They are troubled, instead, by why and how that service is rendered. The motives and methods of Christian benevolence have raised, and continue to raise, substantial questions in Hindu minds.

Gandhi and Inducement

Gandhi, as we saw in Chapter 5, was troubled by the issue of conversion in general, although he allowed that personal conversion was possible. He was adamantly opposed, though, to benevolence as a means to proselytize.

When misrepresented about his views on missionaries and benevolence, Gandhi clarified, "'If instead of confining themselves purely to humanitarian work such as education, medical services to the poor and the like, they would use these activities of theirs *for the purpose of proselytizing*, I would certainly like them to withdraw" (Gandhi 1961, 84; emphasis mine). A further comment articulated the continued concern of many Hindus today, "I hold that *proselytization under the cloak of humanitarian work* is unhealthy to say the least. It is most resented by people here" (ibid.; emphasis mine).

Gandhi once advised *Harijans* (Dalits): "The missionaries have of course the right to preach the Gospel of Christ and to invite non-Christians to embrace Christianity. But every attempt to *press material benefits or attractions in the aid of conversion* should be freely exposed, and the Harijans should be educated to resist these temptations" (Mehta 2002, 18; emphasis mine).

When Christians used benevolence as a cloak, as a material inducement, then Gandhi saw it as unhealthy, a cause for Hindu resentment. These same sentiments repeatedly arise in current Hindu critiques of Christian humanitarian work ninety plus years after Gandhi expressed his concern.

Niyogi Committee on Missionary Activity (1958)

Christians primarily ignored Gandhi's and others' concerns and simply increased their efforts at benevolence for conversion after India's independence (1947). The practice of inducement became so pronounced that the government of Madhya Pradesh ordered an investigation into missionary activity, particularly into benevolence and conversion activity. The 1958 Niyogi Commission Report on missionary activity demonstrated a mix of commendation and concern:

> In all the places visited by the Committee there was unanimity as regards the excellent service rendered by the Missionaries, in the fields of education and medical relief. But on the other hand there was a general complaint from the non-Christian side that the schools and hospitals were being used as means of securing converts. *There was no disparagement of Christianity or of Jesus Christ, and*

no objection to the preaching of Christianity and even to con-
versions to Christianity. The objection was to the illegitimate
methods alleged to be adopted by the Missionaries for this
purpose, such as offering allurements of free education
and other facilities to children attending their schools,
adding some Christian names to their original Indian
names, marriages with Christian girls, money-lending,
distributing Christian literature in hospitals and offering
prayers in the [wards] of in-door patients. (Niyogi 1958,
Volume I, Part I, Chapter 1, Paragraph 6; emphasis mine)

Later in their report, the Niyogi Commission read Christian mission writings extensively. They cited specific examples where Christians
declared benevolent activity as their predominant means of evangelism.
The Commission summary of the evidence was succinct, but clear: "The
media through which the Gospel is propagated are primarily the schools,
hospitals and orphanages" (Niyogi 1958, Volume I, Part III, Chapter 3,
Paragraph 28). These institutions were an "instrument in their task of
Christianizing the whole land." Schools were more for "religious conversions than intellectual improvement" and were primarily "the means
for expansion of the kingdom" (paragraphs 28–33). These and numerous
other quotes from this influential report pointed clearly to a conversion
agenda (see Chapter 5 of this book) among many Christians.

In all fairness, many Christian schools are now careful to not pursue a
conversion agenda at the expense of a quality education. Numerous Hindus, in fact, send their children to Christian schools because of the high
academic standards and testify to the quality education they received, so
the accusation of conversion at the expense of intellectual improvement is
falsified by many Hindu people today.

Hindus Weren't the Only Ones Concerned by Benevolence and Inducement

It is also important to note that the desire to minimize or eliminate inducements has not only been a Hindu concern in India. In the 1930s, according
to the Niyogi report, the Government of India (British at the time) chas-
tised missions for improper benevolence and inducements in Udaipur State.
The problem was so pronounced that the British government required
missions "to maintain a register showing in the case of each new convert,

his name, his father's name and other particulars including *any kind of material benefit given to the converts at the time of their conversion*" (Niyogi 1958, Volume I, Part II, Chapter 2, Paragraph 33; emphasis mine).

Today's anti-inducement laws exist primarily in states where these issues had already been identified as problematic under the British Raj. Colonial administrators passed and enforced similar laws in some of these areas because of the tension raised by conversion practices.

Requirements to register conversions preceded Indian self-rule by over a decade. They were initiated by the "Christian" British government at the time. Modern Christian charges that these laws are Hindu "anti-conversion" laws, ignore the history of these concerns and the laws enacted to address them. When Christians criticize or ignore these laws today, they can appear to Hindus to condone and support the very inducement practices that Hindus find so abhorrent. Their protests can serve to confirm Hindu suspicions that Christians are intent on pursuing dishonest means of buying converts.

In all fairness, it is not anti-Christian to ask believers to examine the motives and agendas that underlie their benevolence efforts. Regrettably, Christian exploitation of benevolence may have been so egregious that the government had to enact accountability measures to restrict the abuses. Surely honest Christians want to do everything possible to demonstrate that they are not using underhanded inducement (allurement) as they seek to introduce people to Jesus.

Religious Freedom Laws Revisited

Chapter 5 briefly discussed the Freedom of Religion laws enacted by several Indian states. Christians often misrepresent these as "anti-conversion laws," but none of the acts forbids conversion. They provide mechanisms to prevent conversions through force, inducement (allurement), or deception. Due to space limitations, this chapter will focus only on the concern for "inducement" to conversion, the issue most commonly raised regarding benevolence.

We must ask why the British, and later the Indians, felt a need to pass such laws in the first place. What social dynamics made them think that these laws were necessary? Is it possible that Indians have wholly misunderstood and misrepresented Christian compassionate benevolence in the name of Jesus? Have Hindus simply misjudged the altruistic motivations of believers to help those in need, no strings attached? If that is the case, then some Christians seem to have substantially failed to demonstrate that their care is offered in such selfless ways. If it is simply a case of misunderstanding, this chapter will suggest some possible alternatives Christians might pursue to address the misperceptions.

We must consider another possibility, though. Christians, in moments of candor, have acknowledged to me that Christian benevolence has not always been purely altruistic and focused only on aiding people. The term "rice Christians" is a well-known concept in Christian circles—some Tamil friends tell me they are called "wheat Christians" in their part of the country. The issues surrounding benevolence with evangelistic agendas have been debated across the Christian world with many different conclusions. Arguments over the "social gospel," "social justice," and Christian social engagement have divided Christians over appropriate responses to the world's challenging needs and how evangelism and conversion relate to those responses.

The Indian religious freedom laws, with their prohibition of inducement, just might be a response to actual Christian misuses of benevolence in manipulative ways. Believers in India and supporters in the US must seriously consider how common benevolence models may unnecessarily perpetuate and aggravate Hindu resistance to Jesus. Believers intend to do these acts of mercy to witness for Christ, but what if their benevolence drives people away from Jesus instead?

HELPING PEOPLE WITH ULTERIOR MOTIVES

Hindus accuse Christians of giving benevolence for ulterior motives, to induce and manipulate people to convert. Sadly, Christians present Hindus with ample evidence, as the following representative examples illustrate.

Praying for "Needy" People or Preying on "Needy" People

We have a Hindu friend who has been very successful in her career. Her family is well-off materially. A Christian woman, who did not know her well, once approached her and asked if she could come to her house and pray. As our friend tells the story, the Christian came into her large, well-appointed home, looked around, and then said, "I cannot pray for you. You have no needs."

"Of course, I have needs," replied our friend. "Please pray for me."

The Christian woman insisted that she could not. After further requests for prayer, the visitor excused herself and left our friend without ever praying.

Why would a Christian not pray in such a situation? Some Christians had coached her in this style of "benevolence" evangelism. In this model, Christians tell me, they identify a target for evangelism. They offer to pray for them to get into their home and assess the situation. Christians then look around for material, medical, or physical needs they can "pray" for and then meet. "Helping" someone is then the gateway for evangelism. Christians may offer to pray, in other words, to prey on people for their conversion agenda.

Given this coaching, the Christian woman's response was natural, even if not Christ-like. Our Hindu friend had no tangible material or physical needs that Christians could capitalize on for their conversion strategy.

Our friend was astonished: "I had family and emotional needs that needed prayer. I would have welcomed being prayed for."

However, a Christian sense of "benevolence" (with an agenda) blinded the Christian woman to the possibility of serving our friend through prayer. Our friend is not the only person who has told us about Christians who offer to pray for people in order to prey on them and spy out "needs" in the name of Jesus. Genuine prayer for the needs and concerns of Hindus can have a powerful influence for good. When Christians are trained, though, to use prayer as an evangelistic gimmick, this simply becomes a barrier to Hindus. They recognize manipulation when they see it. They want nothing to do with a Jesus who is associated with such behavior.

A Christian bias toward only serving the needs of the poor can cause them to focus on visible, material or physical "needs." These are a sure ticket to evangelistic opportunities. This bias is reflected in a book on the conversion debate in India. The author asserts, "All Christian service institutions that serve the upper class and upper middle class are structures without a Christian cause. They have no scriptural warrant to exist" (Raj 2001, 50).

This ignores the example of Jesus and his apostles who clearly served people in all classes and strata of society. Jesus ministered to people with homes and occupations and varying levels of income—people like Matthew, Zacchaeus, Nicodemus, Joseph of Arimathea. He spent time repeatedly at the home of Mary, Martha, and Lazarus. Cornelius was not a pauper when Peter served him (Acts 10). Mary, mother of John Mark, owned a large house and even had servants (Acts 12). Paul served Lydia (a cloth merchant) and stayed with his companions in her home. He worked and probably stayed with Priscilla and Aquila (fellow tentmakers). Paul references others with livelihoods and property like Gaius and Erastus of Corinth (Rom 16:23).

Neither Jesus nor his apostles practiced or taught the anti-wealth bias demonstrated toward our Hindu friend or expressed in the above assertion. Such a spirit confirms to Hindus that Christians are intent on targeting only the "down and out" with their conversion tactics. It's hard not to see inducement, when some Christians practice it so blatantly. An ulterior motive that discriminates against the wealthy and only targets the poor is just as unfaithful to Jesus as one that discriminates against the poor and needy.

Perpetual Benevolence (Rice Christians)

In the US, there is an old ministry truism, "What you win them with, you win them to." That applies equally to benevolence practices in India. One Indian friend, who read this chapter, noted, "At the end of any kind of preaching or teaching, those who receive benefits will continue to expect those benefits . . . Every time any non-Indian evangelist or even an Indian visits local converts or contacts, there is an expectation of some kind of charity at the end. If it is not there, they get disappointed."

My friend further noted that the hearers' desire for more gifts can also seduce those who use benevolence in their preaching. "Every act of charity," he observed, "gives a personal satisfaction and subtle pride . . . to the donors." They seem to get greater results when something is distributed, than when they just preach. In order to "keep a door open for them in the future," Christians continue to go back and give more. This gives the donors a sense of satisfaction, and appears to maintain interest in their preaching by those who keep coming to receive the material benefit.

Some of my Indian friends have described the complications that this can create. If they hand out blankets, they must all be the same size, color, and shape. Otherwise, some of the recipients will feel they have been slighted because they received the wrong size, the wrong color, or the wrong shape compared to someone else. One Indian told me that they made the mistake of getting a certain color of blanket that was offensive to the group they wanted to help. The blankets were rejected and the locals offended by this violation of their sensitivities.

Another Indian friend observed that his own father had "converted" several times before he truly met Jesus. He made the first few "decisions" to get food for his impoverished family.

Perpetual benevolence can feel good to the Christians providing the benevolence and those who financially sponsor their charity work. It can lead, all too easily, to perpetual dependency. This ongoing material support, though, appears to be perpetual inducement in the eyes of Hindu onlookers. Christians, from this perspective, first buy, then continue to support converts who otherwise would not be Christians. For Hindus, permanent inducement not only takes the form of handouts, but even employment by the mission or church can represent inducement (a livelihood the convert would otherwise not have received). When the employment involves hiring as a minister, issues around *dalals* from the last chapter can compound with accusations of inducement (both the hired pastor, and his own financing of new converts).

Believers who truly want to help the needy must examine their own motives in giving and the relationship between benevolence, inducement, and dependency in fundamental ways. Three books in the Bibliography can guide concerned believers to address and avoid the damage of perpetual benevolence (Corbett and Fikkert 2012; R. Reese 2010, Schwartz 2007).

Advertising Benevolence for Further Support

On a regular basis, missions engaged in India report their benevolence activities to donors in the West. They take photographs of donations, medical camps, relief efforts, and trafficking interventions. Sponsors want to know that their contributions are being used to actually help people. Banners may be printed and displayed behind such efforts. These serve a dual purpose. They advertise to the local people those responsible for providing the benevolence, usually a mission name. The banners also provide a great backdrop for Indian missions to show their donors what they are doing. The mission name is front and center in their activity.

The interplay of local desire to help people and Western desire to make a "meaningful difference" can become fertile ground for ulterior motives on either or both sides of the equation—pride, greed, envy, more is better, bigger is better, competition, to mention a few.

The more benevolence becomes marked by marketing glitz and media campaigns, though, the more it resembles what Hindus identify as the "conversion business" (Tracking Evangelism 2014b; Frawley 2008). As in the last chapter, the "Indian conversion agents" report their activities to the clients in the West who fund their benevolence in order to further the conversion services.

Examine the web sites of many Indian ministries. They openly advertise their social service programs: orphanages, schools, poverty alleviation, fresh water, medical care, or trafficking interventions. On many evangelical sites, though, one also finds indications that these activities are a means to a conversion end. Some state it overtly, others only hint at the connection. Many evangelicals have an aversion to the "social gospel" (helping people without evangelism). Consequently, they insist that evangelism must accompany benevolence. Mission websites and informational brochures are expected to clearly articulate this connection for many churches to even consider supporting them.

This mission marketing creates two simultaneous barriers from Hindu perspectives. First, the missions' marketing schemes articulate that their methodologies involve what appears to be inducement in various forms. The message ultimately boils down to some version of, "We help people specifically to evangelize them." How could Hindus who monitor mission publicity not conclude that inducement is fundamental to many missions' strategies? Missions state it in their promotional materials.

Furthermore, the banners, photographs, and constant write-ups of benevolence for Western consumption, can convey another ulterior motive. This publicity appears to solicit greater funding to increase such activities. For many missions, the message seems to be, "See how we helped people. Please give us more money so that we can help more people. Give today!" From the outside looking in, one wonders where the line is crossed from genuinely helping people, to manipulating and stage-managing benevolence to increase contributions.

The benevolence machine can present a barrier, then, when driven by what appear to be self-serving motives. The lines are sometimes blurred between genuine concern to help more people, and a self-centered spirit of aggrandizement disguised under a veneer of benevolence. David Hesselgrave identifies one key indicator, though:

> The people are ready to listen to Christian witnesses who understand and love them. But missionary opportunists who simply preach, take pictures, and write articles for publications in the West will do more harm than good. (Hesselgrave 1991, 634)

The motive of love (genuine concern for the other) must clearly distinguish itself from that of opportunism (using others for institutional gain). In the years since Hesselgrave wrote those words, the opportunists have changed, but the danger has not. Christian opportunists of all kinds (no longer just Western missionaries) may use a variety of schemes, with pictures, letters, websites, and blogs, to get a piece of the benevolence action.

A friend of mine works for a child sponsorship agency in India that is undergoing government scrutiny of its financial dealings. He recently told me of a church they work with that arranged a mass baptism of sponsored children with photographs for donors. Six months later, he visited the same church, and they again held a mass baptism of children. He noticed one child who had been in the previous group and pulled him aside. "You were just baptized," he inquired, "why are you here again?" The child replied, "Pastor told me to get baptized again, so here I am." My friend knew that if he had looked more closely the first time, he would have recognized more "rebaptisms" for the new "photo opportunity."

Indian government clampdowns on non-governmental organizations (NGOs) are a direct response to numerous organizations set up to make money from benevolence opportunities in dishonest ways (Bharata Bharati Admin 2013). Several Christian friends have told me that they see the former and current government crackdowns on NGOs as God's intervention. He is using the Indian governments to clean the Christian house since Christians would not address the issue of ulterior motives and dishonesty in benevolence directly.

Indians, then, are not simply concerned about the *prevalence of inducement* in Christian benevolence, they are also troubled by the *lack of integrity*. Combined, those factors hinder millions of Hindus from even considering the Jesus whose followers condone and follow these ways. Those who serve selflessly and honestly face an uphill battle against the prevailing perceptions such ulterior motives and practices have created in Indian society at large.

Ultimately, Hindu concerns about giving with ulterior motives agree with Jesus' own teaching. After all, he himself taught, "Love your ene-mies, and do good [benevolence], and lend, *expecting nothing in return*, and your reward will be great, and you will be sons of the Most High, for he is kind to the ungrateful and the evil. Be merciful, even as your Father is merciful" (Luke 6:35f., ESV; emphasis mine).

ADDRESSING THE BARRIER OF BENEVOLENCE

Christians themselves know that benevolence can be problematic. So how should believers address the significant concerns Hindus raise about be-nevolence and the possible inducement that it represents? There are no easy answers to this question. The resentment and suspicion aroused by this issue are particularly deep and pervasive. Based on my conversations and research, though, let me suggest several considerations that might help reduce this barrier over time.

"Christian Witness in a Multi-Religious World"

In 2011, a consultation between three major Christian groups issued a joint declaration entitled *Christian Witness in a Multi-Religious World: Recommendations for Conduct*. Crafted over a period of five years, their recommendations include two statements that directly apply to concerns about the misuse of benevolence.

Item 6 under "A basis for Christian witness" states, "If Christians engage in inappropriate methods of exercising mission by resorting to deception and coercive means, they betray the gospel and may cause suf-fering to others. Such departures call for repentance and remind us of our need for God's continuing grace (cf. Rom 3:23)" (World Council of Churches; Pontifical Council for Interreligious Dialogue; World Evan-gelical Alliance 2011, 4). To the extent that benevolence has been used in deceptive or coercive ways (blatantly or subtly), it would be wise for Christians to corporately acknowledge and repent of the harm caused to the good news, to the surrounding community, and even to believers.

Principle 4 ('Acts of Service') again alludes to harmful benevolence practices: "The exploitation of situations of poverty and need has no place in Christian outreach. Christians should denounce and refrain from offering all forms of allurements, including financial incentives and rewards, in their acts of service" (ibid., 4). The fact that they included this statement provides tacit admission that some Christians have resorted to exploitation through benevolence. The call to repentance would apply here also.

A great deal of Hindu resistance to Jesus would subside if Christians seriously addressed and truly repented of benevolence practices related to these two declarations.

Positive Perspectives on "Rice Christians"

D. T. Niles, a Sri Lankan minister and mission executive, has suggested a positive consideration of the common concern about "rice Christians"—people who convert to Christ because of material or social considerations, rather than allegiance to Jesus. He observes,

> These people had not accepted Jesus as Way. They did not know anything about his claim over their lives. But, in their predicament, *Jesus had approached them as the only way open to them.* He had set the Church within reach of their dwellings and they had found in the ministry of the Church a ministry to their need. When we speak about rice-Christians we think that we are speaking about the motives of people: we forget that we are speaking about the methods of Jesus. (Niles 1958, 22; emphasis mine)

Niles provides examples: Dalit Indians who came to the church to find recognition that Brahmins refused them. A widow came and found employment, and education for her children. His own grandfather was taken in as an orphan and raised by a mission in Sri Lanka.

Every day, similar encounters occur, where people seek and find material and social blessings from the followers of Jesus with only the faintest sense initially of who he really is. Yet they come because his people do provide tangible expressions of his compassion and mercy for those who are hurting or helpless. Through his people, his body, they end up meeting him.

No matter how Christians respond to such needs, some skeptics will accuse them of "inducement." They cannot avoid responding to needs, though, just because their motives might be misunderstood. Jesus himself was falsely accused of helping people by the power of Beelzebul, the prince of demons (Matt 12:23). Some levels of misunderstanding may simply be unavoidable.

Christian Benevolence Has Done Significant Good in India

Where possible, believers can also articulate the good that their benevolence has accomplished in India. For instance, *Christianity Today* posted an interview with an Indian doctor entitled "How White Missionaries Helped Birth Modern-Day India" (Gnidovic 2014). The interviewee, Dr. M. A. Raju, called for Indians to recognize the contributions that Western missionaries and Christianity made to Indian society. These benevolent influences included resistance to "widow burning (*sati*), infanticide, and temple prostitution." They called attention to caste discrimination and even led to low-caste people being treated with greater dignity and respect. Hindu groups like the Brahmo Samaj and Arya Samaj initiated Hindu internal reforms in response to Christian calls for justice and equality in various realms. Raju summarizes, "Indian Christians have forgotten the impact their missionary forefathers had, on language, education, Indian identity, health, and the treatment of women, outcasts, the poor" (ibid.). These benefits were made possible by the generosity of Western Christians.

The Niyogi Commission affirmed this positive view of the influence of Christian benevolence at one level, "In all the places visited by the Committee there was unanimity as regards the excellent service rendered by the Missionaries, in the fields of education and medical relief" (Niyogi, et al. 1958, Volume 1, Part I, Chapter 1, Paragraph 6). I personally have met Hindus who gratefully testify to the quality of education they received in Christian schools.

Similarly, in a study of "Religious Philanthropy in India," scholar Amit Kumar Sharma acknowledges that "Christian missionaries have been active in India for nearly two centuries and have contributed greatly in the spheres of education, health delivery, and tribal development, especially in remote areas" (A. K. Sharma 2011, 164).

Believers face a difficult challenge when it comes to benevolence. If they spend too much time touting their record of "selfless" service, they will appear to be self-serving and interested in getting credit. If, however, they say nothing, they run the risk of more skeptical Hindus dominating the conversation and portraying them as always intent on inducement. In addition, if they persist in benevolence practices that overtly appear manipulative, any claims to benefit Indian society will ring hollow in Hindu ears. Only Indians can determine the appropriate balance needed between these alternatives.

Intersecting Barriers

For Hindus, the issue of Christian benevolence is complicated because it intersects with many of the barriers we have already discussed. Many Christians insist that benevolence must be accompanied by evangelism and preaching (Chapter 4). Unless the issues around these two barriers are addressed, their association with benevolence will simply exacerbate Hindu resistance.

Hindu concerns about inducement focus particularly on conversion (Chapter 5). That barrier too provides another lightning rod for Hindu critiques of Christian ministries, especially when they appear to buy or manipulate potential converts. In addition, the foreign financing issues of the last chapter, since they fund much benevolence, compound Hindu concerns about benevolence itself.

Ultimately, benevolence as inducement troubles Hindus because it pays people to separate from and reject their community, culture, and family. In other words, it buys cultural separatism and Christian identity (Chapters 1 and 2). When issues of Hindu "reconversion" (*ghar wapsi*) are discussed, the conversation commonly turns to the material benefits the Christians received or were promised at their "conversion."

More than any other, the barrier of benevolence cannot be addressed in isolation. We must work through solutions for all the barriers previously identified and work them out of consideration for how we serve and help people in the name of Jesus. We must, though, also consider how to best address the benevolence issues themselves.

SCRIPTURAL CONSIDERATIONS FOR THE BARRIER OF BENEVOLENCE

As in earlier chapters, this barrier too is partly the product of human traditions, traditions that ignore or disobey some clear teaching by Jesus concerning giving and benevolence. So, at the close of this chapter let me suggest four scriptural principles that could alleviate various aspects of the barrier of benevolence.

Paul's Concern About Funding Models

As we saw in the previous chapter, Paul looked at the traditional ministry funding model through the eyes and concerns of those with whom he wanted to share Jesus (1 Cor 9:1–18). Their negative view of taking money for teaching led him to adopt a completely different funding model at great personal inconvenience.

As believers, we should follow Paul's approach and examine our funding models for benevolence. We must first ask, "How do Hindus perceive the existing ways that Christians give and fund compassionate care? How seriously do these considerations present an obstacle to the good news of Jesus in India?" To do that we must first consider what troubles Hindus about inducement. We cannot remove the obstacles unless we have a clear idea of how they appear from that outside perspective.

If, as it appears, benevolence is such a significant lightning rod for Hindu opposition, believers must also do as Paul did by developing alternative models. We must ask how we could fundamentally change the ways in which benevolence is offered so that people can see the care and compassion of Jesus, not Western manipulation and inducement.

Some Christians seem to think they have a right to give help in any way they want, but should they insist on that right when it actively keeps a significant proportion of Hindu communities away from Jesus? Instead they should, like Paul, "become all things to all people" even in the way they practice charity and benevolence (1 Cor 9:19–23).

Jesus and Benevolence

After all, Jesus did not say, "Let your light so shine before men that they may see your foreign works and despise your Father in heaven." Neither did he say, "Let your light so shine before men that they may see your good works and be converted." He also did not say, "Let your light so shine before donors that they may see your good works and give you more money."

Believers know what Jesus actually said: "Let your light so shine before men that they may see your good works and glorify your Father who is in heaven" (Matt 5:16). We must therefore prayerfully seek ways of helping that get missions and money and inducement out of the way. This might encourage Hindus instead to clearly see the compassion of Jesus and the glory of God.

How do we do that? By following the teaching of Jesus regarding our benevolence.

NOT TO BE SEEN BY MEN—"DO YOUR CHARITY IN SECRET"

When Christians do benevolence, one can often see signs, banners, or obvious Christian symbols. They want to advertise that they are Christians so that the Hindus know it. In addition, these props provide photo opportunities for publicity to sponsors in the West.

This can be a vicious cycle. Western donors want to see results, to get "bang for their buck." Photos provide evidence of that effectiveness, especially if banners identify the ministry giving the benevolence. Such photos and communications ensure continued and sometimes increased support, so recipients must use these publicity tools to communicate "effectiveness" to donors.

And yet, the Jesus we serve specifically instructs his followers, "When you give to the poor, *do not sound a trumpet before you*, as the hypocrites do in the synagogues and in the streets, so that they may be honored by men. Truly I say to you, they have their reward in full" (Matt 6:2, NASB; emphasis mine). He instead instructs his disciples to give in a way that keeps their benevolence secret, and then their Father who sees in secret will reward them.

In a context where Christians often publicize their generosity and benevolence, both for the sake of converts and for donors, does Jesus' instruction have any application? Given Hindus' deep concern about benevolence being done for show and public display, Jesus actually sides with the Hindus' concerns here. He specifically forbids his followers from advertising their generosity and benevolence. How much Hindu resistance would be reduced, if Christians were more careful about following Matthew 6:1–18 instead of publicly advertising their piety and benevolence to be noticed both by Hindus and supporting Christians?

NOT EXPECTING ANYTHING IN RETURN

Jesus also addresses Hindu concerns about believers who give with an expected return. He taught, "But love your enemies, and do good, and lend, expecting nothing in return; and your reward will be great, and you will be sons of the Most High; for he himself is kind to ungrateful and evil men. Be merciful, just as your Father is merciful" (Luke 6:35f., NASB). Hendricksen comments that this reaffirms what Jesus just said previously, that "one should lend for the sheer joy of helping the person in need and *not for any selfish reason*" (Hendricksen 1978, 353; emphasis mine).

Benevolence as Common Grace

It was January 14, 2012, the first day of the Tamil harvest festival, *Pongal*. Early in the morning, I stood at our hotel window looking out over the city of Chennai, praying. Across the city, and across the entire state, millions of Hindus boiled clay pots of rice and offered a portion to the rising *Surya*, the sun god. This festival is a three-day thanksgiving festival for past sunshine, rain, and harvests.

As I prayed, the sun rose over the eastern horizon and a new day began. The Lord did not withhold the sun because Hindus offered prayers of thanks to it instead of to him. In the years that have followed the Lord continues to bless them with sunshine, rain, and harvests. The words of Jesus in Matthew 5:45 came to mind that morning as the sun's rays shone into the morning's smoky haze: "Be sons of your Father who is in heaven; for he causes his sun to rise on the evil and the good, and sends rain on the righteous and the unrighteous" (NASB).

God does not preach a sermon every time he sends the sun or rain. He does not pass out gospel tracts at the time of every harvest. He simply gives the blessing of sunshine, rain, and harvest as a testimony of his love and care. As Paul observes, "rains and fruitful seasons" have been God's long-term testimony to the nations (Acts 14:17).

God, in other words, blesses people—gives them his benevolence—in an indiscriminate manner. He gently and patiently invites people to know him without forcing himself upon them. He lets the blessing of sunshine, rain, and harvest invite people to recognize his care and provision, whether they acknowledge it or not. Furthermore, Jesus specifically tells us in Matthew 5:45 that we are to follow the example of our heavenly Father in the way we treat those who do not yet know him and who even reject him or us.

I know that this may sound almost heretical to some Christians, but consider the outcome if believers followed Jesus' instruction and the

Father's example. If the followers of Jesus simply gave assistance with no agenda, no forced evangelistic presentation, no imposed message, observing Hindus would be rather surprised and taken aback. If they saw this selfless *seva* simply given out of love for Jesus, but with no overt pressure for evangelism or conversion, it would contrast with what they normally see. They would likely stop and take notice.

CHRISTIAN AND BHAKTA CONSIDERATIONS

Christians

When considering their benevolence practices, Christians need to revisit Paul's approach to funding models. Hindus are deeply concerned about Christian benevolent activity as an inducement to "conversion." Their accusations are not unfounded, since Christians often speak of benevolence for the purpose of evangelism and conversion. In the current political climate, traditional Christian models for benevolence are increasingly scrutinized and questioned. Christian institutions that insist on following the standard benevolence models will likely face increasing suspicion, investigation, and resistance.

What would Paul do, given that the funding model presents such a significant obstacle to the good news of Jesus? He would take whatever steps were necessary to remove the models that present such considerable barriers to the good news of Jesus in the Indian context. He would replace them with scripturally faithful and culturally appropriate alternatives that allowed Hindus to meet and consider Jesus.

Yesu Bhaktas

Yesu bhaktas have several distinct advantages regarding benevolence and the inducement associations. Since they don't extract believers from culture and community, they cannot be accused of inducement or conversion. They encourage Hindus to remain Hindu socially and culturally while following Jesus spiritually.

Additionally, they take no foreign funds, so any charity they give is their own selfless *seva*, not a foreign-funded means to a conversion end. They can honestly say to their fellow Hindus that they do not solicit or use Christian funds for any purpose.

Furthermore, since they are incarnated within the culture, they are more likely aware of the appropriate giving and receiving behaviors of their own people. They can naturally give in appropriate ways that maximize respect and minimize insult, ways that reflect both the Hindu and scriptural ideal of "give expecting nothing in return."

CLOSING REFLECTIONS

Jesus tells his followers not to give benevolence to be seen by men. He tells his followers to give without expecting anything in return, and he specifically tells his followers to give and bless in the way that God gives sunshine and rain—indiscriminately to all, not conditional on the attitude or response of the recipients.

In the aftermath of the 2015 Chennai floods, a church decided to provide needed support for a nearby devastated community. They collected resources, surveyed the community for legitimate needs, then set about collecting and packaging the needed supplies. Some Brahmin families in the neighborhood, who had opposed the church for years, took notice of the selfless way in which they went about serving these people in need. Within a short time, some of the Brahmin family came and even participated in packing relief supplies. The pastor of the church told me that the husband of one of these families waited at the church window until services were finished on Christmas morning. He then handed the pastor twenty thousand rupees, a little over $300, to use in their ongoing community assistance.

This turnaround in spirit was not simply the result of the benevolence. For several years, they had been actively addressing engagement instead of extraction, respect instead of rejection in relation to the surrounding community. They sought to give help in ways that were sensitive to the community around them, instead of just giving in an unconsidered way. The recipients knew the donors were Christians.

They did not create an evangelistic campaign to coincide with the benevolence or do it with publicity banners, as some might have done. By addressing several of the barriers simultaneously, their compassionate care built bridges to more than just the flooded community. It has turned former opponents into friends, built relational bridges where barriers existed just a year earlier.

Hindus have a deep sense that giving should be done selflessly. When they see believers give in a way that reflects that ideal, they will be far more drawn to Jesus. His teaching may resonate more deeply with Hindu giving values than with the publicity-minded benevolence approaches developed and followed by some Christian missions.

May the day come when Indians see our good works, and instead of questioning and challenging believers, they "glorify our Father who is in heaven." I'm thankful for my friends who are following that path!

CHAPTER 10

FINAL OBSERVATIONS

Over my travels in India, I have met a significant number of Hindu-background believers, who wrestle with the disconnect they feel between their Christian identity and their Hindu family and heritage. Some have told of Christians who discriminated against them because they were still considered "Hindus," and not "good" multigenerational Christians. Others described the emotional and relational pain they have experienced, not because of Jesus, but because of their association with the separatist Christian community. Still others recount how they try to worship in Christian ways, but years after their "conversion" the music and expressions still are unnatural and foreign to them. Several have told me, "Following the Christian traditions makes me feel like I am trying to wear someone else's clothes. They don't fit me."

These believers deeply love Jesus and are committed to follow him. Yet the Christian package and culture they are forced to adopt creates deep personal and social dissonance they can't escape. Earlier in the book, I referenced Yesu Das Tiwari, an elderly Christian leader who had followed Jesus for nearly 65 years. His son asked whether he would change anything if he could go back and start over. Tiwari's reply echoes the painful stories I have repeatedly heard and read: "Christ is my 'ishta' [chosen God], he has never left me, I will never leave him, *but I would not have joined the Christian community. I would have lived with my people and my community and been a witness to them*" (Petersen 2007, 87–88; emphasis mine).

I have written this book, in part, because my heart is burdened for so many like Tiwari. They converted and joined the Christian community because they were taught this was the only way to follow Jesus. It is my heartfelt prayer that some Hindu-background "Christians," in reading the preceding, will find the freedom to walk away from unnecessary Christian forms and traditions and follow Jesus as their *ishta* within their

Hindu culture and community. I hope that because of what I have written fewer believers will look back with regret on years of unnecessary separation and conflict with their Hindu family. If this book helps one believer avoid Tiwari's regret, it will have been worth the time and toil.

This book has also clearly articulated my concern for Yesu bhaktas, Hindus who follow only Jesus but within their Hindu culture and community. This book intentionally explains why that incarnational choice is scriptural and faithful to Jesus, despite common Christian claims to the contrary. Most of what is written about following Jesus, worshiping Jesus, and sharing Jesus comes from the pens of Christians who assume many of the traditions I have challenged. Yesu bhaktas, and other incarnational believers, do not often have access to Scripture studies that do not push a Christian agenda of some kind or that do not begin with Western Christian assumptions for their interpretive framework.

My bhakta friends have told me that this book has encouraged them because a Christian has passionately and caringly advocated for the validity of their choices in the face of Christian criticism. My understanding of Scripture and my walk with Jesus has been deeply enriched by my relationship with bhaktas and my consideration of their perspectives and experience. They are not second-class believers or outside the body of Christ, as some Christians seem to imply. I count them as dear brothers and sisters in Jesus.

When all believers gather around the throne to worship the Lord (Rev 7:9), the bhajans of the bhaktas and their worship will be as dear to God's heart as the hymns and choruses of Western Christendom.

For the rest of my readers, I have prayed that this book will help you look more deeply at what it means to follow Jesus and to be a part of his body. If you have made it this far, you have wrestled with significant emotional and spiritual challenges. These ideas are not easy to process and digest. My own life and faith have been both shaken and deepened by these reflections.

So where do we go from here? The analyses in the previous chapters lead me to one troubling conclusion: We as believers have not always examined, at a deep enough level, some fundamental assumptions about what is essential to follow and belong to Jesus. This book is only an opening attempt to model what that deeper analysis needs to entail.

IT'S NOT JUST ABOUT INDIA

When I talk about these barriers with leaders in the US, it doesn't take long before someone says, "This is what we're facing! We need this here." Out of those conversations, let me make two brief observations.

We Created and Perpetuate the Barriers

The barriers we have discussed were often created in the West, are funded by the West, and are often perpetuated by Western church expectations. Increasingly, the assumptions behind some of these barriers (Christian, church institutions, evangelism, worship) present problems for churches in the West and they don't know what to do about them.

Let me summarize the core idea of this book: If we keep holding on to "Christian" and "church" as essential, we aren't really dealing with the root of the problems the Western church faces today. The incarnational believers challenge us to reexamine what is essential for following and belonging to Jesus.

Much of the rest of the world has been left alienated and disconnected from Jesus by the choices and forms that arose from Christian assumptions. In all humility and love, I contend that the time has come to radically reconsider and even relinquish time-worn Christian containers and institutions with which Jesus and his Way have been encased for 1900 years. They are not part of the original Way and Faith of Jesus. They continue to actively stand in the way of his Way for several billion people.

Incarnational Believers in the US

This book has often explored the sometimes-strained relationship between Christians and Hindus. The concerns raised in these pages require US believers to examine their view of the Hindus who live and work around them as neighbors. A 2014 Pew research study asked people of other faiths in the US how many of them had a Christian friend. Only 22 percent of Hindus replied in the affirmative (Pew Research Center 2014; Stocker 2013). It is my prayer that this book will help some believers address that friendship vacuum and learn to address the barriers that contribute to such deep alienation even in the US.

The day is coming when at least some believers in the US will need to step away from Christian identity and church entirely. Many have already left, disillusioned, abused, alienated by the noise, institutionalism, or overt political agendas. They will never return to church. Does that mean they don't or can't love and follow Jesus? I believe the incarnational paradigm offers a non-institutional, less formal alternative (new wineskins). From a shepherding perspective, the possibility intrigues me. The resulting fellowships would likely look much more like the informal network of home groups in the New Testament, without the West's institutional assumptions. These will not be "house churches"—we'll completely work "church" out of our psyche and vocabulary.

The incarnational principles, I believe, also apply to our relationships as believers with people of other cultures and other socioreligious communities. Even in the West we should not start by assuming that all must become Christians and join a church. This forces them into foreign ways of worship and faith that compromise their ability to introduce their own family and society to Jesus in the future.

Take Hindus for example. Based on the New Covenant's incarnational principle, we should encourage new believers to remain as close to their socioreligious community as possible, not extract from it. Western Christians need to understand 1) how much of a barrier Christianity can present to Hindus, and 2) what bridge-building options exist to respectfully introduce them to Jesus on their terms, not ours.

Some believers must wrestle with and address what discipleship and ekklēsia might look like for cultural Hindus who should never join traditional churches. In addition, they need to encourage these culturally appropriate expressions for Hindus as much as they have encouraged traditional or contemporary expressions within their congregations. Those different styles resonate with different cultures. In the same way, Yesu bhaktas should be encouraged to develop expressions of faith, worship, and witness that are biblically faithful and culturally appropriate for their community. These bhaktas already exist and worship in India, in other parts of the world, even in the US. Where they are scattered, they meet in an *e-satsang*[20] every week to encourage one another. Where a number are close by, they gather together to worship and grow.

---

20. E-satsang is an electronic worship and study gathering using Skype or another interactive online tool. This allows believers in various locations to share in worship and study together with fellow believers, a virtual ekklēsia.

A recent volume by Timothy Shultz, *Disciple Making among Hindus: Making Authentic Relationships Grow* provides respectful, wise counsel from years of living among and serving Hindus in the US (Shultz 2016). It is essential reading for anyone interested in incarnational alternatives to traditional, extractive conversion. The resources at Margnetwork.org (MARGNetwork 2016) also provide a growing set of resources for those interested in respectful relationships with the Indian diaspora.

Where Are the Solutions?

This book has introduced several Christian barriers that keep Hindus (and others) from Jesus. It is not an exhaustive treatment of all the barriers. Neither is it a complete treatment of any one of the barriers. Some of my readers have found it frustrating that this book focuses on the barriers and does not provide more specific solutions.

That has been intentional for two fundamental reasons. Unless we own and address the barriers at a deep level, our solutions will perpetuate the barrier-producing traditions and assumptions about Christian "essentials" that are not essentials from the Lord and Scripture. We must spend enough time recognizing and wrestling with these issues that we truly can discern the difference between human invention and scriptural essentials. After eight years, my friends and I are still wrestling with these barriers and their implications. Quickly devised "solutions" will not solve anything. They will only perpetuate or cosmetically change the barriers.

Any solution I might propose for a Hindu context would be laden with my own cultural and unaddressed Christian assumptions. It would, more likely than not, be wrong for believers in that context. I regularly tell those who ask me for solutions, "If I created a solution that felt right to me, it would likely be wrong for them." Whether it's styles of worship or preaching, exact form and words at baptism, prayer traditions, or any other practice, the next section, "Finding the Right Alternatives," provides my primary solution.

FINDING THE RIGHT ALTERNATIVES

How do believers find the most appropriate expressions for their situation? I suggested some key steps in the chapter on worship barriers (see p. 170). Let me reiterate them in closing:

1. Search the Scriptures (Acts 17:11)

If the "Bible is our only rule of faith and practice," then it should be the starting point for any discussion of what believers should do. If it is an essential practice, the Scriptures will describe it. If it's a necessary part of a believer's life, the Scriptures will speak to that.

In Acts 17, these people did not take the Apostle Paul's word for anything he taught. They checked the word of God to see whether his teaching was in line with God's revealed truth. This should be the starting point. Wise leaders will teach their people to read and study God's word and to check whether their teaching agrees with Scripture.

At the same time, Scripture usually does not provide details of practice. It commands the Lord's Supper and baptism, but gives little detail as to who did it, how they did it, when they did it, and more. When the details are not provided, believers must determine how they might best practice this in their context.

Our response to this critical decision point determines whether we perpetuate Christian barriers to Jesus or whether believers build scriptural, cultural bridges to their own socioreligious community. The decisions of other believers in other locations are of little importance in new contexts. Their traditions developed from a different culture, context, and situation.

As familiar as traditions from one culture might be, we must actively and intentionally avoid bringing them and recommending or imposing them on believers in a different culture, context, and situation. Those believers must be as free to develop their own traditions directly from Scripture and their cultural milieu, the way countless other believers have for centuries.

Let me suggest that Jesus is essential (not our packaging of him), Scripture is essential (but not our cultural emphases and interpretations), and the body of Christ is essential (but not "church" forms). We must humbly relinquish anything else and encourage a process whereby new believers in a new town, new city, new community, or new tribe are encouraged to start with these essentials, then build their own appropriate and relevant traditions of faithfulness to the Lord, his Word, and his Body.

2. Ask the Lord for Wisdom (James 1:5)

So, where the Scripture is not clear on an issue, or where it does not address it at all, we don't suggest or provide answers. Instead, believers must, from the very beginning, also be taught to seek the Lord's leading in prayer. This verse in James, "If any of you lacks wisdom, let him ask of God," is not written to missionaries or pastors as the directors of missions and churches. It is written to all of God's people. God listens and still gives his wisdom and guidance today when his people ask.

Leaders, from the beginning of a new group, must teach all believers to ask the Lord for wisdom and direction. They should not simply be mindless sheep dependent on a minster to tell them what to do and how to live. Believers are responsible to seek the Lord's leading for their situations.

Some of the foreign traditions in the barriers arose because this step was ignored or missed. Someone imposed a solution from another culture or location without asking the Lord what he wanted in this situation.

In one sense, this step really should come before, during, and after the Scripture step. Before seeking answers (wisdom) in God's word, believers should ask the Lord to help them find his guidance in the Scriptures.

3. Discuss the Options Together (Acts 15)

In Acts 6 a conflict arose in the congregation that could have led to division. The apostles provided some guidance, but gave responsibility to the congregation to discuss who they wanted to select as new leaders to solve the problem.

In Acts 15 (Jerusalem Council), the fellowships of Jews and Gentiles faced another conflict. The believers examined Scripture and what God had been doing. They talked together for a long time about different aspects of the issue (must Gentiles adopt Jewish culture to follow Jesus?).

When believers have sought the word of God, and sought God's wisdom in prayer, then they can share the ideas they are receiving and find a solution together. This is especially essential in societies where collective decision-making is important. By encouraging participation in these decisions, the fellowship of believers owns the decision together and is better able to follow it.

4. Follow What Seems Good to the Local Ekklesia and the Holy Spirit (Acts 15:28)

Once the group has examined Scripture, prayed, and talked together, they are in a place where the Holy Spirit can lead them to a workable, appropriate solution. This may not look like any solution any Christians have imagined or implemented. It does not have to. As long as these believers have honestly sought and followed the Lord's leading, their solution will be as acceptable to the Lord as anything Christians elsewhere have devised for their contexts.

All of this takes time to process and assimilate. Don't rush it and seek quick fixes and solutions. You'll only perpetuate the barriers or create new ones. I am working alongside Indian colleagues, both Christians and bhaktas, adjusting to their sense of their culture and context, as we continue to explore the barriers and solutions. I'm honestly envisioning at least a decade to work through the deeper issues and find appropriate alternatives. It's a slow process in any culture. On Indian Stretch Time, as my friends call it, things go at a measured, not a hurried pace. We're going a step at a time as the Lord directs. "He is not slow . . . as some count slowness" (2 Pet 3:9).

You now have been introduced to a few of the Christian barriers to Jesus. **Now that you know, what will you do?**

APPENDIX
"HINDUS" AND "HINDUISM"

Since I refer to Hindus regularly, it is important to define "Hindu" and "Hinduism," to clarify how I use those terms. Both defy simple definition. They are foreign-created labels that cannot adequately describe Indian realities, yet they are now utilized by Hindus themselves in diverse ways.

"HINDU"

In one sense, I use "Hindu" as broadly as India's usage allows. I'm tempted to just go with Arvind Sharma's observation, "Fundamentally, a Hindu may be identified as one who does not deny being one" (A. Sharma 1993, 5). The corollary would be "one who claims to be a Hindu," and that is my practical starting point. When a person says, "I am a Hindu," I have a generic understanding of their socioreligious identity, but little details as to what that entails. It would be wrong of me, based on just that statement, to assume what that "Hindu" identity involves, or how much "religion" the individual includes in that understanding. It is not uncommon, for instance, to meet "Hindus" who are agnostic or atheists.

Dayanand Bharati, a follower of Jesus within his Hindu culture and community, has observed, "A Hindu is one who belongs to a particular community, not related to his personal faith in his religious systems. He is more a 'social animal' aiming for personal spirituality rather than one concerned about a religious system" (Bharati 2004, 47). This perspective is important. When a Christian hears "Hindu," they tend to immediately focus on religion and define the person by their understanding of that "religious system." But when "Hindus" self-identify, their primary focus is their sociocultural relationships and communities, which may include widely varying levels of religious observance and practice.

Based on the perspective of Bharati and some others, Dasan Jayaraj suggests, "The word 'Hindu' represents a social system and its cultural practices rather than a religious system. It is only in the recent past that the word has come to mean a religion rather than a social and cultural system" (Jayaraj 2010, 344). This definition makes Hindu simply a socio-cultural identity, with little or no reference to spiritual dimensions of that identity. It certainly makes it easy to understand someone who maintains their social and cultural heritage, while adopting faith in Jesus. It is usually more complex, though, than this would suggest.

Hindu identity is a complex mix of social and religious features, and that must be the starting assumption for understanding. Through conversation and observation, I must determine what that person understands by his or her Hindu identity: this will include aspects of ethnicity, language, geography, socioeconomic status, caste and communal identity, and philosophical orientation. Then mixed in with those identifiers we must add their religious *sampradaya* (traditions or school of belief) if any, and the gods of their village, clan, and personal choice (*ishta devata*). Added to this will be questions of how observant they are to the religious aspects (daily, occasionally, rarely). Some are deeply pious, others have rejected much of the religious faith, even if they go through the motions for family harmony (social identity and obligations can trump religious devotion). Only at this point do you begin to understand, still at a surface level, what "Hindu" means to that individual.

The challenge of definition is highlighted by Hindu scholar, Klaus Klostermaier,

> Hindus are quite often diametrically opposed to one an-
> other on very basic issues. But in an almost indefinable
> way they remain Hindus, in spite of the complexity of
> their peculiarities and prejudices, which as a people they
> will hardly be able to shed or to radically alter. Much of
> Hinduism may be mere tradition and many Hindus may
> disown conventions they have been brought up with,
> yet Hinduism as a whole shows amazing life and vigor.
> (Klostermaier 1989, 42)

I use the term primarily to refer to anyone who identifies with any Hindu socioreligious group or community. Some "Hindus" are deeply religious while others see it as primarily a sociocultural identity. Some are devout and observant, others pay scant attention to the rituals and requirements of the religious aspects of their heritage. Every Hindu can choose preferred gods, paths, and disciplines to some extent. So, in one sense there are as many "Hinduisms" as there are Hindus. Frykenberg reflects this somewhat nebulous sense of Hindu, "There *is* no single or *proper* sense of the term Hindu . . . What one worshiped or how one worshiped, or did not worship, did not make one more or less Hindu" (Frykenberg 1993, 532).

Recently, Timothy Shultz explored why the higher castes and socio-economic strata of Hindu society have not responded significantly to the good news of Jesus:

> This raises a question that we must all take at least a moment to ponder. Do higher caste Hindu people fail to respond to the gospel and therefore receive little or no ministry, or do higher caste Hindu people receive very little ministry and therefore fail to respond? Regardless how one answers this question, higher caste Hindus are at the epicenter of the least reached peoples of the earth, and they may number as many as 400 million. That's a truly staggering figure. (Shultz 2016, 7)

I share with Shultz a particular concern for this segment of Hindu society. The barriers explored in my book have especially served to keep these Hindu communities alienated from Jesus in significant ways. That will likely not change unless the fundamental issues this book raises are addressed deeply, so when I refer to Hindus, often I have these mostly distanced Hindus expressly in mind.

"HINDUISM"

In this book, I usually refer to "Hindu traditions," because Hinduism is not one monolithic religious system. It is, rather, an outsiders' label for a widely diverse and complex accumulation of social, cultural, philosophical, and religious traditions rooted in Indian soil and life. H. L. Richard has suggested that we should refer to this complex of beliefs and practices as "Hindu traditions" (private conversations).

At the same time, even Hindus refer to Hinduism, so I will not be overly pedantic. Where I speak of Christians or Muslims criticizing or condemning Hinduism, I will use the term, since that is how they speak, and how Hindus report it. Where Hindu websites and publicity use Hinduism (e.g., *Hinduism Today*), they themselves use the term to identify what they believe and practice.

Klaus Klostermaier additionally suggests,

> One is tempted to see not so much a parallel between Hinduism and other religions but between Hinduism and what one could call, for the moment, Europeanism or Americanism. . . Hinduism has always been more than mere religion in the modern Western sense, and it aims at being a comprehensive way of life as well today, a tradition by which people can live. (Klostermaier 1989, 1, 3)

Shultz, who works incarnationally with Hindus in the United States, has summarized the issues succinctly, "Since there are one billion Hindus in the world, we also need to understand Hinduism as it is experienced in the lives of contemporary Hindus. *This approach will reveal that Hinduism is actually a comprehensive way of life within which the gospel may be translated, rather than a religion that people need to reject in order to confess Christ*" (Shultz 2016, 7–8; emphasis mine).

"Hinduism," then, refers to a socioreligious way of life, one that means very different things to different communities and societies, even individuals, within its ambit. Spiritual, cultural, and social elements are intricately mixed and cannot be artificially separated.

In the New Testament, believers did not reject and abandon their Roman or Greek way of life just because there were elements of religion mixed with the social, cultural, and political components. They too incarnated the Way of Jesus within their socioreligious milieu. Jesus led them to change and reject aspects of their culture that did not conform to his Way, but they did not abandon and forsake their entire way of life to do so. Neither should Hindus today.

Christians, Indian and foreign, create unnecessary misunderstanding when they identify the entire Hindu way of life as religion, then demand that Hindus abandon this way of life and heritage to follow Jesus.

My Yesu bhakta friends, devout followers of Jesus, remain as members of their Hindu socioreligious community. Like many modern, urban Hindus, they do not allow caste prejudice and discrimination to interfere with friendship and other human relationships. They own their Hindu cultural and social identity, and acknowledge there are religious elements woven in with which they must wrestle. By faith, though, they worship and share Jesus as their only God (*ishta devata*), but in culturally Hindu ways.

"In the end," writes Klostermaier, "it is Hindus alone who determine what Hinduism is and what it is not. The Hindu community is large and diverse and has room for many different individuals and schools of thought" (Klostermaier 2003, 14). Bhaktas are part of that community.

When I speak of Christian barriers that keep "Hindus" from Jesus, I am referring to those members of Hindu socioreligious communities who do not know or do not follow Jesus. When I refer to Yesu bhaktas, I mean followers of Jesus who remain within their Hindu socioreligious community and culture. This book will explain how that is possible, scriptural, and preferable for many, probably the majority, of Hindus.

GLOSSARY

Biblical Terms

Adelphoi Plural of *adelphos* (brother). Commonly meant "brothers and sisters" when used of mixed groups. Used of the "members of a community" (Deissmann 1980, 107). Early believers used this of themselves and of fellow Jews.

Aphiēmi Release, leave, forgive. Used synonymously with *kataleipō* in Matthew 19 and Mark 12.

Baptizō Greek word for immerse, submerge, dip, plunge. From which churches created the word baptize. Done in the New Testament "in the name of Jesus," and in water, to indicate a believer's faith and participation in the core of the good news, the death, burial, and resurrection of Jesus. Baptism carries the same ideas. These words, however, are deeply encrusted with Western church and conversion baggage that makes them lightning rods for Hindu resistance. Using accurate translation and careful exegesis can free these words to mean what they meant in the New Testament and to build an understandable bridge to Hindus instead of turning them away.

Basileia Kingdom. Can mean geographical territory of a king, but usually in the New Testament it refers to the reign of God and Jesus within human hearts, the reign of heaven or the reign of God. When "kingdom" is used in the Middle East or India it suggests imperial power and colonial intentions, something Jesus wants nothing to do with. We must clearly explain God's rule in men's hearts versus Euro-American imperial intentions.

Christianos Christian. A Latin (Roman) derived label for those associated with "Christ," first coined in Antioch of Syria around AD 47 (Acts 11:26).

Does not mean "Christ-follower" any more than Asian means Asia follower, Indian means India follower. It simply implied association.

Ekklēsia The Greek word usually translated "church." It did not have a sense of institution or building in the Greek world, but of people assembled or gathered for a purpose.

Epistrophē Turning around. Only used in the New Testament in Acts 15:3 to describe the Gentiles turning to God. Translated "conversion" in some Bibles. The only occurrence of "conversion" in Scripture.

Euangelion Good news. Often translated "gospel" in English, which now hides its original meaning. I always read "good news" when I see gospel for this reason, both to myself and in public reading of Scripture.

Euangelistēs One who brings good news, messenger of good news. Translated "evangelist" in the Bible, which carries all kinds of Western assumptions not assumed in this word at all. Timothy and Titus were "evangelists" not pastors (2 Tim 4:5). This role (Eph 4:11) seems to include bringing the good news and helping set fledgling ekklēsias in order with healthy, responsible local leadership (1 Tim 3; Titus 1).

Euangelizomai Bring, tell, announce good news. Often translated "evangelize" or "preach the gospel"; but preach is not in this word.

Hagioi Plural of *hagios* meaning holy, dedicated, consecrated, devoted people who have been made holy by Jesus, not by their own piety. All believers are called this in the New Testament. English Bibles use "saint" which has unscriptural, confusing ideas of especially holy people, often based on their extraordinary piety.

Hodos Road, way, path. The Way is one common designation for the person and teaching of Jesus. The Faith (see Pistis) is also used this way.

Kataleipō Leave. Used synonymously with *aphiēmi* in Matthew 19 and Mark 12.

Kērussō Proclaim, report, announce an authoritative message. Sometimes used in Greek of a news reporter. Translated commonly in English as "preach," but the Western church has layered "preach" with many traditions, expectations, and postures that the original has nothing to do with. This forces believers to follow Western "preaching" instead of appropriate, natural expressions of *kērussō* in their own context.

Koinōnia Greek word usually translated "fellowship," but also partnership (Phil 1:5). Signifies sharing, togetherness, and comradeship on multiple levels, not just sharing food (e.g., fellowship dinner).

Mathētes Disciple, student. *Shishya* or *chela* commonly in India.

Mathēteuo "Make disciples" as in Matthew 28:19

Petros/Kephas Greek (Peter) and Aramaic (Cephas) respectively for stone. Used by Jesus to name Peter (stone). He then said, "Upon this rock (petra)," speaking of Peter's confession as the bedrock on which he would build his ekklēsia. Some churches misread this and say that Peter was the foundation. Jesus, however, distinguishes the two clearly.

Pistis Faith, the Faith. A common term for the Way and Faith of Jesus used in the New Testament. "Christianity" did not exist as a term until invented by Ignatius after the New Testament (see *Christianismos*, next section).

Pistoi Plural of *pistos*, believer, one who believes (typically in Jesus).

Prosēlutos Proselyte. A convert from the Gentile world to Judaism. The only actual "convert" word in the New Testament and *never* used of the followers of Jesus. Only those who changed culture to Judaism. The related proselytize refers to converting people from one culture to another, rather than just to discipleship in Jesus within one's own culture.

Extra-Biblical Christian Terms

Adiaphoran Optional, not necessarily required.

Christianismos Literally Christianism. Separatist term Ignatius termed that is now commonly called Christianity. Jacques Ellul's *Subversion of Christianity*, in the original French, makes much of the divisive sense that -ism carries.

Cultural Separatism My term for the Christian spirit of extraction and separation from one's birth culture, rejection of that culture, and adoption of a separate, isolated Christian culture. Contradicts the incarnational way of Jesus.

Ecclesia Latin form of Greek ekklēsia because Latin had no equivalent term. Used in the sense of political gatherings long before the New Testament or "church." The Latin church, though, invested *ecclesia* with all the institutional and hierarchical sense that church has in English today. It is not equivalent to the original Greek ekklēsia.

Kuriakon Greek for "of the Lord" or "the Lord's." Used in Constantinian era and after for "The Lord's house." Word from which "church" is derived.

Plantatio Ecclesiae Latin for planting churches in the Catholic sense.

Indian Terms

Aarti Hindu fire ritual performed by waving a plate with burning oil or camphor in a clockwise motion in front of the *murti* (god-image) at certain *pujas* (worship rituals).

Aryan (Pronounced Ar-yawn, not Aree-an). Sometimes used by older Europeans for Indians in general (as with Rudyard Kipling). Sometimes figures into caste and regional distinctions where some north Indians of Hindu roots are considered Aryans as opposed to south Indians who come from Dravidian cultures instead. The North–South division between Hindi and Dravidian languages is rooted in this distinction (one more layer of challenge).

Bhagavata/Bhagawan One term for the supreme God.

Bhagavatars Story-tellers of God (Rowe 2013, 61).

Bhajan Worship song sung by groups in which a leader usually sings a line and then the worshipers repeat or respond. This Hindu style of worship song is used with Jesus-focused lyrics by some Indian believers also, both Christian and bhakta.

Bhakta One who follows God through the path of bhakti (devotion). A person who deeply loves, worships, and follows God. Incarnational believers in India commonly call themselves Yesu bhaktas, devoted followers exclusively of Jesus. Since the Bible word *hagios* (saint) means someone devoted to God, *bhakta* provides a possible understandable alternative to the misunderstood "saint."

Bhakti Deep religious devotion, heart religion, seeking for direct, personal connection and experience with the divine. This devotion can be exclusive to one *sampradaya* (tradition) and God.

Bindi/Pottu Dot Indian women commonly wear on their forehead. Often a sign of a married woman, but now also worn by married and single as decoration. This is seen by some Christians as a Hindu symbol that women must remove to show their devotion to Jesus. Doing so is more offensive, however, than a Western woman removing her wedding ring.

Brahma The Creator. One of the three main gods of the Hindus, but rarely worshiped in comparison to Shiva and Vishnu.

Brahman The ultimate divine reality behind and permeating all things.

Caste This is not the Indian term, but provides a helpful location to explain related terms. Hindu society is divided into four main castes (*varnas*): Brahmin (priests), Kshatriya (soldier-ruler), Vaisya (merchant-traders), Sudra (workers). Below this are the Dalits (considered outcastes by Hindus, called Harijans by Gandhi), officially termed Scheduled Castes today (Richard 2007b, 53). Within each of these *varnas* exist numerous subcastes (*jatis* lineage or birth-group). These are further divided into several thousand *gotras* or clans (Klostermaier 2003, 77, 90).

Chela Student, disciple.

Dalal Tout, broker, pimp, panderer, carnival bar ker, shyster, huckster. A pejorative term used by Hindus sometimes to refer to Christian pastors who purvey spiritual things for monetary gain from foreign-funded missions.

Dasa/Dass/Doss Servant, slave.

Desi/Deshi Culturally or naturally from India, belonging to India.

Dharma Teaching. "Duty, righteousness, order, that which sustains society, etc." (Richard 2007b, 54). While used in various senses, Kane in his compendious *History of Dharmasastra*, concludes that "ultimately its most prominent significance came to be 'the privileges, duties and obligations of a man . . .'" (Kane 1930, 2).

Dhoti Picture Gandhi's cloth wrap-around, and you have the dhoti. Sometimes worn short like his, and sometimes, on formal occasions, it's worn long. Traditional Indian dress forsaken by many Indian Christians for pants. Some Christians do not even know how to wear their own national dress, don't even want to. A symbol of "cultural separatism." Rejecting the dhoti led to south Indians calling Christianity "the pants religion." Jesus and his followers wore robes (more like *dhotis*) than pants.

Diksha Initiation or dedication rite, often into relationship to a guru (spiritual teacher), as in *guru diksha*. When understood from New Testament, immersion (baptism) is *diksha* into Jesus as Lord and Teacher (Guru).

Gayatri Mantra A verse from the Rig Veda (3.62.10) recited by many Hindus at least at sunrise and often at other times of the day. Called the *Veda Mata* or "Mother of the Vedas" it is said to encapsulate all Hindu scripture somewhat like "Love the Lord your God . . ." does for "all the Law and Prophets" according to Jesus. It is a prayer to experience God's glory and for him to guide the petitioner's thoughts (guidance).

Ghar Wapsi Literally "home coming." Emotionally charged term (for Hindus and Christians) used for reconverting Christians and Muslims to Hinduism. From a Hindu perspective it involves bringing them back to their Hindu faith and home.

Ghats Bathing steps along the banks of holy rivers in India, as the Asi Ghat in Varanasi. A place, usually considered holy, where people can come to bathe to remove their sins.

Gram Panchayat Village-level administrative councils. Lowest level of decision-making in India's multi-tiered political system.

Guru Religious teacher or leader. Highest ones are often revered as a god. Yesu bhaktas consider Jesus their Maha Guru (great or supreme Teacher), among other terms.

Harmonium Small hand-pumped musical instrument with organ keyboard and sound.

Hindutva Hindu-ness. Used to advocate for a Hindu nation where one must honor India as a holy land (Hindu *rashtra*) and participate in Hindu culture (*sanskriti*) to be truly Indian.

Ishta/Ishta Devata One's chosen deity. Hindu tradition allows individuals and families to select the particular god or gods they most identify with. Yesu bhaktas explain to Hindus that Jesus is their ishta devata–their one and only chosen God. [Note: Please don't do false etymology and relate the Sanskrit *ishta* (chosen) to Ishtar the Middle Eastern fertility goddess. The two are not related in any way.]

Jal Sanskar Water ritual or sacrament into relationship with a guru or God. Exactly what New Testament baptism symbolized connection to the person of Jesus, not into an institution.

Karatala/Karatalam Small hand cymbals commonly used in *satsangs* and various Indian music forms.

Karma "1. In the general sense, good works; religious, moral, and caste duties. (One of the three traditional ways to attain salvation.) 2. The principle that reward or punishment infallibly follows every deed. At times the recompense comes in the present life; always the situation and fate of the coming life are determined by one's *karma*" (Richard 2007b, 35). Sometimes viewed as inescapable consequence, but Hindu tradition has many ways to adjust levels of good and bad karma.

Kurta Indian shirt of varying lengths (hem can be from waist down to ankles depending on how formal).

Lok Sabha Lower Assembly or House of the Indian parliament system.

Mandali Fellowship, circle, group. A worship meeting of a *mandali* is often called a *satsang*. Sometimes used by Yesu bhaktas of their Indian expression of ekklēsia.

Marg/Panth Way, path.

Masala Indian spice mix.

Mangalsutra/Mangalyam/Thali Wedding chain placed around bride's neck at a wedding. Some Christians require women to remove this as a Hindu symbol, again offending family in a worse way than removing a wedding ring. Other Christians practice this as the Indian alternative to Western wedding rings.

Mela Mass gathering, festival.

Mridangam Two ended drum held and played horizontally.

Muktinath Sanskrit for "Salvation Lord." This captures the original meaning of Jesus or the Hebrew original Yeshua/Joshua, which meant "the Lord saves." This explains why the angel told Joseph to call Jesus by this name, "because he will save his people from their sins."

Murti Image. Hindu term for the images they use for worship.

Paap Hindu word for sin, wrongdoing. Much of Hindu ritual and practices seeks to remove sin and its consequences from one's life. A deeply significant concept in Hindu traditions, unlike what many Christians claim ("Hindus don't know sin").

Pongal A three-day harvest festival celebrated by Indians of Tamil culture and background in January each year. It expresses thanks to the gods, especially Surya, the sun, for the previous harvest, and seeks divine blessings for the coming year. Tamil version of Makar Sankranti celebrated around the same time by Hindus in other parts of India.

Prasad/Prasadam Sanskrit word for grace. Food that has been offered to a deity, then eaten or shared with others later. How to deal with this arises from Paul's discussions of "food sacrificed to idols" (Rom 14–15; 1 Cor 8–10). This term, though, is also used by some believers, Christian and Hindu, to refer to the Lord's Supper a meal or ordinance that shares in the Lord's grace and blessing with his followers.

Prayaschitta Act of penance or expiation done to remove the offense and shame caused by offensive acts. These acts can also serve an atoning effect, because paying for the cause of shame and offense allows reconciliation and restoration to God or the community.

Puja Worship ritual.

Pujari Priest, one who presides over or performs a puja on behalf of observing devotees.

Pukka Genuine, real.

Qaum Urdu word for a nation or community.

Rajya Sabha Upper Assembly or House of the Indian parliament system.

Roti, Chapatti, Naan Types of Indian flat breads baked and eaten in different parts of the country.

Sabha Assembly, meeting, sometimes political as Lok Sabha or Rajya Sabha. One legitimate alternative for ekklēsia. Some Indian translations use *sabha* for ekklēsia, which is much better than church if we explain it and don't turn *sabha* into "church."

Sadguru Truth-teacher. Term used by some Christians and many *bhaktas* for Jesus, a term of respect and submission to his ultimate authority.

Sampradaya Literally means "tradition," as we would say, for example, "in the Methodist tradition." Used for the sects and orders of Hinduism, equivalent to religious schools or denominations.

Samsara Cycle of birth, death, rebirth, commonly known as reincarnation. One is repeatedly reborn ("born again" confusion) until all bad karma is eliminated and one can attain deliverance (*moksha*) from the cycle. Disagreement over what happens then is the source of different *sampradayas*.

Sanatana Dharma "Eternal way of life." This is their term. They believe they belong to the eternal way of life, or "the eternal ordinances" (Kane 1930, 1). Hinduism is an outsiders' word for the beliefs of Hindus.

Sanskrit Language of the Hindu scriptures, spoken and read by some religious scholars.

Sanskriti Sanskrit and Hindi word for culture and civilization. Generic word for culture, not just Indian culture.

Sati Widow burning. Voluntarily going onto the funeral pyre of her husband to be burned with him and stay with him. A highly-valued practice at one time among caste Hindus.

Satsang/Satsangh Literally "truth gathering or fellowship." Common Indian word, used by Hindus and Christians, for spiritual or religious gatherings.

Seva Service, as in the act of serving people or God.

Shaadi Marriage.

Shiva The Destroyer, one of the three main gods of the Hindus (along with Brahma and Vishnu). His worshipers are called *Shaivites*.

Sisya/Shishya Student, disciple.

Sindoor/Sindur Red strip of paste worn by a woman in the middle part of her hair as a sign of marriage. Some Christians call this Hindu and require women to remove it. See *bindi* for the same offensive issues.

Sitar, Veena Indian stringed instruments.

Sloka Verse of scripture.

Snan/Snanam Ritual bathing, often to remove spiritual impurity and sin.

Surya One name for the sun god.

Swadeshi "One's own nation, local" (Bharati 2005, 319; Gandhi 2003).

Swami A spiritual religious leader, sometimes used as term of respect for one's guru.

Tabla Two headed, side-by-side percussive instrument that looks something like bongos.

Tilak/Tilaka Mark on forehead that indicates one's *sampradaya*. Vertical strokes generally indicate *Shaivite* (worshipers of Shiva), while horizontal indicate *Vaishnavite* (worshipers of Vishnu).

Trimarga Three paths considered the ways to salvation in Hindu traditions: *Karma* (works), *Jñana* (knowledge), *Bhakti* (devotion, worship).

Upanishad One of a set of Hindu scriptures that provides commentary and added insight from the original Vedas.

Veda Scripture, writing. The earliest Hindu scriptures are called the *Vedas*. More generally, Hindu scriptures are also called *Shastras*. Some *bhaktas* refer to the Bible as *Muktiveda* (salvation Scripture). They call the Old Testament, *Purva Veda* (Old Scripture) and the New Testament, *Uttara Veda* (New Scripture).

Villu Pattu Literally bow song. A Tamil folk art that uses a large bow shaped, one-string instrument, along with other accompanying instruments. The player sings and tells stories in a highly interactive way, using give and take with the fellow players and the audience.

Vishnu The Sustainer. One of the three main gods of Hindu religions. Vishnu has taken multiple *avatars* (incarnations) to help humanity in times of crisis. The two most popular in which he is often worshiped are Ram and Krishna.

Yatra Pilgrimage, religious journey.

BIBLIOGRAPHY

Ali, Akhtar. 2016. "India Rejects US Religious Freedom Report." *Religion News.* Accessed Nov 11, 2016. http://religionnews .com/2016/05/05/india-rejects-us-religious-freedom-report/

All India People's Forum. 2016. *"Bastar: Where the Constitution Stands Suspended."* All India People's Forum. Accessed Feb 7, 2017. https:// www.scribd.com/document/320141424/Bastar-Where-the -Constitution-Stands-Suspended-AIPF-report#download &from_embed

Allen, Roland. 1962. *The Spontaneous Expansion of the Church.* Grand Rapids, MI: William B. Eerdmans.

———. 1972. *Missionary Methods: St. Paul's or Ours?* Grand Rapids, MI: William B. Eerdmans.

Anderson, Rufus. 1869. *Foreign Mission: Their Relations and Claims.* New York, NY: Charles Scribner and Company. Accessed Dec 10, 2013. https://archive.org/stream/foreignmissionst00andc

Anonymous. 2013. "Wish We Had Known." *PioneerBible.org.* Accessed Dec 17, 2013. https://pioneerbible.org/articles/wish-we-had-known

Appasamy, A. J. 1927. *Christianity as Bhakti Marga: A Study in the Mysticism of the Johannine Writings.* Reprint (Kessinger Publishing). London, UK: MacMillan and Co, Ltd.

Appasamy, Dewan Bahadur A. S. 1924. "Fifty Years Pilgrimage of a Convert: Sequel to My Conversion." *Archive.org.* Accessed Oct 14, 2014. https://archive.org/details/MN41587ucmf_3

Arora, Tehmina. 2012. *"India's Defiance of Religious Freedom: A Briefing on 'Anti-Conversion' Laws."* Bonn, Germany: International Institute for Religious Freedom. Accessed Apr 14, 2016. http://www.iirf .eu/fileadmin/user_upload/IIRF_Reports/iirf_rep_2_1_india .pdf

————. 2016. "The Spread of Anti-conversion Laws from India: A Threat to the Religious Freedom of Minorities." *Lausanne Global Analysis* 5(3). Accessed May 20, 2016. https://www.lausanne.org/content /lga/2016-05/anti-conversion-laws-india

Arora, Vishal. 2015. "Sixth Indian State Seeks to Adopt 'Anti-Conversion' Law." *WorldWatch Monitor.* Accessed Nov 11, 2016. https://www .worldwatchmonitor.org/2015/09/4008146/

Ayer, Pradip. 2001. "Conversion or Regeneration: A Brief Discussion." *International Journal of Frontier Missions* 18(4): 183–185. Accessed Jan 15, 2015. http://www.ijfm.org/PDFs_IJFM/18_4_PDFs/183 185 Ayer.pdf

Baker Publishing Group. 2012. *You Lost Me by David Kinnaman.* YouTube Video, 2:54. Posted Aug 2012. https://www.youtube .com/watch?v=jitHsBPGtUY

Barclay, William. 1965. *The Letters of James and Peter.* Edinburgh, Scotland: The Saint Andrews Press.

————. 1972. *The Gospel of John, Volume 2.* Reprint, Edinburgh, Scotland: The Saint Andrew Press.

Barnett, P. W. 1993. "Tentmaking." In *Dictionary of Paul and His Letters,* edited by Gerald F. Hawthorne, Ralph P. Martin and Daniel G. Reid, 925–927. Downers Grove, IL: InterVarsity Press.

Bauer, Walter, William F. Arndt, F. Wilbur Gingrich, and Frederick W. Danker. 1979. *A Greek–English Lexicon of the New Testament and Other Early Christian Literature.* Chicago, IL: The University of Chicago Press.

Bauman, Chad M. 2013. "Hindu-Christian Conflict in India: Globalization, Conversion, and the Coterminal Castes and Tribes." 72(3): 633–653. Accessed Nov 7, 2014. http://digitalcommons.butler.edu/cgi /viewcontent.cgi?article=1271&context=facsch_papers

Beasley-Murray, George Raymond. 1962. *Baptism in the New Testament.* Grand Rapids, MI: William B. Eerdmans.

Bharata Bharati Admin. 2013. "Government cracks down on foreign funding of Christian NGOs – News Bharati." *Bharata Bharati.* Accessed Sep 12, 2015. https://bharatabharati.wordpress .com/2013/08/27/government-cracks-down-on-foreign-funding -of-christian-ngos-newsbharati/

Bharati, Dayanand. 2004. *Living Water and Indian Bowl.* Pasadena, CA: William Carey Library.

———. 2005. *Understanding Hinduism.* New Delhi, India: Munshiram Manoharlal Publishers, Pvt. Ltd.

———. Interview with J. Paul Pennington, Apr 6–9, 2015, interview notes.

Bonk, Jonathan J., ed. 2005. "Editorial: Can There Be Christianity Without Church?" *International Bulletin of Missionary Research* 29(4): 169–170. Accessed Mar 29, 2016. http://www.internationalbulletin .org/issues/2005-04/2005-04-ibmr.pdf

Bosch, David J. 1996. *Transforming Mission: Paradigm Shifts in Theology of Mission.* Maryknoll, NY: Orbis Books.

Breen, Mike. 2013. *The Great Disappearance.* Exponential Resources. https:// exponential.org/resource-ebooks/the-great-disappearance/

Bromiley, Geoffrey W. 1986. *Theological Dictionary of the New Testament: Abridged in One Volume.* Grand Rapids, MI: William B. Eerdmans.

Bruce, F. F. 1987. *New Testament Development of Old Testament Themes.* Reprint, Grand Rapids, MI: William B. Eerdmans.

———. 1988. *The Book of Acts (NICNT).* Grand Rapids, MI: William B. Eerdmans.

———. 1990. *The Acts of the Apostles: Greek Text with Introduction and Commentary.* Third Revised and Enlarged Edition. Grand Rapids, MI: William B. Eerdmans.

Center for the Study of Global Christianity. 2013. *"Christianity in its Global Context, 1970–2020: Society, Religion, and Mission."* South Hamilton, MA. Accessed Nov 1, 2013. http:// www.gordonconwell.com/netcommunity/CSGCResources /ChristianityinitsGlobalContext.pdf

Corbett, Steve, and Brian Fikkert. 2012. *When Helping Hurts: How to Alleviate Poverty without Hurting the Poor . . . and Yourself.* Expanded edition. Chicago, IL: Moody Publishers.

Cottrell, Jack. 1990. *Baptism: A Biblical Study.* Joplin, MO: College Press.

Dahat, Pavan. 2014. "In Bastar, 50 villages ban non-Hindu missionaries." *The Hindu.* Accessed Jan 25, 2015. http://www.thehindu .com/news/national/In-Bastar-50-villages-ban-non-Hindu -missionaries/article11254725.ece

Daniell, David. 1994. *William Tyndale: A Biography*. New Haven, CT: Yale University Press.

Darden, Robert. 2015. "Remembering Andrae Crouch, Dead at 72." *Christianity Today*. Accessed Jan 18, 2015. http://www .christianitytoday.com/ct/2015/january-web-only/remembering -andrae-crouch-dead-at-72.html

Das, R.C. 1999. *R. C. Das: Evangelical Prophet for Contextual Christianity*, edited by H.L. Richard. Delhi, India: ISPCK.

de Waard, Jan, and Eugene A. Nida. 1986. *From One Language to Another: Functional Equivalence in Bible Translating*. Nashville, TN: Thomas Nelson Publishers.

Deissmann, Adolf. 1980. *Light from the Ancient East*. Grand Rapids, MI: Baker Book House.

Dhar, Aarti. 2015. "Mother Teresa's aim was conversion, says Bhagwat." *The Hindu website*. Accessed Dec 16, 2015. http://www.thehindu .com/news/national/mother-teresas-aim-was-conversion-says -bhagwat/article6926462.ece?ref=relatedNews

Duerksen, Darren. 2012. "Must Insiders Be Churchless? Exploring Insiders' Models of 'Church.'" *International Journal of Frontier Missiology* 29(4): 161–167. Accessed Sep 15, 2015. http://www .ijfm.org/PDFs_IJFM/29_4_PDFs/IJFM_29_4-Duerksen.pdf

———. 2015. *Ecclesial Identities in a Multi-Faith Context: Jesus Truth-Gatherings (Yeshu Satsangs) among Hindus and Sikhs in Northwest India*. Vol. 22 American Society of Missiology Monograph Series. Eugene, OR: PICKWICK Publications.

Edersheim, Alfred. 1980. *The Life and Times of Jesus the Messiah*. Reprint. Grand Rapids, MI: William B. Eerdmans.

Editorial. 1985. "Declaration on Caste and the Church (EFI and ATA, 1984)." *Transformation: An International Journal of Holistic Mission* 2(2): 1. Accessed Jan 29, 2016. http://trn.sagepub.com /content/2/2/1.full.pdf+html

Ellul, Jacques. 2011. *The Subversion of Christianity*. Eugene, OR: Wipf & Stock.

Encyclopedia Britannica. 2016a. "Bhimrao Ramji Ambedkar." *Encyclopedia Britannica online*. Accessed Mar 25, 2016. http://www.britannica .com/biography/Bhimrao-Ramji-Ambedkar

———. 2016b. "Christian Caste." *Encyclopedia Britannica online*. Accessed Apr 29, 2016. http://www.britannica.com/topic/Christian-caste

Ferguson, Everett. 2008. "Why and When Did Christians Start Constructing Special Buildings for Worship?" *Christianity Today*. Accessed Oct 12, 2015. http://www.christianitytoday.com/ch/asktheexpert/ask_churchbuildings.html

Fikkert, Brian, and Russell Mask. 2015. *From Dependence to Dignity: How to Alleviate Poverty Through Church-Centered Microfinance*. Grand Rapids, MI: Zondervan.

Frawley, David. 2008. "Hindu Front: A Fraudulent Mission: Exposing False Premises and Dangerous Notions behind Christian Missionary Activity." *Hinduism Today* 30(4): 35–36. Accessed Nov 7, 2013. http://www.hinduismtoday.com/archives/2008/10-12/pdf/Hinduism-Today_Oct-Nov-Dec_2008.pdf

Frazier, Jessica. 2011. *"Bridges and Barriers to Hindu-Christian Relations."* Oxford, UK: Oxford Center for Hindu Studies. Accessed Jun 19, 2014. http://www.ochs.org.uk/sites/g/files/g383876/f/building-bridges.pdf

Friedrich, G. 1985. "Euangelizomai, Euangelion." In *Theological Dictionary of the New Testament: Abridged in One Volume*, edited by Geoffrey D. Bromiley, 267–273. Grand Rapids, MI: William B. Eerdmans.

Frykenberg, Robert Eric. 1993. "Constructions of Hinduism at the Nexus of History and Religion." *The Journal of Interdisciplinary History* (The MIT Press) 23(3): 523–550. Accessed Nov 11, 2016. http://www.jstor.org/stable/206101

——. 2003. "Introduction." In *Christians and Missionaries in India: Cross-Cultural Communication since 1500*, edited by Robert Eric Frykenberg, 1–32. Grand Rapids, MI: William B. Eerdmans.

———. 2004. "Gospel, Globalization, and Hindutva: The Politics of "Conversion" in India." In *Christianity Reborn: The Global Expansion of Evangelicalism in the Twentieth Century*, 108–132. Grand Rapids, MI: William B. Eerdmans.

Gandhi, Mahatma K. 1929. "The Complete Works, Volume 45." *Gandhiserve.org*. Accessed Feb 24, 2016. http://www.gandhiserve.org/cwmg/VOL045.PDF

———. 1931. "The Complete Works, Volume 51." *Gandhiserve.org.* Accessed Feb 24, 2016. http://www.gandhiserve.org/cwmg /VOL051.PDF

———. 1961. "In Search of Supreme. Volume III." *MKGandhi.org.* July. Accessed Dec 18, 2015. http://www.mkgandhi.org/ebks/in -search-of-the-supreme-III.pdf

Gandhi, Mohandas K. 2003. *Indian Home Rule or Hind Swaraj.* Translation. Reprint, Yann Forget. Accessed Nov 30, 2014. https://docs.google.com/file/d/0B2GRozT38B1eYWU0OTc5 N2UtNGQyZC00YTlmLWI4N2UtZjQ2ZTg4MzY3NTM5 /edit?ddrp=1&pli=1&hl=en#

Georges, Jayson. 2014. *The 3D Gospel: Ministry in Guilt, Shame, and Fear Cultures.* HonorShame.com

Ghatwai, Milind. 2016. "Blind couple among 13 in Madhya Pradesh held for 'conversion.'" *The Indian Express.* Accessed Feb 10, 2016. http://indianexpress.com/article/india/india-news-india/blind -couple-among-13-in-madhya-pradesh-held-for-conversion/

Gill, Brad. 2009. "Exploring the Process of Contextualization: A Panel Discussion." *International Journal of Frontier Missions* 26(4): 183–187. Accessed Jan 28, 2015. http://www.ijfm.org/PDFs _IJFM/26_4_PDFs/Panel%20Discussion_galley.pdf

Gnaniah, N. J. 2011. "Caste, Christianity, and Cross-Cultural Evangelism Revisited." *International Journal of Frontier Missiology* 28(4): 161–167. Accessed Apr 29, 2016. http://www.ijfm.org/PDFs _IJFM/28_4_PDFs/IJFM_28_4-Gnaniah.pdf

Gnidovic, Gary. 2014. "How White Missionaries Helped Birth Modern-Day India." *Christianity Today.* Accessed Feb 5, 2014. http:// www.christianitytoday.com/ct/2014/february-web-only/how -white-missionaries-helped-birth-modern-day-india.html

Goel, Sita Ram. n.d. "Catholic Ashrams." *Voice of Dharma.* Accessed Aug 25, 2014. http://www.voiceofdharma.org/books/ca/index.htm

———. 1989. "Chapter 2: Indigenisation, A Predatory Enterprise from Catholic Ashrams." Accessed Apr 20, 2014. http://www .voiceofdharma.org/books/ca/ch02.htm

———. 1996. *History of Hindu-Christian Encounters (AD 304 to 1996).* Delhi: Voice of India. Accessed Dec 12, 2015. http:// voiceofdharma.org/books/hhce/

Government of India. 1860. "India Penal Code, 1860." *India Code Legislative Department.* Accessed Sep 1, 2015. http://indiacode .nic.in/

———. 2007. "Constitution of India." *India Law Ministry.* Accessed Dec 9, 2014. http://lawmin.nic.in/coi/coiason29july08.pdf

———. 2011. "Personal Law." *India.gov.in.* Accessed May 6, 2016. http:// www.archive.india.gov.in/citizen/lawnorder.php?id=16

———. 2014. "Verification of the Claims of Scheduled Castes, Scheduled Tribes and Other Backward Classes." *Ministry of Personnel.* http://persmin.gov.in/DOPT/Brochure_Reservation _SCSTBackward/Ch-08_2014.pdf

Graham, Carol. 1985. "The Legacy of V. S. Azariah." *International Bulletin of Missionary Research* 9(1): 16–19. Accessed Nov 13, 2016. http:// journals.sagepub.com/doi/pdf/10.1177/239693938500900106

Guder, Darrell L. 2000. *The Continuing Conversion of the Church.* Grand Rapids, MI: William B. Eerdmans.

Hale, Chris. 2011. "Reclaiming the Bhajan." In *Rethinking Hindu Ministry: Papers from the Rethinking Forum,* 119–121. Pasadena, CA: William Carey Library.

Halley, Henry H. 1965. *Halley's Bible Handbook: An Abbreviated Bible Commentary.* 24th ed. Grand Rapids, MI: Zondervan Publishing House.

Harper, Susan Billington. 1995. "Ironies of Indigenization: Some Cultural Repercussions of Missions in South India." *International Bulletin of Missionary Research* 19(1): 13–20. Accessed April 20, 2016 at http:// journals.sagepub.com/doi/pdf/10.1177/239693939501900103

———. 2000. *In the Shadow of the Mahatma: Bishop V.S. Azariah and the Travails of Christianity in British India.* Grand Rapids: MI: William B. Eerdmans.

Harris, Robin P. 2013. "The Great Misconception: Why Music is Not a Universal Language." In *Worship and Mission for the Global Church: An Ethnodoxology Manual,* 82–89. Pasadena, CA: William Carey Library.

Hauser, I. L. 1884. "Missionary Music." *The Heathen Woman's Friend*, 235–237. Accessed Nov 2, 2016. https://books.google.com /books?id=SYFIAAAAYAAJ&pg=RA1-PA237&lpg= RA1-PA237&dq=Why+do+Christians+sing+Western+songs+in +India&source=bl&ots=GNlngHaFAy&sig=-JrGORZBxq9cs px4eAlQQ2K8zvo&hl=en&sa=X&ved=0ahUKEwjvrdGTmY _QAhUs1oMKHcQiBTAQ6AEINzAE#v=onepage&q&f=fals

Hawley, John Stratton. 2015. *A Storm of Songs: India and the Idea of the Bhakti Movement.* Cambridge, MA: Harvard University Press.

Hendricksen, William. 1978. *The Gospel of Luke (New Testament Commentary).* Grand Rapids, MI: Baker Book House.

Hesselgrave, David J. 1991. *Communicating Christ Cross-Culturally: An Introduction to Christian Communication.* 2nd ed. Grand Rapids, MI: Zondervan Publishing House.

Hian, Chua Wee. 1999. "Evangelization of Whole Familes." In *Perspectives on the World Christian Movement: A Reader*, edited by Ralph D. Winter and Steven C. Hawthorne, 613–616. Pasadena, CA: William Carey Library.

Hinkhoj. 2015. *Hinkhoj Hindi Dictionary.* Accessed Feb 12, 2015. http:// dict.hinkhoj.com/.

Hoefer, Herbert E. 2001a. "The Conversion Confusion." *International Journal of Frontier Missiology* 18(1): 47–49. Accessed Apr 19, 2016. http://www.ijfm.org/PDFs_IJFM/18_1_PDFs/hh_conversion .pdf

———. 2001b. *Churchless Christianity.* Pasadena, CA: William Carey Library.

Hort, Fenton John Anthony. 1914. *The Christian Ecclesia: A Course of Lectures on the Early History and Early Conceptions of the Ecclesia.* London, UK: MacMillan and Co., Limited. Accessed August 27, 2014. https://archive.org/details/christianecclesi00hort

Houssney, Georges. 2010. "Position Paper on the Insider Movement." *Biblical Missiology Website.* May 3. Accessed Nov 18, 2014. http://biblicalmissiology.org/2010/05/03 /position-paper-on-the-insider-movement/

Hout, Michael, and Tom W. Smith. 2015. "Fewer Americans Affiliate with Organized Religions, Belief and Practice Unchanged." *General Social Survey Site of NORC, University of Chicago.* March 10. Accessed Apr 29, 2016. http://www.norc.org/PDFs/GSS%20 Reports/GSS_Religion_2014.pdf

Hunter, Alan. 2007. "Forgiveness: Hindu and Western Perspectives." *Journal of Hindu-Christian Studies* 20(11): 1–8. Accessed Feb 16, 2016. http://digitalcommons.butler.edu/cgi/viewcontent .cgi?article=1386&context=jhcs

IDSN. 2013. "India: Official Dalit Population Exceeds 200 Million." *International Dalit Solidarity Network.* Accessed Nov 18, 2015. http://idsn.org/news-resources/idsn-news/read/article /india-official-dalit-population-exceeds-200-million/128/

Ignatius, Peter. 2016. *Identifying and Teaching on Psycho-social Issues to the Assimilation Groups in an Urban Indian Church. Unpublished DMin project. Deerfield, IL: Trinity Evangelical Divinity School.*

India Census. 2001. "Census and You: Religion." *CensusIndia.gov.in.* Accessed Feb 27, 2015. http://censusindia.gov.in/Census_And _You/religion.aspx

———. 2011. *Distribution of Population by Religions.* Delhi, NCP. Accessed Aug 23, 2013. http://censusindia.gov.in/Ad_Campaign /drop_in_articles/04-Distribution_by_Religion.pdf

IndiaFacts Staff. 2014. "Exposing Evangelism: IndiaFacts Impact Stories." *IndiaFacts.org.* Accessed Apr 6, 2016. http://indiafacts .org/exposing-evangelism-indiafacts-impact-stories/

InterFaithShaadi Admin. 2014a. "Follow Jesus, Not the Church: A Message to Interfaith Couple." *InterfaithShaadi.* Accessed Feb 21, 2016. http://www.interfaithshaadi.org/blog/?p=7914

———. 2014b. "After conversion, will I be able to follow my Hindu religion?" *InterfaithShaadi.* Accessed Dec 5, 2014. http://www .interfaithshaadi.org/blog/?p=8694

Jain, Sandhya. 2007. "Is There Imperial Design behind Conversion Overdrive?" *Crusadewatch.* Accessed Oct 22, 2015. http:// www.crusadewatch.org/index.php?option=com_content&task =view&id=765&Itemid=9

———. 2008. "Buta Singh Has a Point on Religious Reservation." *Ascent of Asia Blogspot*. Accessed Apr 20, 2015. http://ascent-of-asia .blogspot.com/2009/01/sandhya-jain_23.html

Jayaraj, Dasan. 2010. *Followers of Christ Outside the Church in Chennai, India: A Socio-Historical Study of a Non-Church Movement.* Hyderabad, India: KEEANS.

Johnson, Mark. 2002. "Church in a Box." *Voice of Bhakti* 1(3). Accessed Feb 14, 2015. http://www.bhaktivani.com/volume1/number3 /box.html

Johnson, Todd M., Gina A. Zurlo, Albert W. Hickman, and Peter F. Crossing. 2016. "Christianity 2016: Latin America and Projecting Religions to 2050." *International Bulletin of Mission Research.* 40(1): 22–29. Accessed Mar 7, 2016. http://ibm.sagepub.com /content/40/1/22.full.pdf+html

Jones, E. Stanley. 1926. *Christ of the Indian Road.* Reprint, New York, NY: The Abingdon Press. Accessed Feb 20, 2015. https:// open.bu.edu/bitstream/handle/2144/926/Jones%2c%20E.%20 Stanley%2c%20The%20Christ%20Of%20The%20Indian%20 Road.pdf?sequence=1

———. 1948. *Gandhi: Portrayal of a Friend.* Nashville, TN: Abingdon Press.

Joseph, Jacob. 2013. "The Challenge of Indigenizing Christian Worship: An Example from India." In *Worship and Mission for the Global Church: An Ethnodoxology Handbook*, edited by James R. Krabill, 137–140. Pasadena, CA: William Carey Library.

Joshua Project. 2016a. "Country: China." *Joshua Project.* Accessed Feb 15, 2016. https://joshuaproject.net/countries/CH

———. 2016b. "Country: India." *Joshua Project.* Accessed Feb 15, 2016. http://joshuaproject.net/people-profile.php

———. 2016c. "Global Statistics." *Joshua Project (2016).* Accessed Feb 15, 2016. http://joshuaproject.net/global_statistics

Kane, Pandurang Vaman. 1930. "History of Dharmasastra, Volume 1." *Archive.org.* Accessed Oct 24, 2016. https://archive.org/details /HistoryOfDharmasastraancientAndMediaevalReligiousAnd CivilLawV.1

Kannan, P., and S. Kannan. 2001. "A Survey of Disciples of Christ from Non-Dalit Hindu Homes." *International Journal of Frontier Missions* 18(4): 165–169. Accessed Nov 10, 2013. http://www.ijfm.org/PDFs_IJFM/18_4_PDFs/165%20170%20Kannan.pdf

Kim, Sebastian C. H. 2005. "Hindutva, Secular India, and the Report of the Christian Missionary Activities Enquiry Committee: 1954–1957." In *Nationalism and Hindutva: A Christian Response: Papers from the 10th CMS Consultation*, edited by Mark T. B. Laing, 108–144. Delhi, India: CMS/UBS/ISPCK

———. 2013. "'Mass Movements' In the 1930s and Their Impact on Indian Politics and the Church." *Dharma Deepika* 17(2): 6–26.

Kinnaman, David. 2011. *You Lost Me: Why Young Christians Are Leaving Church . . . And Rethinking Faith.* Grand Rapids, MI: Baker Books.

Kinnaman, David, and Gabe Lyons. 2007. *unChristian: What a New Generation Really Thinks about Christianity.* Grand Rapids, MI: Baker Books.

Klostermaier, Klaus K. 1989. *A Survey of Hinduism.* Albany, NY: State University of New York Press.

———. 2003. *A Concise Encyclopedia of Hinduism.* Oxford, UK: ONEWORLD.

Knight, William. 1880. *Memoir of the Rev. H. Venn: The Missionary Secretariat of Henry Venn, B. D.* London, UK: Longmans, Green, and Co. Accessed Apr 19, 2016. https://archive.org/details/memoirofrevhvenn00knig

Kornfeld, William J. 1997. "What Hath Our Western Money and Our Western Gospel Wrought?" *Mission Frontiers* 19(1). Accessed Sep 10, 2015. http://www.missionfrontiers.org/issue/article/what-hath-our-western-money-and-our-western-gospel-wrought

Kuhn, K. G. 1985. "Proselutos." In *Theological Dictionary of the New Testament: Abridged in One Volume*, by Geoffrey W. Bromiley, 943–946. Grand Rapids, MI: William B. Eerdmans.

Kuppa, Padma. 2012. "Predatory Proselytism." *Hinduism Today.* Accessed Jan 20, 2015. http://www.hinduismtoday.com/archives/2012/10-12/pdf/Hinduism-Today_Oct-Nov-Dec_2012.pdf

Liddell, Henry George, Robert Scott, and Sir Henry Stuart Jones. 1940. *A Greek–English Lexicon: Revised and Augmented.* Oxford, England: Clarendon Press. http://www.perseus.tufts.edu/hopper /text?doc=Perseus:text:1999.04.0057

Malhotra, Rajiv. 2000. "The Ethics of Proselytizing." *Infinity Foundation.* Accessed May 26, 2016. http://www.infinityfoundation.com /ECITproselytizingframeset.htm

———. 2011a. *Breaking India: About the Book.* http://www.breakingindia .com/introduction/

———. 2011b. *Dharma's Good News: You Are Not a Sinner!* Accessed Dec 4, 2014. http://www.huffingtonpost.com/rajiv-malhotra/the -hindu-good-news-you-a_b_854904.html

———. 2011c. "How Evangelists Invented 'Dravidian Christianity.'" *The Blog, Religion Section, Huffington Post.* Accessed Dec 15, 2014. http://www.huffingtonpost.com/rajiv-malhotra/how-evangelists -are-inven_b_841606.html

———. 2012. "The Tiger And The Deer: Is Dharma Being Digested Into The West?" *RajivMalhotra.com.* Accessed Mar 25, 2015. http://rajivmalhotra.com/library/articles /tiger-deer-dharma-digested-west/.

———. 2015. "Christian Good News vs Hindu Good News (Video Presentation)." *Decolonising Indians channel YouTube Video, 3:36. Posted Mar 2015.* https://www.youtube.com/watch?v =gtyWUe-MjzY

MARGNetwork. 2016. *Marg Network.* margnetwork.org

Marshall, I. Howard. 1980. *Acts (Tyndale NT Commentaries).* Grand Rapids, MI: William B. Eerdmans.

McGavran, Donald A. 1961. *The Bridges of God: A Study in the Strategy of Missions.* London, England: World Dominion Press.

———. 1979. *Ethnic Realities and the Church: Lessons from India.* Pasadena, CA: William Carey Library.

McKnight, Scot. 2010. "Jesus vs. Paul." *Christianity Today.* Accessed Feb 16, 2016. http://www.christianitytoday.com/ct/2010 /december/9.25.html

McLaren, Brian D. 2012. *Why Did Jesus, Moses, the Buddha, and Mohammed Cross the Road? Christian Identity in a Multi-Faith World.* New York, NY: Jericho Books.

McTague, Corey. 2013. "Witnessing to Hindus." *firstBibleInternational.* Accessed Jan 27, 2017. http://www.firstbible.net/uwj/15-fall2013 /54-witnessing-to-hindus

Meeks, Wayne A. 1983. *The First Urban Christians: The Social World of the Apostle Paul.* New Haven, CN: Yale University Press.

Mehta, Sandhya. 2002. "Gandhiji on Religious Conversion." *MKGandhi. org.* Accessed Dec 8, 2014. http://www.mkgandhi.org/ebks /Gandhiji-on-Religious-Conversion.pdf

Menezes, Saira, and Venu Menon. 1999. "The Zealots Who Would Inherit." *Outlook.* Accessed Mar 17, 2016. http://www.outlookindia.com /magazine/story/the-zealots-who-would-inherit/207018

Minear, Paul Sevier. 2004. *Images of the Church in the New Testament.* Louisville, KY: Westminster John Knox Press.

Morris, Leon. 1988. *The Epistle to the Romans.* Grand Rapids, MI: William B. Eerdmans.

Moulton, W. F., A. S. Geden, and H. K. Moulton. 1978. *A Concordance of the Greek Testament.* 3rd ed. Edinburgh, Scotland: T. & T. Clark.

MWD. 2014. "Church." *Merriam-Webster.com.* Accessed Jan 27, 2014. http://www.merriam-webster.com

Nash, Donald A. n.d. "Why the Churches of Christ are Not a Denomination." *Christian Restoration Association Site.* Accessed Feb 15, 2015. http://thecra.org/files/WhyNotDenom.pdf

National Bureau. 2015. "Ruckus over comments on Mother Teresa; Rajya Sabha adjourned." *The Hindu online.* Accessed Dec 16, 2015. http://www.thehindu.com/news/national/ruckus-over-comments -on-mother-teresa-rajya-sabha-adjourned/article6936447 .ece?ref=relatedNews

Naugle, David K. 2002. *Worldview: The History of a Concept.* Grand Rapids, MI: William B. Eerdmans.

Neill, Stephen. 1990. *A History of Christian Missions.* London, UK: Penguin Books.

Netland, Harold. 2000. "World Religions." In *Evangelical Dictionary of World Missions,* edited by A. Scott Moreau, 1029–1031. Grand Rapids, MI: Baker Books.

Nevius, John. 1899. *The Planting and Development of Missionary Churches.* New York, NY: Foreign Mission Library. Accessed Dec 16, 2014. https://archive.org/details/plantingdevelopm00nevi.

Nida, Eugene A. 1954. *Customs and Cultures: Anthropology for Christian Missions*. Pasadena, CA: William Carey Library.

Niles, Daniel T. 1958. *The Preacher's Task and the Stone of Stumbling*. New York, NY: Harper & Brothers.

Niyogi, M. B. S., Ghanshyam Singh Gupta, Ratanlal Malviya, B. G. R. S. Deo, S. K. George, and B. P. Pathak. 1958. *Report of the Christian Missionary Activities Enquiry Committee, Madhya Pradesh, Vol I*. Voice of Dharma. Accessed Nov 6, 2014. http://voiceofdharma .org/books/ncr/index.htm

North, James B. 1991. *A History of the Church: From Pentecost to Present*. Joplin, MO: College Press.

OED. 2014. "Church." *Oxford English Dictionary*. Accessed January 28, 2014. http://www.oxforddictionaries.com

———. 2015a. "Gospel." *Oxford English Dictionary*. Accessed Nov 18, 2015. http://www.oxforddictionaries.com/us/definition/american _english/gospel?q=Gospel.

———. 2015b. "Preach." *Oxford English Dictionary*. Accessed Nov 10, 2015. http://www.oxforddictionaries.com/us/definition/american _english/preach

———. 2016. "Christianity." *Oxford English Dictionary*. Oxford University Press. Accessed Mar 24, 2016. http://www.oxforddictionaries .com/definition/english/christianity

Pani, D. D. 2001a. "Fatal Hindu Gospel Stumbling Blocks." *International Journal of Frontier Missions* 18(1): 23–32. Accessed Nov 20, 2013. http://www.ijfm.org/PDFs_IJFM/18_1_PDFs/dp_stumbling _blocks.pdf

———. 2001b. "Submission to Oppression in India: Lessons from History." *International Journal of Frontier Missions* 18(1): 33–41. Accessed Mar 2, 2016. http://www.ijfm.org/PDFs_IJFM/18_1 _PDFs/dp_submission.pdf

Patterson, George, and Richard Scoggins. 2002. *Church Multiplication Guide: The Miracle of Church Reproduction*. Revised edition. Pasadena, CA: William Carey Library.

Paul, Timothy. 2011. "The Cultural Core of Hinduism." In *Rethinking Hindu Ministry: Papers from the Rethinking Forum*, 11–14. Pasadena, CA: William Carey Library.

Pennington, J. Paul. 2015. "Christian Encouragement for Following Jesus in Non-Christian Ways: A Case Study." 32(3): 129–137. Accessed Jan 1, 2016. http://www.ijfm.org/PDFs_IJFM/32_3_PDFs /IJFM_32_3-Pennington.pdf

Petersen, Brian K. 2007. "The Possibility of a Hindu Christ-Follower: Hans Staffner's Proposal for the Dual Identity of Disciples of Christ within High Caste Hindu Communities." *International Journal of Frontier Missiology* 24(2): 87–97. Accessed Sep 30, 2014. http://www.ijfm.org/PDFs_IJFM/24_2_PDFs/24_2_Petersen .pdf

Pew Research Center. 2012. "'Nones' On the Rise." *PewResearchCenter: Religion & Public Life Project.* Accessed Feb 10, 2016. http://www .pewforum.org/2012/10/09/nones-on-the-rise/

————. 2014. "How Americans Feel About Religious Groups." *Pew Research: Religion & Public Life Project.* Accessed Nov 6, 2014. http:// www.pewforum.org/2014/07/16/how-americans-feel-about -religious-groups/

Philostratus, Flavius. 1912. *Life of Apollonius.* London, England: William Heinemann. Accessed Oct 22, 2015. https://ryanfb.github.io /loebolus-data/L016N.pdf

Pickett, Jarrell Waskom. 1938. *Christ's Way to India's Heart.* Lucknow, India: Lucknow Publishing House.

Piper, John. 2015. "I Will Not Leave Jesus—But I'm Done with the Church." *DesiringGod.org.* Accessed May 26, 2016. http://www .desiringgod.org/interviews/i-will-not-leave-jesus-but-i-m -done-with-the-church

Priest, Robert J. 2012. "'Who Am I?' Theology and Identity for Children of the Dragon." In *After Imperialism: Christian Identity in China and the Global Evangelical Movement,* edited by Richard R. Cook and David W. Pao, 175–192. Cambridge, England: The Lutterworth Press.

Puniyani, Ram. 2013. "Religious Conversion and Violence in India: A Secular Perspective." Edited by P. Daniel Jeyaraj. *Dharma Deepika* 17(2): 26–36.

Raj, Ebe Sunder. 2001. *National Debate on Conversion.* Chennai, India: Bharat Jyoti.

Ramachandran, Jayakumar. 2013. "Reconversion: Some Challenging Questions and Implications." Edited by P. Daniel Jeyaraj. *Dharma Deepika* 17(2): 37–51

Rao, Madhusudhan. 2001. "Brahmabandhab Upadhyay and the Failure of Hindu Christianity." *International Journal of Frontier Missions* 18(4): 195–200. Accessed Mar 2, 2016. http://www.ijfm.org /PDFs_IJFM/18_4_PDFs/195%20200%20Rao.pdf

Reese, Gareth L. 1971. *A Critical and Exegetical Commentary on the Book of Acts.* Ann Arbor, MI: Braun-Brumfield, Inc.

Reese, Robert. 2010. *Roots & Remedies of the Dependency Syndrome in World Missions.* Pasadena, CA: William Carey Library.

Richard, H. L. 1998. *Following Jesus in the Hindu Context: The Intriguing Implications of N.V. Tilak's Life and Thought.* Pasadena, CA: William Carey Library.

———. 2001a. "A Brahmin's Pilgrimage in Christ: Lessons from N. V. Tilak." *International Journal of Frontier Missions* 18(4): 191–194. Accessed Mar 12, 2016. http://www.ijfm.org/PDFs _IJFM/18_4_PDFs/191%20194%20Richard.pdf

———. 2001b. "Evangelical Approaches to Hindus." *Missiology* 29(3): 307–316. Accessed Apr 27, 2016. ATLA Religion Database, EBSCOhost

———. 2007a. "Community Dynamics in India and the Praxis of 'Church.'" *International Journal of Frontier Missiology* 24(4): 185–194. Accessed Mar 28, 2016. http://www.ijfm.org/PDFs _IJFM/24_4_PDFs/185_Richard.pdf

———. 2007b. *Hinduism.* Pasadena, CA: William Carey Library.

Richards, E. Randolph, and Brandon J. O'Brien. 2012. *Misreading Scripture with Western Eyes.* Downers Grove, IL: IVP Books.

Robinson, John A. T. 1976. *Redating the New Testament.* London, England: SCM Press Ltd.

Rohr, Richard. 2016. "Your Life Is Not about You." *Center for Action and Contemplation.* Accessed May 25, 2016. https://cac.org /your-life-is-not-about-you-2016-05-25/

Rowe, Julisa. 2013. "Ethnodramatology for Community Engagement." In *Worship and Mission for the Global Church: An Ethnodoxology Handbook*, edited by James R. Krabill, 61–63. Pasadena, CA: William Carey Library.

Rutz, James H. 1992. *The Open Church*. Auburn, ME: The SeedSowers.

Saraswati, Dayananda. 1999. "Conversion is Violence." *jaiabharati. org*. Accessed Dec 9, 2014. http://www.jaia-bharati.org/anglais /swami-conviolence.htm

Savarkar, V. D. 1921–22. "Essentials of Hindutva." *Savarkar.org*. Accessed Nov 6, 2014. http://www.savarkar.org/content/pdfs/en /essentials_of_hindutva.v001.pdf

Schaff, Philip. 1870. *History of the Christian Church, Volume 1*. New York, NY: Charles Scribner & Co. Accessed Feb 7, 2016. https:// archive.org/stream/historyofchris01scha

Schmidt, K. L. 1985. "Ekklesia." In *Theological Dictionary of the New Testament (Abridged in One Volume)*, edited by Gerhard Kittel and Gerhard Friedrich, 397–402. Grand Rapids, MI: William B. Eerdmans.

Schwartz, Glenn J. 2007. *When Charity Destroys Dignity: Overcoming Unhealthy Dependency in the Christian Movement*. Lancaster, PA: World Mission Associates.

Sen, Amartya. 2005. "Contrary India." *The Economist*. Accessed Nov 20, 2015. http://www.economist.com/node/5133493

Sen, Keshab Chandra. 1884. "Selected Portions from the Lectures, Sermons &c. of Chandra Sen." In *Keshab Chandra Sen and the Brahma Samaj*, by Thomas Ebenezer Slater, 197–344 (renumbered from page 1). Madras, India: Society for Promoting Christian Knowledge. Accessed Apr 13, 2016. https://play.google.com/books/reader ?id=_SEaAAAAMAAJ&printsec=frontcover&output=reader &hl=en&pg=GBS.PP1

Sharma, Amit Kumar. 2011. "Religious Philanthropy in India." In *Religion and Culture in Indian Civilization: Essays in Honor of Prof. C. N. Venugopal*, edited by Amit Kumar Sharma, 153–180. Delhi, India: D. K. Printworld (P) Ltd.

Sharma, Arvind. 1993. "Hinduism." In *Our Religions*, edited by Arvind Sharma, 1–68. San Francisco, CA: HarperSanFrancisco.

Sharma, Supriya. 2014. "A BJP MP in Bastar is washing people's feet and stirring resentment against Christians." *Scroll.in*. Accessed Jan 7, 2015. http://scroll.in/article/686484/A-BJP-MP-in -Bastar-is-washing-people's-feet-and-stirring-resentment -against-Christians

Sharpe, Eric J. 2003. *The Riddle of Sadhu Sundar Singh.* New Delhi, India: Intercultural Publishers.

Shashikumar, VK. 2004. "Preparing for the Harvest." *Tehelka.* Accessed Feb 25, 2016. http://archive.tehelka.com/story_main .asp?filename=ts013004shashi.asp&id=1.

Shultz, Timothy. 2016. *Disciple Making among Hindus: Making Authentic Relationships Grow.* Pasadena, CA: William Carey Library.

Siemens, Ruth E. 1999. "Tentmakers Needed for World Evangelization." In *Perspectives on the World Christian Movement: A Reader,* edited by Ralph D. Winter and Steven C. Hawthorne. Pasadena, CA: William Carey Library.

Singh, Shiv Sahay. 2015. "Mother Teresa above religion: Missionaries of Charity." *The Hindu website.* Accessed Dec 16, 2015. http://www .thehindu.com/news/cities/kolkata/mother-teresa-above -religion-missionaries-of-charity/article6929037.ece

Snopes. 2010. "Snopes Messages." *Snopes.com.* Accessed Nov 3, 2015. http://message.snopes.com/showthread.php?t=61900

Soundaraj, Joseph. 2016. "Ethnomusicology and Scripture Translation." Presentation at Ethno-Arts Workshop, Chennai, India: Lakeview Bible College and Seminary.

Srawley, J. H. 1910. *The Epistles of St. Ignatius, Vol I.* London: Society for Promoting Christian Knowledge. Accessed Mar 21, 2016. https://archive.org/details/theepistlesofsti01srawuoft

Staff Reporter. 2015. "Bhagwat has spoken bitter truth: Sena." *The Hindu website.* Accessed Dec 16, 2015. http://www.thehindu.com /todays-paper/tp-national/bhagwat-has-spoken-bitter-truth -sena/article6934552.ece

Stocker, Abby. 2013. "The Craziest Statistic You'll Read About North American Missions." *Christianity Today.* Accessed Aug 21, 2013. http://www.christianitytoday.com/ct/2013/august-web-only /non-christians-who-dont-know-christians.html?start=1

Storti, Craig. 2007. *Speaking of India: Bridging the Communication Gap when Working with Indians.* Boston, MA: Intercultural Press.

Stott, John R. W. 1976. *Christ the Controversialist.* Downer's Grove, IL: InterVarsity Press.

———. 1990. *The Message of Acts.* Leicester, England: InterVarsity Press.

Subbamma, B. V. 2011. "Smoothing the Paths: A Caste Hindu Tells Her Story." In *Rethinking Hindu Ministry: Papers from the Rethinking Forum*, edited by H. L. Richard, 115–118. Pasadena, CA: William Carey Library.

Sumithra, Sunand. 1990. *Christian Theologies from an Indian Perspective.* Bangalore: Theological Book Trust.

Talman, Harley, and John Jay Travis. 2015. *Understanding Insider Movements: Disciples of Jesus within Diverse Religious Communities.* Pasadena, CA: William Carey Library.

Tracking Evangelism. 2014a. "Fundamentalism, Hatred and Aggression—a trip by [Name Withheld] group." *Tracking Evangelism Blogspot.* Accessed May 1, 2016. http://trackingevangelism.blogspot. com/2014_09_01_archive.html

———. 2014b. "Onsite-Offshore Model of Soul Harvesting Business." *Tracking Evangelism Website.* Accessed Dec 12, 2014. http:// trackingevangelism.blogspot.com/2014/08/onsite-offshore -model-of-soul.html

Trench, Richard C. 1978. *Synonyms of the New Testament: Studies in the Greek New Testament (10th Printing).* Grand Rapids, MI: William B. Eerdmans.

Van Rheenen, Gailyn. 2006. *Contextualization and Syncretism: Navigating Cultural Currents.* Pasadena, CA: William Carey Library.

Vedantham, Major T. R., Ram Swarup, and Sita Ram Goel. 1983. "Christianity: An Imperialist Ideology." *Voice of India.com.* Accessed Apr 24, 2016. http://www.voiceofin.com/pic/pdf/51.pdf

Viola, Frank, and George Barna. 2012. *Pagan Christianity? Exploring the Roots of Our Church Practices.* Carol Stream, IL: Tyndale House Publishers.

Wan, Enoch. 2000. "Practical Contextualization: A Case Study of Evangelizing Contemporary Chinese." *Enoch Wan Site.* Accessed Jan 24, 2015. http://www.enochwan.com/english/articles/pdf /Practical%20Contextualization%20Evangel%20Chinese.pdf

———. 2004. "Ethnic Receptivity and Intercultural Ministries." *Global Missiology* 1(2). Accessed May 24, 2016. http://ojs. globalmissiology.org/index.php/english/article/viewFile/128/371

Wansborough, Henry. 2015. *Introducing the New Testament.* New York, NY: Bloomsbury.

Webster, John C. B. 2007. *A Social History of Christianity: North-west India Since 1800*. New Delhi, India: Oxford University Press.

Wenham, David. 1995. *Paul: Follower of Jesus or Founder of Christianity?* Grand Rapids: MI: William B. Eerdmans.

Wilken, Robert L. 1984. *The Christians as the Romans Saw Them*. New Haven, CT: Yale University Press.

Williams, Thomas D. 2016. "India: 12 Arrested for Converting to Christianity." *Breitbart.com*. Accessed Jan 27, 2016. http://www.breitbart.com/national-security/2016/01/19/india-12-arrested-for-converting-to-christianity/

Winter, Ralph D. 2008. "Living with Ill-Defined Words: A Response to Herbert Hoefer and Rick Love." *International Journal of Frontier Missiology* 25(1): 38–41. Accessed Apr 25, 2016. http://www.ijfm.org/PDFs_IJFM/25_1_PDFs/25_1Winter.pdf

Witherington III, Ben. 1995. *Conflict and Community in Corinth: A Socio-Rhetorical Commentary on 1 and 2 Corinthians*. Grand Rapids, MI: William B. Eerdmans.

———. 1998. *The Acts of the Apostles: A Socio-Rhetorical Commentary*. Grand Rapids: MI: William B. Eerdmans.

Wolfsdorf, David. 2015. "Sophistic Method and Practice." In *Wiley Companion to Ancient Education*, 63–76. Wiley-Blackwell. Accessed Oct 15, 2015. http://astro.temple.edu/~dwolfsdo/Sophists%20chapter%20revised%20(7.19).pdf

World Council of Churches; Pontifical Council for Interreligious Dialogue; World Evangelical Alliance. 2011. "Christian Witness in a Multi-Religious World: Recommendations for Conduct." *Oikomene.org*. Accessed Apr 19, 2016. http://www.oikoumene.org/en/resources/documents/wcc-programmes/interreligious-dialogue-and-cooperation/christian-identity-in-pluralistic-societies/christian-witness-in-a-multi-religious-world

Worthington, Ian. 2010. "Rhetoric and Politics in Classical Greece: Rise of the Rhetores." In *A Companion to Greek Rhetoric*, edited by Ian Worthington, 255–271. Chichester, UK: Blackwell Publishing Ltd.